Communities

Ca~~lderdale~~ Council

Libraries and Information Services

Items should be returned on or before the last date shown below.

Any item **not required** by another reader may be renewed at any library, by phone, or on-line at www.calderdale.gov.uk.

To renew, please give your library membership number.

DATE DUE FOR RETURN

3 0 NOV 2020		
1 1 FEB 2022		
0 8 AUG 2023		

Anthropological Studies of Creativity and Perception

Series Editor: Tim Ingold, University of Aberdeen, UK

The books in this series explore the relations, in human social and cultural life, between perception, creativity and skill. Their common aim is to move beyond established approaches in anthropology and material culture studies that treat the inhabited world as a repository of complete objects, already present and available for analysis. Instead these works focus on the creative processes that continually bring these objects into being, along with the persons in whose lives they are entangled.

All creative activities entail movement or gesture, and the books in this series are particularly concerned to understand the relations between these creative movements and the inscriptions they yield. Likewise in considering the histories of artefacts, these studies foreground the skills of their makers-cum-users, and the transformations that ensue, rather than tracking their incorporation as finished objects within networks of interpersonal relations.

The books in this series will be interdisciplinary in orientation, their concern being always with the practice of interdisciplinarity: on ways of doing anthropology *with* other disciplines, rather than doing an anthropology *of* these subjects. Through this anthropology *with*, they aim to achieve an understanding that is at once holistic and processual, dedicated not so much to the achievement of a final synthesis as to opening up lines of inquiry.

Ways of Walking
Ethnography and Practice on Foot

Edited by

TIM INGOLD and JO LEE VERGUNST
University of Aberdeen, UK

LONDON AND NEW YORK

First published 2008 by Ashgate Publishing

Published 2016 by Routledge
2 Park Square, Milton Park, Abingdon, Oxfordshire OX14 4RN
711 Third Avenue, New York, NY 10017, USA

First issued in paperback 2016

Routledge is an imprint of the Taylor & Francis Group, an informa business

British Library Cataloguing in Publication Data
Ways of walking : ethnography and practice on foot. -
(Anthropological studies of creativity and perception)
1. Human beings - Effect of environment on 2. Walking -
Cross-cultural studies 3. Geographical perception -
Cross-cultural studies
I. Ingold, Tim, 1948- II. Vergunst, Jo Lee
304.2

Library of Congress Cataloging in Publication Data
Ways of walking : ethnography and practice on foot / [edited] by Tim Ingold and Jo Lee Vergunst.
p. cm. -- (Anthropological studies of creativity and perception)
Includes bibliographical references and index.
ISBN 978-0-7546-7374-3
1. Human beings--Effect of environment on. 2. Walking--Cross-cultural studies. 3. Geographical perception--Cross-cultural studies. I. Ingold, Tim, 1948- II. Vergunst, Jo Lee.

GF51.W38 2008
304.2--dc22
2007051241
ISBN 13: 978-1-138-24462-7 (pbk)
ISBN 13: 978-0-7546-7374-3 (hbk)

Transferred to Digital Printing

Contents

List of Figures[1]

---

1   Figures listed indicate those with captions in the text.

Notes on Contributors

Elizabeth Curtis is a Lecturer in the School of Education at the University of Aberdeen.

Tim Edensor is Reader in Cultural Geography at Manchester Metropolitan University.

Pernille Gooch is a Senior Lecturer in the Human Ecology Division at Lund University.

Tim Ingold is Professor of Social Anthropology at the University of Aberdeen.

Sonia Lavadinho is a Research Fellow in the Department of Territorial Development at the Swiss Federal Institute of Technology in Lausanne.

Allice Legat is a PhD Graduate from the Department of Anthropology at the University of Aberdeen.

Hayden Lorimer is Senior Lecturer in Human Geography, Department of Geographical and Earth Sciences, University of Glasgow.

Raymond Lucas is a Research Fellow in the Department of Architecture at the University of Strathclyde.

Katrín Lund is a Lecturer at the Department of Geology and Geography, University of Iceland.

Kenneth R. Olwig is Professor in the Department of Landscape Architecture at SLU-Alnarp, the Swedish University of Agricultural Science.

Lye Tuck-Po is an environmental anthropologist affiliated with the Naga Research Group and HeritageWatch.

Jo Lee Vergunst is an RCUK Academic Fellow in the Department of Anthropology at the University of Aberdeen.

Thomas Widlok is Senior Researcher at the Max Planck Institute for Psycholinguistics in Nijmegen and Professor of Anthropology at the Department of Anthropology, Radboud University Nijmegen, The Netherlands.

Yves Winkin is Professor of Social Sciences at the École Normale Supérieure Lettres et Sciences Humaines in Lyon (France).

Preface and Acknowledgements

Let's get going then. In September 2005 we held a three-day event at the University of Aberdeen that was simply called the walking seminar. Although for much of the time we were sitting in a traditional seminar room, the journeys recounted by the participants left us feeling well-travelled indeed, through places both near and far, both extraordinary and everyday. In our free afternoon we went to Bennachie, Aberdeen's own mountain, and climbed up through the forest and out to the open hillside. We moved from quiet pine needles underfoot to rough boulders, heather and a buffeting wind, at which point we mostly gave up talking, but carried on walking.

The purpose of the seminar was to begin to explore the diversity of walking practices in the places where anthropologists and others work. We felt that although this topic – of ways of walking – is probably one that crops up frequently in ethnographers' fieldnotes, it rarely sees the light of day in the articles and books that they eventually write and publish. It rather seems to be pushed into the wings, by way of a separation of *what* is being purposefully done (arriving somewhere, say) from *how* it is done (by getting there, step by step, along a path). We wanted to find out what insights might be had through paying attention to both. So we invited participants to bring to the seminar the actual walking experiences of the people with whom they had spent time, in order to explore how life is led on the ground, along paths. They responded to the task with enthusiasm. In the papers they presented they not only described the ways that people walk through their inhabited places, but also reflected on walking as a technique of ethnographic research. For as researchers, we are inhabitants of the world like everyone else and need to find ways to get around in it as best we can. For everyone, learning how to do so is a process that has no clear beginning or end. Likewise the end – really a pause – of one walk, or one journey, usually marks the beginning of another. So let's carry on, going along.

We heartily thank all the seminar participants for their efforts. With the one exception of Paul Basu, all are included among the contributors to this volume. We also wish to thank the many members and friends of the Department of Anthropology at the University of Aberdeen who also joined in the discussions. The seminar was made possible thanks to an award from the UK Economic and Social Research Council for a two-year (2004-06) project of research entitled *Culture from the ground: walking, movement and placemaking* (RES-000-23-0312). Some of the results of this research are reported in Chapter 8. Finally, we are proud to launch, with this book, the first volume in a new series of *Anthropological Studies of Creativity and Perception*, and we would like to thank Neil Jordan, of Ashgate Publishing, for his encouragement and help in getting the series off the ground.

Jo Lee Vergunst and Tim Ingold
Aberdeen, May 2007

Chapter 1

Introduction

Tim Ingold and Jo Lee Vergunst

When did our walk begin? When will it ever end? We cannot remember, and will never know. Walking, in this regard, is much like talking, and both are quintessential features of what we take to be a human form of life. We are already talking by the time we realize that this is what we are doing; and only those who remain after we are gone will know which words will have been our last. So it is, too, with our first and last steps. Life itself is as much a long walk as it is a long conversation, and the ways along which we walk are those along which we live. There are beginnings and endings, of course. But every moment of beginning is itself in the midst of things and must, for that reason, be also a moment of ending in relation to whatever went before. Likewise, every step faces both ways: it is both the ending, or tip, of a trail that leads back through our past life, and a new beginning that moves us forward towards future destinations unknown. The same goes for the words we read and write. We begin to write, and you begin to read, in the thick of things, and only because we have set aside other tasks for the time being. We do not, however, travel alone. Our principal contention is that walking is a profoundly social activity: that in their timings, rhythms and inflections, the feet respond as much as does the voice to the presence and activity of others. Social relations, we maintain, are not enacted *in situ* but are paced out along the ground.

With this book we draw together several lines of thinking in contemporary social science: about the human body and its movements; about perception and the work of the senses; about education, enskillment and the formation of knowledge; about the constitution of space and place; about wayfaring and storytelling; and about the relations between humans and non-humans. We follow in the footsteps of Marcel Mauss who, in his famous essay of 1934 on *Techniques of the Body*, was perhaps the first to put walking on the agenda as a serious topic for comparative ethnological inquiry (Mauss 1979, 95-135). As in so many of his writings, Mauss left no more than a fragmentary and unfinished sketch for a programme of work that had still to be undertaken, and one that was so anachronistic in its formulation – with its lists of customs from around the world – and yet so far ahead of its time in the questions it opened up, that for long it fell on deaf ears. So thoroughly had it been forgotten that when, some four decades later, Pierre Bourdieu (1977) launched his theory of practice centred on the bodily dispositions of the *habitus*, few recalled that Mauss had already introduced the *habitus* to anthropology, as the key to his understanding of the social formation of body techniques, taking care to distinguish it from the merely idiosyncratic 'habits' of individuals, and illustrating it by way of a narrative of walking. Significantly, the narrative was about the arms and hands:

I think I can recognize a girl who has been raised in a convent. In general, she will walk with her fists closed. And I can still remember my third-form teacher shouting at me: "Idiot! why do you walk around the whole time with your hands flapping wide open?" Thus there exists an education in walking too (Mauss 1979, 100).

Indeed, walking is an accomplishment of the whole body in motion, as much the work of the hands and lungs as of the feet.

Of course Bourdieu's understanding of the *habitus* was far removed from that of Mauss. For Mauss was still enough of a disciple of his mentor, Emile Durkheim, to give pride of place in his thinking to systems of collective representations. His point was simply that to be enacted or given physical expression, these representations must call upon some material means, and for human beings these means are furnished, first and foremost, by the body – whether or not extended by extra-somatic instruments. The body thus plays object to the collective subject otherwise known as 'society'. Refusing such subject/object dichotomies, Bourdieu placed the *habitus* firmly in the space of the body's active engagement in its surroundings, in the 'practical mastery' of everyday tasks involving characteristic postures and gestures, or a particular body *hexis* (Bourdieu 1977, 87). A way of walking, for example, does not merely express thoughts and feelings that have already been imparted through an education in cultural precepts and proprieties. It is itself a way of thinking and of feeling, through which, in the practice of pedestrian movement, these cultural forms are continually generated (ibid., 93-4).

But could we not also put this proposition in reverse, to argue that thinking and feeling are ways of walking? This would, admittedly, be to interpret the notion of walking more broadly than is usual, as a paradigmatic instance of what Maxine Sheets-Johnstone (1999) has called 'thinking in movement'. Taking this step, however, obliges us to acknowledge that to think and feel is not to set up a relation of external contact or correspondence between subjective states of mind and objectively given conditions of the material world, but rather to make one's way *through* a world-in-formation, in a movement that is both rhythmically resonant with the movements of others around us – whose journeys we share or whose paths we cross – and open-ended, having neither a point of origin nor any final destination. Not only, then, do we walk because we are social beings, we are also social beings because we walk. That walking is social may seem obvious, although it is all the more remarkable, in this light, that social scientists have devoted so little attention to it. However to hold – as we do – that social life is walked is to make a far stronger claim, namely for the rooting of the social in the actual ground of lived experience, where the earth we tread interfaces with the air we breathe. It is along this ground, and not in some ethereal realm of discursively constructed significance, over and above the material world, that lives are paced out in their mutual relations. Thus careful, ethnographic analysis of walking, we suggest, can help us rethink what being social actually means. This is a task that remains to be done. Amidst the clamour of calls to understand the body as an existential ground for the production of cultural form, rather than only as a source of physical and metaphorical means for its expression (Csordas 1990, 5), we tend to forget that the body itself is grounded in movement. Walking is not just what a body *does*; it is what a body *is*. And if the body is foundational to culture, then walking – or thinking in movement – is 'foundational to being a body' (Sheets-Johnstone 1999, 494).

Ethnographers, as we have noted elsewhere (Lee and Ingold 2006), are accustomed to carrying out much of their work on foot. But while living with a group of people usually means walking around with them, it is rare to find ethnography that reflects on walking itself, least of all from the kind of comparative perspective that we offer in this book. No doubt the topic of walking figures often enough in ethnographers' fieldnotes. Once they come to write up their results, however, it tends to be sidelined in favour of 'what really matters', such as the destinations towards which people were bound or the conversations that happened en route. Even multi-sited fieldwork (Marcus 1998) focuses on the sites themselves, as though life were lived at a scatter of fixed locales rather than along the highways and byways upon which they lie. But *how* people go along on foot (as the vast majority of human beings have done, throughout history) is important. How do they prepare and set out, and how do they carry on through places in which, for any number of reasons, it may be difficult to walk? How do they arrive? Drawing on a phenomenological tradition (Jackson 1996), we aim to embed our ideas of the social and the symbolic within the immediate day-to-day activities that bind practice and representation, doing, thinking and talking, and to show that everything takes place, in one way or the other, on the move. In describing their own trails or those of the people in many lands with whom they have walked, the contributors to this book – though they come from a variety of disciplines and represent more than one theoretical perspective – share an ambition to pay attention to experiences of tactile, feet-first, engagement with the world. By way of introduction we will go around to meet them, eventually returning, as befits a tour, to where we began.

Setting out

As we embark on our walk, our eyes are not upon a distant horizon. The first steps we take are tentative, even experimental, and time passes slowly as we attempt them. As yet unsure of our bearing or direction, each step feels like our first: a one-off that may lead to a second, a third, and so on, but that may just as well come to nothing. We do not, in other words, *start* to walk as the athlete starts to run, at the shot of a pistol, springing into action at the instant. For it is only after quite a few steps, when the feet have found their rhythm and the body its momentum, that we discover – without having been aware of any moment of commencement – that we are already walking. In this respect setting out recapitulates, albeit in a highly abbreviated form, what happens in infancy. The infant's attention, too, is on the close-at-hand. Seeking to reach it by whatever means possible, he or she will improvise a mode of locomotion that mixes steps and tumbles – quaintly known as 'toddling' – until, after what seems like an age, it matures into a fully-fledged walk. Rarely, of course, do infants walk alone, as parents or older siblings give a helping hand. Between whiles, they may be carried, and it is surely while sitting astride or behind the shoulders of a grown-up that the infant first experiences walking as a rhythmic activity in which the eyes can set their sights on more expansive vistas while leaving the feet to look after themselves. Before that, of course, the unborn baby will have experienced something of the same rhythmic movement while carried in the womb.

Even when they have found their feet, small children's focus on the near-at-hand and their boundless curiosity in everything in the vicinity – which they want to reach out and touch as well as look at – can continually thwart the intentions of the adults with whom they walk. Nowhere is this more so than in a modern Western city where rules of orderliness and proper conduct on the street combine with real risks from passing traffic or of becoming separated in the throng. Tightly held hands can mediate something approaching a tug-of-war in which the adult, due to superior strength and stature, invariably wins out while the child has to put one foot before the other simply to avoid falling flat on the face. For younger children, of course, the ultimate penalty for insubordination is to be forcibly strapped into a push-chair, wheeled with steely determination by the victorious adult. Older children are dragged along behind. Sociologist Michael Wolff has described how city parents treat under-sevens like baggage to be pulled like a suitcase on wheels (Wolff 1973). While the adult looks ahead, negotiating a path through eye-to-eye contact with oncomers, the child's eyes are resolutely downcast. By the time the child has reached school age, he or she is supposed to have been trained by such discipline, and already to 'know' how to walk.

Meet Elizabeth Curtis (Chapter 10), as she escorts classes of primary schoolchildren by foot along the streets of the city of Aberdeen, in north-east Scotland. The purpose of these educational outings is to enhance children's awareness of the architectural heritage of the city. They follow a pre-planned trail linking a series of sites of special interest. At each successive site they stop to make and record their observations. These may be auditory and tactile as well as visual, such as the sound of running water in a concealed gully or the texture of cut stone. So far as their teachers are concerned, however, walking itself is not understood as a practice of observation, nor do the trail booklets they use make any reference to it. Observations are to be made from a stationary position, not on the move. Walking, then, is considered simply as a means to get from one site to the next. During walks, children are expected to behave sensibly and to follow the rules of road safety. Ideally they should march two abreast in a neat line, a formation traditionally known as the 'crocodile'. Though instructed to look and listen, attention is to be focused on traffic and passers-by, in order to avoid accident, rather than on such things as the wind, rain or sunshine, the flight of birds and the barking of dogs, puddles and autumn leaves, and the myriad trifles from snails to conkers, and from dropped coins to telltale litter, that make every street a place of such absorbing interest to the miniature detective whose eyes are still close to the ground. For every child is such a detective, especially as – unsupervised – they make their way on foot to school and back, absorbing as they do the sights, sounds, feel, and smells of their surroundings through varying weather and changing seasons.

Learning the way

The supervised heritage trail, as Curtis shows, transforms the streets into a classroom. It does so by taking outdoors an axiom fundamental to the constitution of the classroom as an indoor learning environment, namely, that knowledge is to be pieced together through the work of head and hands, from information obtained at diverse locations, rather than grown along the paths children take as they make their ways on foot, from place to place, through the world about which they learn. Such a division between knowledge and movement would seem strange to the Batek of Malaysia, forest-dwelling hunter-gatherers described by Lye Tuck-Po (Chapter 2). We come across Lye fumbling her way through the tropical forest, an environment that could not be more different from the paved streetscape of her childhood, when the jungle was remembered as an alien and fearsome place. Now, living with the Batek, she finds herself slipping and slithering through a dense tangle of roots, vines, ooze and debris, where one can never be sure of one's footing and where to hang on to vegetation risks bringing the whole lot down on one's head. In this highly dynamic environment nothing is ever quite the same from one moment to the next. Batek 'train' their children in the arts of negotiating the forest not through the imposition of discipline, or by keeping them on a leash, but rather by leaving them as much as possible to their own devices. Adults follow from the rear rather than taking the lead, and allow children to find their own ways, at their own pace, while keeping them under close but benign observation. For the Batek, as Lye shows, walking comprises a suite of bodily performances that include observing, monitoring, remembering, listening, touching, crouching and climbing. And it is through these performances, *along the way*, that their knowledge is forged.

Movement, here, is not adjunct to knowledge, as it is in the educational theory that underwrites classroom practice. Rather, the movement of walking is itself a way of knowing. A knowledgeable person is distinguished from a novice not by the sheer amount of information packed into his or her head – information that would in any case be perpetually obsolescent in an ever-changing environment – but by observational acuity and an awareness of the consequences of actions. Let us join Allice Legat (Chapter 3) as she walks with hunter-gatherers from the other side of the world, the Tłıchǫ (Dogrib) people of northwest Canada, in their boreal forest environment. Here too, walking is as much a movement of pensive observation – of thinking as you watch and watching as you think – as it is a way of getting around. Someone who has walked knows the ways of the world. To know, here, means to be able to take action, with a reasonable knowledge of what its consequences will be. Knowledgeable people, in short, can *tell*, in all senses of the word. As discerning observers, they can tell what is going on in the world around them, such as the movements of animals or impending changes in the weather. But they can also tell the stories that, for Tłıchǫ people, are fundamental to all understanding. And by relating their observations, taken while walking, to the appropriate narratives, they can tell what will come to pass.

Tłıchǫ adults are compulsive storytellers. Whatever the matter at hand, they can always find a story stretching back to old times but extended and embellished through their own experience, by which its significance can be interpreted. Children grow up hearing these stories almost every day. This storytelling is not however invested with didactic purpose or understood, as it might be by Western educationalists, as a child-centred way of conveying valued knowledge and information. Stories are stories, not coded messages. As Legat shows, simply having heard the stories is not enough to make an individual knowledgeable in the sense of having the capacity to take action. True knowledge depends on the confirmation of stories in personal experience, and to achieve this one must travel the trails and visit the places of which they tell, in the company of already knowledgeable elders. Between hearing the stories and walking the land, there is therefore a transitional stage in children's learning. At this stage children know the stories but do not yet know what they mean, and so cannot be guided by them in their action. This carries a crucial implication regarding the inter-generational transmission of knowledge, which is of great concern to Tłįchǫ elders. It is that the continuity of knowledge can be secured only by ensuring that generations overlap in their actual experience of walking the land. An intermediate generation that has heard the stories but has not had those stories validated by experience will not be able to guide its successors. That is why Tłįchǫ elders attach such importance to providing opportunities for young people to walk with them. Far from being accessory to the conveyance of knowledge by means of stories, walking is in their view the very means by which stories are converted into knowledge.

Leaving footprints

In this conversion – in walking their stories – predecessors leave footprints for successors to follow. Tłįchǫ people regard knowledge and footprints as part and parcel of the same action, and often speak of them as though they were one and the same. Readers accustomed to the discourses of modernity may be perplexed by this equivalence. Is not knowledge a property of the mind? And are footprints not marks in the physical world? Knowledge and footprints, it would seem, lie on opposite sides of a division between the mental and the material: on the one side the mental content that we take with us into our encounter with the world; on the other the marks left after we are gone. This view, however, betrays an assumption that underwrites the entire project of colonial expansion, namely that the surface of the earth is presented to encompassing humanity as a space to be occupied, and subsequently perhaps abandoned once its resources are used up. As Friedrich Engels famously put it, humans are destined in their imperial ambition to 'impress the stamp of their will upon the earth' (Engels 1934, 179). Something of this ambition is evident in the project of the 'confluencers' documented by Thomas Widlok (Chapter 4), who aim to visit every site on the terrestrial surface where whole degree lines of latitude and longitude intersect, and thereby to obtain 'an organised sampling of the world'. Though the resource that confluencers seek is more symbolic than real, there is the same concern with the occupation of space, with 'getting there first' and leaving one's mark. And the procedure of organized sampling, which the confluence movement shares with the field sciences and cartography, likewise has as its aim to make the unknown known by assembling data collected from multiple locations into a comprehensive survey. Confluencers stamp the earth at predetermined points rather than leaving their footprints along paths of habitation, as do people indigenous to the lands they visit. For them the whole world is a classroom – a full-sized replica of the classroom globe.

We meet Widlok in northern Namibia, a region he knows well from his fieldwork among the Akhoe Hai//om hunter-gatherers who have always lived there. To find out how the indigenous perspective compares with that of the prospecting confluencer, he has decided to register as a confluencer himself and to visit three sites of full degree intersection of latitude and longitude in the region. Unsurprisingly, he finds that the places and paths that are salient to the Akhoe Hai//om, and paced out in their everyday lives, fall through the grid of confluence sites. From the perspective of confluencers, these places and paths are all but invisible. It is as though, in reaching and taking possession of their sites, they were setting foot in a world as yet unoccupied. For the Akhoe Hai//om, on the other hand, confluence sites are of no significance unless they can be incorporated into local narratives of walking and place-making. For their task in life is not to *occupy* the world but to *inhabit* it (Ingold 2007, 81-4). In the pursuit of this task the footprints left by both human and non-human inhabitants of the land serve as useful clues to the whereabouts of local resources. Their footprints, however, are formed by walking within the world rather than tramping upon its exterior surface. These prints are not stamps but impressions. Moreover, as Legat observes of the Tłįchǫ, even after people have left a place where they have walked, something of themselves remains there. That is why treading in predecessors' footprints, so that they mingle with one's own, is enough to establish a relationship of co-presence. For inhabitants' footprints are traces of memory. Knowledge and footprints are not then opposed as mental to material. The relation between them is rather tantamount to one between bodily movement and its impression. If knowledge and footprints appear equivalent, it is because knowing is doing, doing is carrying out tasks, and carrying out tasks is remembering the way they are done.

Making an impression

Evidently, leaving footprints is not at all like printmaking. The printer stamps a design that has already been engraved or set, upon an absolutely flat, homogeneous and resistant surface. The surface itself is not deformed by this movement, which leaves a mark only because the plate or type has been inked. The surfaces on which inhabitants walk, however, are neither flat nor homogeneous. As Jo Vergunst explains in Chapter 8, they are *textured*. Joining him on his walks in the city of Aberdeen and the surrounding countryside, we become aware of the delicate footwork by which people negotiate the minor hazards of textured ground, and of the trips and slips that threaten to lay them low. Hardwearing surfaces such as of gravel, bedrock, cobblestone or asphalt are unmarked by this footwork, though they may be gradually eroded by it. Paths that have been worn in vegetation through the regular passage of feet, as on a grassy meadow, are revealed not as an accumulation of prints but in the stunted or bent growth of trampled plant stems. Actual, distinct footprints show up most clearly in surfaces that, being soft and malleable, are easily impressed, such as of snow, sand, mud or moss. Yet precisely because surfaces of this kind do not readily hold their form, such prints tend to be relatively ephemeral. Snow may be covered by further falls or may eventually melt away, sand may be sculpted anew by the wind or washed by the tide, mud may be dissolved by the rain, and moss may grow over again. Footprints thus have a temporal existence, a duration, which is bound to the very dynamics of the landscape to which they belong: to the cycles of organic growth and decay, of weather, and of the seasons. As Kenneth Olwig argues in Chapter 6, the landscape of inhabitants should be compared not to a stage that they perform *upon* but to a tapestry *within* which their own lives are interwoven. Footprints are part of the weave.

In all these ways – in their texture, their temporality and their literal embeddedness in a landscape of habitation – footprints differ from stamps. Perhaps, then, they should be likened to inscriptions, to lines traced in a surface rather than stamped upon it. This, after all, is how handwriting is distinguished from print: whereas in printing there is no relation between the technically effective gesture and the graphic forms it serves to deliver, on a manuscript the letter, word or character is revealed as the actual trace of a gestural movement of the hand. Yet here again, footprints differ. One can read a pedestrian movement from footprints, as one can a manual gesture from the written line (Ingold 2004, 333). But whereas the writing hand with its inscribing tool glides across the surface, leaving a sinuous mark, the treading foot falls upon it so as to leave a dent with a certain outline and surface conformation. It is from these latter clues that the detective or tracker can 'read' the movements and possible intentions of previous passers-by. Footprints are, in short, im*pressions* rather than in*scriptions*, and the movement they register is one of changing pressure distributions at the interface between the body and the ground. The sensory experience of such pressure is commonly described as touch. For this reason, as Vergunst points out, ground texture is intrinsically linked to tactility.

Just as word follows word along a line of text, however, so print follows print along a track. In both cases it is from reading the marks in sequence, rather than inspecting each individually, that the narrative thread unfolds. The analogy between narrative writing and walking is indeed a beguiling one. Michel de Certeau describes writing as 'an itinerant, progressive and regulated practice', or in a nutshell, as a 'walk' (1984, 134). Rebecca Solnit, taking up the same theme, argues that narrative writing is closely bound up with walking precisely because, just as with following footsteps, it allows one to read the words of someone – the author – who has gone before (Solnit 2001, 72). Whether reading words or following footsteps, however, the narrative trail is revealed on the surface as a series of discontinuous marks or imprints rather than a continuous line. On paper, written words are separated by spaces, as are footprints on the ground. Yet although the traces are discontinuous, the movement they register is a continuous one. Even with a cursive script, handwriters have to lift the pen from time to time from the paper surface, between words and sometimes between letters. So too, walkers have to lift their feet between steps. But the writer does not cease to write on lifting the pen, nor does the walker cease to walk on lifting each foot, alternately, from the ground. Nor, for that matter, does the singer or storyteller cease his recitation every time he pauses for breath. 'Stories walk', writes John Berger, 'like animals and men. And their steps are not only between narrated events but between each sentence, sometimes each word. Every step is a stride over something not said' (Berger 1982, 284-5).

Stories on foot

But this leaves us with a tricky question. If, with Berger, we compare narrative writing or oral storytelling to pedestrian walking, then does every footfall correspond to a word or to a space between words? Are footprints akin to words or to punctuation? Originally, punctuation was introduced into written texts in order to assist their oral delivery, to show where the narrator could pause for breath (Parkes 1992). Does every step, then, correspond to a sounded word or to a silent inhalation? Is the narrative of the walk revealed in the footprints of the walker, or does it fall through the spaces between them, as spoken words fall through the spaces between successive intakes of breath? Consider a concrete instance. From her vantage point in the church belltower, high above the village of Bubión in Andalusia, Spain, Katrín Lund (Chapter 7) is watching the annual procession of San Sebastian in which a statue of the saint is carried around the village along a circuitous route that begins and ends at the church square. Villagers tell of how the statue was returned to the village following its absence during the Spanish Civil War. Then, too, it had been carried in procession from a neighbouring village where, in the panic of the war, the statue was found to have been mislaid. The story of the statue, however, is not yet over, which is why villagers themselves do not call it a story but simply 'what people say'. And what people say – the *narration* – is continually carried onwards not just in their spoken words but in their pacing feet which, in the saint's annual fiesta, carry the statue itself, onwards through and around the village. The procession, in short, does not *re-enact* a story that is already finished, but rather *keeps it going*. And in so doing, it momentarily fuses or brings into phase the otherwise divergent and unsynchronized life trajectories of individual participants into a unified tale of belonging to this place.

Lund, on this occasion, is not at street level with the procession but assisting three companions with the task of ringing the church bells. The bells ring while feet walk, and when the procession pauses, or reaches its climax back in the square, the bells fall silent. Are the bells, then, the footsteps of the saint, sounding in the air as human feet, in unison, tread the ground? If every word of a story, like every peal of a bell, corresponded to a footfall, then what would the story sound like? In her account of the Batek, Lye provides an example. Walking and talking, she observes, are inseparable for the Batek. Here, an old man recounts a walk he made to visit a sick grandson: ' … *and I walked, walked, walked, I thought. I thought, thought, thought in my mind, I walked. I walked, walked, walked, I thought. I thought …* '. Where, as in this example, word follows word as foot follows foot, what is passed over is everything about where the man has been, what incidents occurred or what he observed along the way, and what thoughts were going through his mind: everything, in brief, that would comprise a narrative. This man's talking is like the pealing of bells. His breathing is voiced as words, while his actual narrative remains silent and unspoken: it lies in the spaces in between the words he utters. In Bubión, likewise, the events of the story unfold in the spaces between the peals of the bells, and it is precisely when the bells fall silent that the most climactic events occur.

All this is not to question the analogy between walking and storytelling or narrative. It is merely to observe that there is far more to walking than what is registered on the ground in the monotonous tread of feet. But by the same token, to concentrate exclusively on the spaces in between would yield an equally reductive account, as Tim Edensor shows in Chapter 9. We find him walking around in the ruins of abandoned industrial buildings. The ruin offers a labyrinthine tangle of pathways through what was once an intensely regulated space, in which normal entrances and exits such as doorways are often blocked, while openings appear in broken walls and windows, and the fallen beams of collapsed ceilings rather than staircases allow access to higher levels. As he improvises a path through the rubble, Edensor is accosted by a barrage of tactile, auditory and olfactory as well as visual sensations, triggering a jumble of alarms and surprises, memories and feelings. Narrative writing, he argues, can never capture more than a tiny proportion of the sensuality, affectivity, materiality and entropy of such a walk. Although the ruin may represent an extreme case, it highlights what he takes to be a general limitation of the narrative form. A purely verbal account of events or observations along a walk can convey little or nothing of the embodied experience of the walker, from which they have been abstracted for the purposes of the narrative plot. It is important to bear in mind, however, that just as there is more to walking than the iteration of footsteps, so there is more to narration than the concatenation of words. If the elements of narrative fall through the gaps between the walker's steps, there is a contrary tendency for the bodily experience of the storyteller or writer to fall through the intervals between words. In practice, the storyteller harnesses the power of the voice and lungs to deliver a performance no less visceral and muscular than that of walking. Nor should our familiarity with words as they appear on the printed page or the computer screen lead us to forget the deeply sensual, embodied and improvisatory effort of writing by hand, the sheer physical effort involved, and the expressivity of the inscribed lines themselves, quite apart from the words written in them (Ingold 2007, 146).

Walking with non-humans

Human beings are not the only inhabitants of the urban industrial landscape. The city teems with non-human forms of animal life, from dogs, cats, foxes and rodents to birds, insects and spiders. Apart from domestic animals with which urban dwellers knowingly share their homes, these non-humans are normally sequestered in concealed or confined spaces where they do not significantly impinge on everyday human lives. In ruins, however, they have the upper hand. To walk through a ruin, as Edensor did, is at once to recognize the limitations of ordinary bipedal locomotion and to admit this modality of movement as just one of a much broader range, more often on four feet than two, by which the legs are deployed alongside other limbs in creeping, crawling, climbing and burrowing over and under the crumbling infrastructure of industrial society. Indeed Edensor's account has much in common with Lye's of moving through the rainforest, and it would probably not be far-fetched to regard the ruin as the rainforest's urban equivalent. In both environments ground can give way underfoot, debris can trip you up, and whatever you might cling to for support is liable to come crashing down along with everything to which it is attached. Getting around under these conditions frequently involves copying, so far as is practically feasible, modalities of movement routinely employed by other creatures, and in so doing, perceiving the environment in ways similar to theirs.

Among hunting and gathering people such as the Batek and the Tłįchǫ, it is generally acknowledged that successful tracking calls for a precise understanding of the way the target animal moves about, and of how these movements mark the ground. To anticipate what the animal will do the hunter has to move like it, and therefore to perceive the world as it does; to reconstruct what it has done, he has to be able to read back from its traces to the movements that gave rise to them. In this way, Kenneth Olwig (Chapter 6) suggests, hunters and gatherers develop a feel for the land that is mediated as much by the feet of the animals they follow as by their own. And if this is true of hunters, then it is even more so of pastoralists who ordinarily walk *with* their animals in their practice of herding. Through an etymological excursion into the possessive verb 'to have' and its cognates, Olwig finds a link with the herding of sheep. As they roam the hill pastures, sheep are said to bond with the land. By way of their four-footed movement, they *heft* (or *haft*) onto it. These pastures, by extension, are known as the 'heft' of the farm, and so people will say of themselves that they are 'hefted' to the land to which they belong and that, by the same token, belongs to them. It is a belonging, however, that is established primarily through the quadrupedal perambulations of the sheep, and only derivatively through the movements of the human bipeds who herd them. Every shepherd knows that to manage a flock one must be able to see the world, as it were, through the eyes of the sheep, to understand their rhythms of grazing on the move, and to be alert to their moods and motivations.

Pernille Gooch (Chapter 5) recalls her experience, from three decades ago, of herding goats in the hills and woods around her home in northern Sweden. As soon as the animals became restless, she would call them to her and lead the way to a new spot, with the swift-footed goats following behind. But she could do this only because she had usurped the position of the she-goat that would otherwise have led the flock, becoming – at least in the eyes of her caprine charges – something of a goat herself. But when we meet her some twenty years later, on the trail of the Van Gujjars of the Central Indian Himalayas as they wend their way, at the end of the summer, on their annual migration from mountain pastures near the tree line to the forests in the foothills where they will spend the winter, everything seems, to her, back to front. The Van Gujjars are herders of large, ponderous and extremely slow-moving buffalo. You cannot, as Gooch discovered, take a buffalo for a walk. The animals know the way, and will go at their own speed. They are in the lead. The herders can only follow along behind, on the tails of their animals, adjusting their pace to that of their charges not by reducing the length of their stride but by increasing its duration, as though walking in slow motion. Who then is walking, and who being walked? Are the buffaloes, as they make their way down from the mountains, taking their minders for a walk?

With such a close, centaurian synergy of human and beast, it is difficult to assign agency unequivocally to one side or the other. The Van Gujjars on migration become, in effect, 'buffalo-people' – human-animal hybrids whose combined feet and hooves move in unison and whose perception is attuned to features of the world of common concern to such compound beings. Their walking, then, manifests a compound agency: it is what 'buffalo-people' do. On migration, however, the buffaloes with their herders move ahead of the rest of the household, including women, children and pack animals (bullocks and ponies). Moving more quickly, the latter can catch up later at the next halt. In these household movements, people of all ages, along with the animals, walk side by side. Each, in this case, is a separate agent; each walks. But the pace of walking is adjusted to that of the slowest member of the group, whether human or animal. In these adjustments we can see not only that walking is a social activity, but also that the social relations of walking crosscut the divide between humans and animals, and between the pacing of two feet and of four. The same can be readily observed of any domestic group in a Western society – including members of all ages and statures, along with the family dog – as they stroll at leisure. Sometimes they are physically connected: the child gripped by an adult's hand, the dog held on a leash. So long as they walk in harmony, mutually 'tuning' their steps of different amplitude, the grip is relaxed and the leash slack. As in the case of adult and child described earlier, however, so with human and dog: tautness in the leash is an index of conflicting agencies as first one and then the other, digging in the heels or leaning backwards to retain stability, is induced to step forward in order to remain upright. The balance of power, in this case, can swing like a see-saw as first the human and then the animal gains the upper hand. Each, alternately, 'walks' the other.

Crossing the road

The Van Gujjars are no longer free to choose the routes of their transhumance. Their room for manoeuvre is tightly curtailed by a government that wants to see them settled and to that end is intent on putting ever more hurdles in their path. They are forced to take their buffaloes along roads now busy with trucks and tourist vehicles whose noise and lights can scare the animals. Roads are dangerous. Along them, powerful people move in their motorized vehicles. To walk the roads, with feet and hooves, amounts for the Van Gujjars to a form of political resistance. For the Akhoe Hai//om of Namibia, prior to independence when the country was administered by South Africa, anyone seen crossing a road, or whose tracks remained as evidence, risked being shot. As Widlok explains (Chapter 4), the South African army had cut a grid of roads through the territory, in order to protect land occupied by White settlers from infiltration by fighters of the independence movement SWAPO. These roads served a dual purpose. On the one hand, they allowed the rapid deployment of troops into the area; on the other, they functioned as clearings in the bush that would expose anyone attempting to cross and thus deter them from doing so. They are, like all military roads, lines of occupation. Riding roughshod over the meandrine lines of habitation that indigenous people thread in their everyday lives, they both *open up* land to the forces of colonization, channelling the import of personnel into the area and the export of resources from it, and, at the same time, *close it off* to its inhabitants, for whom they are not so much thoroughfares as boundaries. Such roads, in short, are just as much a way of keeping inhabitants out as of bringing occupants in.

Generally speaking, powerful colonizers ride rather than going about on foot, as inhabitants usually do. In the past, as Widlok reminds us, they rode on horseback or in ox-drawn wagons, or were even carried by servants on a palanquin. Nowadays they use motor vehicles such as the ubiquitous jeep or truck. It would however be a mistake to conclude that colonization is invariably conducted by vehicle, and habitation invariably on foot. The Roman occupation of Britain, for example, was undertaken principally by pedestrian means, along dead-straight roads specially constructed for the purpose. However the footwork of colonial occupation is of a peculiar kind, namely the *march*. Characteristic of marching is that the body is propelled on a predetermined course by a mechanical movement that is unresponsive to any kind of interaction with the environment that opens up along the way. Soldiers on the march are expected to keep to the steady beat of a drum, but not to look where they are going. Before their unswerving gaze and in their deafened ears the world passes by unnoticed and unheard. In this regard their pedestrian movement contrasts markedly with that of inhabitants whose gait, pace and posture respond with sensitivity and precision to a close and continual perceptual monitoring of the country through which they pass and which offers them sustenance for life. But if colonists do not always ride, nor do inhabitants go about only on foot. They may use vehicles of many kinds, from bicycles to automobiles. They ride these vehicles, however, as often off-road as on them, and in ways that are as improvisational as they are inventive in answering to the ever-changing conditions of their surroundings (Ingold 2007, 78-9).

Whereas occupants march along roads, inhabitants more usually step across them – if they can without being run over or shot at. For both human and non-human inhabitants, the business of life lies not at end of the road but in the lands on either side of it, and in carrying on they may have no alternative but to cross over from time to time. They do so at considerable risk to life and limb, and have no reason to linger there for any longer than necessary. For all kinds of creatures, great and small, the road can be a killing field. For parents and teachers with responsibilities towards children, as Curtis shows in Chapter 10, the road is perceived primarily as a place of peril where safety has to take precedence over all other considerations. The road itself is a desert; nothing can live or grow there. Uncovered by ground vegetation and unprotected by bushes or trees, the road can be a bleak, open space: tiring to walk on, prone to mudslides and with its own micro-climate characterized by extremes of wind, solar radiation, aridity or frost. This is especially true of a road that has been surfaced, such as with asphalt. While in the eyes of the transport engineer the point of surfacing a road is to enable it to withstand the impact of the heavy traffic that rolls on top, for inhabitants it may seem to have another purpose altogether, more repressive than enabling, which is to prevent any growth from below. Life binds the substances of the earth with the medium of air, on exposure to sunlight. Thus to *surface* the earth – to separate it from air by means of an impenetrable barrier – is tantamount to the suppression of life itself.

Of course, roads of occupation and paths of habitation are not always as starkly opposed as in the sands of Namibia or the Himalayan forests. Over time, paths can become roads and vice versa. In Britain, for example, the routes of many modern trunk roads follow the byways of previous inhabitants while, conversely, residual fragments of roads built long ago for the purposes of occupation are frequently incorporated by rural inhabitants into countryside walks. In the city, the layout of streets has often emerged organically, and over a considerable period, as an irregular mesh of lines of habitation, and may differ only in degree from the more planned and arterial roads that connect the city to its hinterlands. Moreover moves are afoot in many European cities to re-establish parity between the lines of occupation and habitation, or more simply, between roads and streets, through policies of pedestrian empowerment. Sonia Lavadinho and Yves Winkin (Chapter 11) have been mingling with pedestrians in the city of Geneva, which is currently in the process of implementing a Pedestrian Masterplan intended to promote walking within the urban environment. One key to the plan is the establishment of so-called 'encounter areas', in which pedestrians, motorists and other users of civic space jostle on equal terms, finding a way through the throng, as pedestrians have always done with one another, through the ceaseless negotiation of their right of way with oncomers from all directions. In an encounter area there is no longer any need for such artefacts as pavements and zebra-crossings, designed to segregate the flow of pedestrian and vehicular traffic, whether spatially or temporally. There is probably greater safety, and certainly greater enjoyment, in a free-for-all where no-one can move much faster than walking pace, and where everyone – whatever their mode of locomotion – has to keep their eyes and ears open for everyone else.

Collecting life

In a densely populated encounter area, civic space is transformed from a static array of geometrically circumscribed zones and structures into something more like a whirlpool of humanity-on-the-move. For the individual pedestrian, surrounded on all sides by the ebb and flow of the crowd, it takes on the character of a labyrinth. The wonder is how people routinely manage to find a way through the labyrinth without becoming hopelessly lost and disoriented. Ray Lucas (Chapter 12) went to Tokyo, one of the most crowded cities in the world, to find out, and we can join him there as he attempts to navigate the vast subway interchange station of Shinjuku. Having walked counter to the flow, both in and out of rush hours, Lucas recalls his own movements from a body-centred perspective, initially by comparing his walking to dance. This allows him to record these bodily movements by means of standardized dance notation. The record reveals a number of recurrent motifs, which he can then re-describe using the conventions of architectural drawing. Each motif takes the form of a corridor whose lineal axis corresponds to the passage of time. In this way Lucas is able to reconstruct the actual architectural experience of individual subway walkers as they deal with the movements of crowds, the distractions of advertising and signage, and the many obstacles placed in their path. Instead of regarding walking as a practice of occupation, channelled within the confines of a predetermined architectural space, he can show us how for the inhabitant of the subway, walking is itself a practice of architecture that generates its own forms, out of which emerges the totality of the labyrinth. Corresponding to nothing that could ever be shown on an official plan or map of the station, these are the forms through which people really move as they make their everyday journeys around the city.

It was in this labyrinthine form that the city also appeared, and appealed, to the flâneur, much celebrated both in the poetry of Charles Baudelaire and subsequently in the writings of the philosopher and critic, Walter Benjamin. A wanderer who impresses the byways of the city with his feet, the flâneur finds in its passing details an endless source of fascination. The character he performs, as Benjamin observes, is that of the detective. With his eyes and ears open and alert to any fortuitous but revealing incident, his interest in every little clue to the myriad lives around him resembles that of the small child on his way to school. As Curtis shows us in Chapter 10, there is a world of difference between urban children's unsupervised explorations and their experience of being marched in crocodile formation from point to point, in their organized excursions on the city streets. Likewise, the *flâneur* is the exact opposite of the marcher on parade who, as he strides along, sees and hears nothing of what is going on. So, too, in contrast to Edensor's (Chapter 9) depiction of the regulated, signposted and monitored circulation of pedestrians in the modern city, with its walkways, conveyors and surveillance cameras, Lavadinho and Winkin (Chapter 11) describe the delight that urban dwellers take in the incorporation of little places of their own – a garden, a bench, or a bridge over a stream – where they may linger for a moment to wonder, to dream, to remember and possibly to be astonished by the unexpected. These places are not destinations or sites of special interest to be made the occasion of a separate visit. They are but resting places along the paths that people take on their everyday walks around their homes and offices: places to pause and take stock.

As a collector and recollector of the passing incidents of life, the flâneur bears comparison with another pedestrian character to whom we are introduced, in Chapter 13, by Hayden Lorimer and Katrín Lund. This character is the 'Munro-bagger'. But the things the Munro-bagger collects are not small or ephemeral. They are *mountains* – or more specifically, summits in Scotland rising at least three thousand feet above sea level. Every mountain climbed is another Munro in the bag, and the ambition of the true enthusiast is to bag them all. Like the *flâneur*, the Munroist collects things with his feet rather than his hands, that is, by *going about*. Mountains can be collected in any order, under all sorts of weather conditions, yielding a trail that, were it mapped out, would be as haphazard, labyrinthine and contingent upon circumstance as that of the *flâneur*, and, if retold, as replete with the apparently trivial and the incidental. The parallel ends there, however. For Munroists are nothing if not methodical. Though their ambition is driven more by national than global ideals, they otherwise resemble the confluencers described by Widlok in that the summits they seek are picked out by an arbitrary criterion that nevertheless carries the imprimatur of scientific measurement: here of altitude rather than of latitude and longitude. The bagging of a Munro resembles the registration of a confluence, and a collection of Munros offers an 'organised sampling' of views of the Scottish Highlands not unlike what the collection of confluences is supposed to offer of the entire terrestrial world.

However as Lorimer and Lund show, although in one sense every conquered mountaintop can be 'brought back' and catalogued alongside the others as a kind of trophy, in a logbook or on a wallchart, in the pedestrian practice of Munroists themselves collections are not so much assembled as grown. In so far as they are experienced and remembered rather than merely logged and tabulated, summits are not just objects but *topics*, each a way-station along a path where walkers can pause to rest, relax, wander about, chat with companions, and take stock of their achievements so far. They are, in that sense, rather similar in function – though entirely different in scale, accessibility and the physical demands placed on walkers – to the little places of enchantment placed around the city, described by Lavadinho and Winkin (Chapter 11). Collecting on foot, for Munroists, is a kind of gathering or 'pulling together': at once a gathering of narratives into a coherent story of personal growth and fulfilment, and a gathering of the peaks of which they tell into a seamless landscape. Standing on the final summit, and viewing others he has climbed arrayed all around, the Munroist has the satisfaction of seeing a lifetime's effort laid out in the terrain. His 'collection' is none other than the landscape itself. As they collect their mountains, Munroists collect themselves.

Coming and going

Compressed into the preceding pages are many lives of walking, paced out at greater length in the following chapters. Setting out from the first steps of infancy we have gone to school and walked with the class, listened to the stories of elders, followed their trails and left footprints in our wake, clambered through ruins and slithered in the rainforest, joined a religious procession, herded sheep, goats and buffalo, tracked across sands and scaled mountains, wandered city streets and breasted rush-hour crowds, and now – older, wiser, and perhaps a little foot-weary – we are coming home. Not that there is any finishing line. Just as no definite point marks where we start to walk, so there is no point, on homecoming, at which we come to a stop. Rather, in an almost exact inversion of setting out, the stride is gradually shortened to a shuffle, and as the body loses its forward momentum there is no longer any certainty of follow-through from one step to the next. Each becomes a separate movement. Indeed if setting out recapitulates in brief the development of walking in infancy, then coming home presages the decline of walking late in life. Barring accident, older people do not, of an instant, stop walking. However as muscles waste and the body's centre of gravity consequently rises, old age generally brings reductions in both strength and stability. With every step becoming more tentative, auxiliary means have to be improvised for getting around, often involving the co-option of sticks, frames and other people for support. Time slows, and attention lowers from the horizon to the ever nearer at hand. Gradually and imperceptibly, pedestrian movement drifts into the grey area between walking and non-walking commonly described by such terms as 'tottering', 'doddering' or even – in the flagrant infantilization of old age characteristic of modern Western society – 'toddling'.

Growing older, however, is a lifelong process, and people have continually to readjust the patterns and styles of their walking in order to accommodate the changes undergone not only by their own developing bodies but also by the bodies of those, including young children or the elderly, whom they walk *with*. It is not as though these adjustments were limited to early childhood and old age. They go on all the time. One has constantly, as it were, to go back to the beginning, learning and relearning to walk along the way, in order to cope with ever-changing bodily capacities and environmental conditions. For the long walk of life is not a unidirectional progress from start to finish, or from cradle to grave. It does not go *from* A to B. With no discernible beginning or ending, it rather goes *around* A, B, C, D, E and any number of further places, in a circuitous movement. Leaving any place, in such a movement, is part of the process of returning to it. Far from leading inexorably from the past on a one-way march into the future, it is a movement that keeps itself going by picking up and carrying onward the trails of earlier life. Since to follow a trail is to remember how it goes, making one's way in the present is itself a recollection of the past. Thus every move forwards, as Lye reminds us (Chapter 2), takes one back to old haunts and pathways, the past and history.

To the extent that onward movement is itself a return, walkers are able to resolve what Widlok, in Chapter 4, calls the 'coming is going' dilemma, namely that to turn towards some place is necessarily to turn away from some place else. The dilemma, Widlok shows, concerns not just the walker but other people as well, for it implies a renunciation of relationships with those remaining in the place whence one has turned, and the initiation of relationships with those in the place whither one is bound. Granted that no-one can be everywhere at once, the dilemma can never be fully resolved. Nevertheless, by leaving in every place a token of continuing presence that carries the promise of eventual return, a person can turn his or her back on others and head towards them at the same time. In a roundabout movement, as Widlok points out, there can be no distinction – no marked point of separation – between 'going out' and 'coming back'. People whose lives are caught up in such a movement, including most of us for most of the time, are neither coming nor going but perpetually 'coming and going'. For example in the regions they inhabit, the Van Gujjars described by Gooch (Chapter 5) are known as 'coming-going people' (*ana-jana lok*), as they make their ways back and forth between summer and winter pastures and, at each end of the transhumance orbit, between the camp and the spots where the animals will graze. These latter movements are to the main seasonal migration like the loose, frayed ends of a single knotted rope. During the winter months in the forest, the buffaloes feed overnight on the leaves of branches lopped from trees, starting with trees furthest from the camp and then coming ever closer as the season progresses. Every evening and morning, animals go and come between the camp and the lopped trees, guided by the sounds of human voices. The coming and going of both human and buffalo feet, as Gooch shows, creates an intricate web of paths, fanning out from the camp into the forest.

For the Batek, too, the coming and going of camp life – in Lye's words 'a constantly iterated process of walking here, there and everywhere' – enacts in microcosm a more expansive pattern of movement. Thus in their foraging expeditions, people will go fairly directly to the furthest point from the camp, and then wend their ways back along innumerable detours as they search for and harvest the bounty of the forest. As Lye explains, both coming and going are combined in the Batek term *lew*, which means both 'to leave' and 'to arrive'. Yet the confidence the Batek display in finding their ways through the tangle of the forest is laced with uncertainty. Even when following a path, every step forward is a step into the unknown. As in a labyrinth, the path may turn out to be deceptive, to come to a dead-end, or to lead one astray. One may leave and *not* arrive. Thus the Batek are not unafraid of the forest. Fear and confidence are, for them as for people everywhere, two sides of the same coin. Occasionally people *do* get lost, just as they sometimes fall sick, especially if they are overconfident and fail to observe proper precautions or watch where they are going as carefully as they should. In Chapter 8, Vergunst describes what it felt like to become lost while walking with his companions in the hills of north-east Scotland. It was an unsettling experience. Life seemed more tenuous than usual, and the ground less firm underfoot. Losing the way is like falling asleep: amounting to a temporary loss of consciousness, you can have no awareness of it at the moment when it happens. By the time any kind of awareness dawns, that moment is already long past. And what if you never wake? What if you never find your way back to your walk of life? In an uncertain world, the only thing of which each of us can be sure is that we will eventually die. As we walk through life, with greater or lesser degrees of confidence, we do so with care and concern, and with the knowledge that the ultimate question is not *whether* we will eventually lose the way, but *when*. But even as we mourn those whom we have lost, they live on in the memories of those who follow in their footsteps. As one journey ends, others begin, and life goes on.

References

Berger, J. (1982), 'Stories', in Berger and Mohr (eds) (1982), *Another Way of Telling* (New York: Vintage Books).

Bourdieu, P. (1977), *Outline of a Theory of Practice*, trans. R. Nice (Cambridge: Cambridge University Press).

Certeau, M. de (1984), *The Practice of Everyday Life* (Berkeley: University of California Press).

Csordas, T. (1990), 'Embodiment as a Paradigm for Anthropology', *Ethos* 18, 5-47.

Engels, F. (1934), *Dialectics of Nature*, trans. C. Dutton (Moscow: Progress).

Ingold, T. (2004), 'Culture on the Ground: The World Perceived Through the Feet', *Journal of Material Culture* 9:3, 315-40.

—— (2007), *Lines: A Brief History* (London: Routledge).

Jackson, M. (ed.) (1996), *Things as They Are: New Directions in Phenomenological Anthropology* (Bloomington and Indianapolis: Indiana University Press).

Lee, J. and Ingold, T. (2006), 'Fieldwork on Foot: Perceiving, Routing, Socializing', in Coleman, S. and Collins, P. (eds) (2006), *Locating the Field: Space, Place and Context in Anthropology* (Oxford: Berg).

Marcus, G. (1998), *Ethnography Through Thick and Thin* (Princeton: Princeton University Press).

Mauss, M. (1979), *Sociology and Psychology: Essays*, trans. B. Brewster (London: Routledge and Kegan Paul).

Parkes, M. (1992), *Pause and Effect: An Introduction to the History of Punctuation in the West* (Aldershot: Scolar Press).

Sheets-Johnstone, M. (1999), *The Primacy of Movement* (Amsterdam: John Benjamins).

Solnit, R. (2001), *Wanderlust: A History of Walking* (London and New York: Verso).

Wolff, M. (1973), 'Notes on the Behaviour of Pedestrians', in Birenbaum, A. and Sagarin, E. (eds) (1973), *People and Places: The Sociology of the Familiar* (New York: Praeger).

Chapter 2

Before a Step Too Far: Walking with Batek Hunter-Gatherers in the Forests of Pahang, Malaysia

Lye Tuck-Po

This chapter explores a seeming paradox in the walking practices of the Batek of Malaysia.[1] They are forest-dwelling hunter-gatherers who, at least in Pahang state where I have done all my work, are largely mobile. By 'mobile' I mean that the Batek are always on the move, whether from camp to forest and back again in the course of a day's activities, from camp to camp as they shift locations around their traditional territories, or from forest to the outside as they seek purchased goods, work opportunities, or excitement in local villages and small towns (Lye 1997; 2004; 2005). Even in a sedentary settlement, they move sleeping places and houses around as they do in a forest camp (Lye 1997, 390-428). If anyone can be said to have a walking life, they can.

The paradox is this. On the one hand, the Batek are confident and even proud of their ability to make their way around the forest. They walk with the assurance of people who are comfortably at ease in their home ambience. On the other hand, listening to Batek talk about their emotions, what is most commonly voiced is fear (*?əɲtəɲ*)[2] – of specific dangers in the forest, and of particular kinds of walking experiences – giving the impression that fear is everywhere around and even inside them as well. How, then, can we reconcile these expressions of fear and confidence? Is fear a deterrent? If it does deter the Batek from walking in the forest, then it is operating very subtly indeed! Walking is one of the primary means for interacting with the forest, but it also engenders an awareness of its dangers. Where walking takes the body forward, fear draws it back, and it is this tug between opposing directions of movement that characterizes the practices of hunting and gathering.

The problematic I have set up implies an analytical disjunction between body and mind, knowing and fearing, self and environment, and coming and going. My

1   The research on which this paper is based was funded variously by grants from the Wenner-Gren Foundation for Anthropological Research, the East-West Center, the John D. and Catherine T. MacArthur Foundation, and the Japanese Ministry of Education. I would like to thank Bion Griffin for sharing insights on the walking practices of Agta hunter-gatherers of the Philippines. Finally, I thank my Batek hosts, from the very young to the very old, for showing me what a difficult accomplishment walking is.
2   The word is both a transitive and an intransitive verb but is not, to my knowledge, a noun.

ethnography, however, suggests that this is a false disjunction, or that the dichotomies at least need revision. I will nevertheless hold to it, at least provisionally, in order to clarify what walking in the rainforest is all about and what it means to these hunter-gatherers. Like many indigenous peoples, the Batek are excellent ethnologists (compare Benjamin 1966 on the Temiar) and so, following their habitual way of stressing a point, I shall use my own experiences for illustration and comparison.

In step with the forest

Lest I give the impression of isolation and remoteness, I should first point out that Batek are primarily lowland peoples, and much of the remaining lowland forest in Peninsular Malaysia is fragmented and bordered by roads. In my experience Batek camps are always within walking distance of a Malay village where supplies may be bought and jobs may be offered.[3] Batek walking practices include visits to such villages and Batek paths often join onto logging and access roads, village paths, and surfaced roads (Lye 2005). The largest unbroken tract of Batek forest lies within the national park, Taman Negara (4,343 sq. km) – most of which sits astride their traditional territories – and there Batek and tourist trails often intersect. While acknowledging the implications of landscape fragmentation, in this chapter I am most concerned with what happens *in* the forest, which is what the Batek know most about.

Some 120 years ago, Miklucho-Maclay offered the following description of the Batek of Kelantan. It is still largely accurate:

> Knowing the direction in which he is to go and keeping it in view, he tries to find out the lighter places in the wood. Without breaking them, he bends aside with his hand the younger trees, which he cannot avoid; he stoops or creeps below the larger ones. He will never tear off or cut away a liana hanging in his way, he prefers holding it in his hand and crawling under it; and in spite of this constant stooping, creeping, picking his way, and running zigzag, he advances with great rapidity (Miklucho-Maclay 1878, 212-13).

Walking remains the primary mode of locomotion in the tropical forest.[4] My first question concerns what this entails – and demands. (A corollary question would be whether and how walking in the tropical forest is different from any other kind of walking, but I am not qualified to address this directly.) One response is to think of walking practices as a set of culturally developed adjustments to constraints of climate, environment, and geography. However, this approach suggests that the 'culture' of people is needed to overcome the 'nature' of the forest and risks enshrining an image of the forest as 'ancient', 'primeval', or 'pristine' jungle untouched by humans, and of human interaction with it as disturbance that is bound to destabilize the ecology and destroy the 'wilderness' (for problems with this model, see for

---

3   Malays comprise the ethnic and political majority in Malaysia. For more on the Batek-Malay relationship, see Lye (2004, 102-10).

4   The prospect of walking *in* the tropical forest – and temporary relief from the urban environment – is of course a major source of appeal for tourists and trekkers.

example Botkin 1990; Cronon 1996; Dove, Sajise, and Doolittle 2005; Ellen and Fukui 1996). Current orthodoxy stresses that local communities have a long history of manipulating natural vegetation (Latinis 1999; Yen 1989): such disturbances are often integral to the maintenance of forest cover (Ellen 1998; Fairhead and Leach 1996; Rambo 1979). For example, the Batek monitor and intervene in the life process of favoured food-sources like wild yams and seasonal fruits, return to harvest upon regrowth and regeneration, and track all-round availability of supplies by following each other's movements through the landscape (Lye 2004). They alter the environment, improve its productivity on their behalf, and 'look back' to evaluate the effects of their predation on biological populations. Another kind of disturbance, often overshadowed by more dramatic instances but as old as human history (Tilley 1994), is that brought about through millennia of human movement: the creation of paths in the forest. I will start from here.

The Batek *halbəw* is a central cultural symbol. Walking is not possible without it. Whether one is following an established trail or going off-trail (for example as a shortcut), one follows the *halbəw*: it is both path and route, both the way followed and the way *of* movement. Concepts of path and movement are closely related in other ways (Lye 2004, 59). For example, the same path will become a (*halbəw*) *cəniwəh* on an upward slope (derived from the verb *cwəh* 'to ascend') and a (*halbəw*) *pənisar* on the downward slope (derived from *sar* 'to descend'). The infixation in the verbs turns them into nouns: or, to express this differently, the movement creates the path. Following from this, the path is not just a means of getting from here to there, nor is walking just about covering the distance.

Let us consider the most straightforward example of a Batek walk: from camp (*hayã?*) to forest (*həp*). *Cip ba-həp* (literally, 'go to-forest') is one of the most common tropes of everyday life; it is what people normally expect to do when they wake up in the morning. But the preamble to such a walk can be most tortuous (and torturous to the impatient).

30/12/95, Taŋuy / Tələm

I was in the lean-to watching the morning bustle. This morning, ?eyCəncəŋ's[5] *hayã?* was the focal point for some of the men. Could hear some discussion. ?eyNon walked out. ?eyGk walks in. Kayə? and Bəhi?, etc, come over. They walk in. Finally, the group leaves: ?eyCəncəŋ, ?eyN0n, ?eyPayol, Bəhi?.

I go over to na?Non's. The women urge me to go over to the village with them. I'm reluctant. They say they're afraid of *gob ?o? ŋaw* (mad Malay woman) and I'm brave. Finally I agree and go over to collect my things. Na?Gk [my then host] had already left, having decided to go digging with na?Alor. ?eyGk had also left. When I emerge, ready, the group at na?Non's had already left – had gone over to Taŋuy [the adjoining camp] to wait. I follow. Arrived there 10:20am.

The campsite is full. ?eyGk and ?eyKadoy are fussing over the two chainsaws. ?eyPaliy's sitting around. Na?Gk and na?Alor and their kids to one corner. The *kəradah* [single

---

5   The adults' names are teknonyms. *?ey* means 'father' and *na?* means 'mother'. Thus ?eyAlor and na?Alor are, respectively 'father' and 'mother' of Alor.

women] to another corner. I sit down at na?Gk's old lean-to. I still don't know who's supposed to go where, though I'd thought only na?Non and na?Payol were coming to the shops. The men are going to '*təbɛs te? gob*' (clear-cut Malay field).

Ten minutes later, we set off for the shops. Na?Non, na?Payol, Ciwat, kids. Na?Kadoy was supposed to have come with us, but when we call out to her, she says she's not coming. We had made it to the first turning when we hear more calls behind us. The *kəradah* Non, Yip, and Gol are joining us.

Only after we had got back from our trip did the comings and goings become clear.

Two characteristics of this scene are relevant to my discussion. The first lies in the 'comings and goings': a constantly iterated process of walking here there and everywhere in camp discussing plans and trajectories with campmates and revising them frequently – often spontaneously. This scene is, indeed, a microcosm of movement in Batek society more generally. Every joining of one activity means not joining another, and people may become quite exercised as they evaluate their options and desires (Lye 2004; Widlok this volume). The second characteristic lies in the 'improvisation' (Rosaldo 1993, 109-26) by which events unfold; they do not have the certainties of formal programming and scheduling. Improvisation is the context before a walk, and it affects the context *of* a walk as conversations continue and grievances with folks left behind are expressed in the privacy of the trail. Improvisation also continues along the trail: some people may straggle, some may dart off for a quick try at some other pursuit, the group's desired harvest may not materialize, other stuff may be sighted (or heard), and new opportunities to harvest may appear.

27/09/95, Tom Tabɛn, Taman Negara national park

Fruit collection

10:04am   Left camp. Took the tourist trail to Lata Berkoh. I managed to cross the creek with the narrow bridge though with some help. The pathway follows the Tahan upriver, occasionally we are walking on the bankside. Up one rather steep hill and then it levels off, and another climb downhill. We were leapfrogging tourists – two pairs of men. We feasted off the remains from a previously harvested *payit* tree [Nephelium spp.] then did a circle, walking past an old campsite that's situated on the escarpment close to the Tahan river. Here the path opened up – obviously a well-used trail in the past. The path meets the tourist trail again at the point where the latter ends at the river (tourists using the trail have to cross the river there). We crossed the tourist trail to the other side, and walked a few minutes to get to the *payit* tree. While they started to *tutoh* (lop off the branches), two of the women looked for another tree, that 'people' said were there, but no luck. Two of the women climbed up a smaller tree – tossed down the fruits.

10:11   Stopped for the rest of the group to catch up. Hear sound of tourists at back of us.

11:21	Waiting for Heŋ [only man in the group]. He had lagged behind, probably to try and get an animal (he brought his blowpipe along).
12:00pm	Having finished off the *payit* harvest, we went up the creek – Tom Lawit. Heŋ's gone upriver by himself to look for more trees. We're waiting.
2:00	Collect from a third tree. Still in the same vicinity.
2:20	Return trip starts.
2:29	Stop on the way back.
2:49	Stop for *kapɛs* [unidentified fruit]. Tree is off the trail on the way up the hill. Heŋ climbs up. Women rest. Spot *buloh akar*.[6] We stopped there less than an hour.

By 4-4:30pm   Back at camp.

However assiduously I was noting the time of each of these fragments, I was clearly too engaged in the activities (or too engorged with fruits) to write too much. I wonder now, for example, what was occupying us on that long stretch from noon to 2pm. As I wrote at the end of another fieldnote, 'As usual, I was impressed how easy it was to pass the time in the forest'. I began by scribbling down the characteristics of the trail as we walked purposefully to the first of our planned stops; then, as the day wore on, directions and destinations became muddled as our explorations threw up new options and new activities were thrown into the repertoire (as I recall, the initial statement of intention had been 'let's go look for *payit* fruit'). Time, which I was using as an activity marker, was passing me by. Not the right setting for clear-headed writing!

This note illustrates how forest expeditions tend to proceed: first walk to the farthest point using a series of shortcuts, then begin the search and harvest – which necessitates detours and sideturnings – back in the direction of camp. In this, a complex suite of bodily performances is involved. Along the way, we were (to list some obvious examples from my descriptions) observing, monitoring, remembering, listening, touching, crouching, and climbing (this last without my participation), in addition to stepping on the ground, wading across rivers, pushing vegetation aside, cutting fruit-laden boughs, eating the fruits, navigating the way, orienting ourselves to the camp, the Tahan River, and the stands of fruit trees, and, of course, talking and discussing the fruit harvest. We might have looked ahead most of the time (*birəy*) but we were also scanning the tree-tops (*bilay*, 'to look up') and looking sideways and backwards (*kihley*) for signs of fruits and the fauna associated with them. At least one of us, the blowpipe-ready Heŋ, was also listening and looking hard for the calls and traces of game animals.

Some parts of the trail, especially in overgrown forest, are not easy to remember, and the entire route probably should not be undertaken alone by a first-timer. Even experienced navigators have been known to lose their way. Having done such a

---

6   A multifunctional species of bamboo; it is identified with hillslopes.

trip, though, the experience becomes integrated into one's knowledge of the forest landscape and through 'topographic gossip' (Widlok 1997) into the collective memory of the group. Recall in my note the fruitless search for a second *payit* tree. Information about that tree had come from 'people': rather, '*gən kədəh*' ('they said') it was there. Never mind that the information in this case was faulty in its details. Many expeditions are prompted by such gossip. Talking and walking are inseparable, and this brings me back to my initial point. If walking creates the path and if walking itself is an act of sociality, then can the path have any meaning without the stories of the people using it? Whenever I ask the Batek to talk about the ecology and classification of pathways, the results are not very productive. A little patience, however, and the stories of movements and travels will roll. Paths are social phenomena, and are remembered in relation to social events.

15/09/95, Tərŋin

> Ta?Raŋləs was chattering away beside me. It was pitch black, very late, and I desperately wanted to sleep. But the old man babbled on. Once I jolted awake to hear him say that he had just returned from a trip somewhere, gone to see a child up near Kelantan – his grandson. The child had been sick. What stuck in my head: ... *and I walked, walked, walked, I thought. I thought, thought, thought in my mind, I walked. I walked, walked, walked, I thought. I thought* ... I did not 'catch' what was preoccupying him so. What remains of that evening's talk is the image of walking, and thinking, and walking, a rhythmic joining of place, movement, and thought.

I want to turn now to some linguistic discussion. Though many of the bodily movements I noted above are recognized by distinctive verbs, the entire performance can be labelled *cip bahəp* (go to the forest). The verb *cip*, in turn, means both 'to walk' and 'to go'. Thus walking defines movement. Walking is also associated with *wek* (to come back): *cip ba-həp* and *wek ba-hayã?* (return to camp) are commonly contrasted. As with similar oppositions elsewhere in Batek thought and imagery, the contrast also implies equivalence (Lye 2004, Chapters 3 and 4; Dentan 2002). You cannot come back if you do not go in the first place, nor can you think of one without thinking of the other. The two concepts, coming and going, are joined together in a third verb, *lew*, which has the dual meaning of leaving *and* arriving. Again, one is meaningless without the other; walking to one place implies walking from another (Widlok, this volume). Finally, there is another key identity symbol, the action of *jok*, to move residential location, and signally the camp. The meaning of *jok* suggests one-way movement; it is sometimes contrasted to *ləp*, which is usually associated with resource-harvesting trips that require several days' absence from camp and was defined for me as a move from which there will be a return. However, as Tebu said, even after one has *jok* from one place, one remembers it, one feels longing (*ha?ip*), and accordingly one returns. All of this suggests something important about the phenomenology of walking for Batek, and possibly other hunter-gatherers: it is not really where one goes that is ultimately important; it is where one can return to. Moving forward in time and space is also about moving back – to old camps and pathways, the past, and history.

The year of walking clumsily

My own history with the Batek may give some insight into other aspects of the question I asked earlier: what walking in the tropical forest entails. Like the confluencers described by Widlok (this volume), I will highlight the romance of hardship.

Having begun participant observation before considering that walking might be a research topic in its own right, much of my understanding is by way of introspective and retrospective analysis. One source of insight is quantitative. During the 15½ months of fieldwork in 1995-96,[7] I moved residential locations approximately 80 times (averaging six days per location). Of these moves, maybe one-third were done exclusively on foot; these were short-distance movements within forest bounds. On other occasions we moved to camps farther off, which were more accessible with vehicular transport (the traders' four-wheel drives and lorries). With the Batek, I stayed in at least 32 different campsites and two settlements, averaging about two weeks per location. On my own I also made frequent visits to family in Ipoh or to Kuala Lumpur to deal with official paperwork, and these might require travel by some combination of walking with land and water transport (boats, buses, lorries, cars, taxis, and trains). I had certainly anticipated a lot of movement, but these numbers are astonishing to me. The extensive travelling and walking was not an ordeal at the time (or I would not need statistics to remind me of it), but it did create practical challenges. I will discuss two that *were* prominent: dealing with physical loads and learning to walk competently.

Walking does move us forward in one direction and away from another. Yet the two places must be bridged in some way, otherwise there could be no anthropology. One critical bridge is the stuff that we bring to the field with us; for the student of walking hunter-gatherers, this is a bridge that we must make and learn to unmake. So far I have not seen a fieldwork methods manual that teaches how to do this. It is largely a learn-to-make-do issue. Here was the practical problem: participating in Batek life meant that I had to be as ready to move around as they were, so I had to keep my possessions to the minimum. But I was a *participant observer*, and needed the tools not only of observation (notebooks, pens, camera, cassette recorders, tapes, films, batteries, maps, species identification manuals, compass, GPS receiver, and so on) but also for survival in that particular environment (machete, digging blade, fishing line and hooks, backpack, sleeping mat, flashlight, sleeping bag, eating utensils, food rations, medical kit, etc.). Thus my main concern was how to equip myself adequately but sustainably.

The Batek themselves were also loaded down with stuff. The difference is that unless enfeebled or very young, they could walk sturdily with all their stuff – and mount the occasional child on top of everything on their backs, *and* wearing the minimum of clothes and more often than not barefoot – whereas I could not. Furthermore, they always had the option to come back: they could use left-behind

---

7   Though much of the data for this chapter comes from that year's work, I have visited the Batek at other times (1993, 1998, 1999, 2001, 2003, 2004, 2005); the sum total of time spent with them is about two years.

camps as 'storage closets'. Initially, I thought I could afford a small carrying bag for some of the overflow, but I quickly realized that I needed all four limbs unencumbered if I were to stay upright for at least some of the fieldwork. And I did not want to load other people down with my stuff – besides, the usual porters, the young men, were in such general demand and so creative at absenting themselves at set-off time, that I really had no choice but to carry my own gear. Packing became a high art with me; with experience I learned to do without.[8] The farther along this process, the more I was unmaking the metaphorical bridge: less observation, more participation.

Lightening the packload is one thing. Knowing how to control the body is another. I am used to the comforting texture of hard solid concrete and suspicious of unstable surfaces such as muddy ooze and vegetation-concealed pits and dips. Stepping on Batek paths meant dealing with the ecology of these paths, such as their slopes and the profusion of roots and vines that grew over and across them, and with the Batek treatment of them. There are also visual constraints: it is rarely possible to see further than a few tens of metres in any direction, and there is never a truly broad vista or view. Batek and other forest dwellers adapt by being hyper-alert to sound shifts and changes (Gell 1999; Ichikawa 1998). Needless to say, I struggled to achieve this. The tropical forest, moreover, is a highly dynamic environment. It has a way of changing when one is not looking. There is always new growth, and new forms of decay. As people move, they may cut new openings, or find ways of bypassing fresh obstructions such as a fallen tree. Compared to other pathways found in the area (logging roads, tourist trails, village trails, and so on), a Batek path is recognizable by one singular characteristic: it is usually far narrower and not maintained. Foraging trails, especially, are just 'ways' through the forest rather than distinctive 'paths'. Their muddy, slopey, slidey, and rooty characteristics are more pronounced after rainfall, which is frequent in Malaysia.

Walking on these trails, I had to learn a whole new vocabulary for the body: such as where to step and how to step (for example, toes pointed outward and not down into the crevices between thorny roots), adjusting my pace to the demands of the topography rather than to following my natural rhythms, keeping my arms close to avoid brushing against piercing thorns, and – resigning myself to the inevitable – falling lightly rather than hard on the joints. I developed my own innovations. Where a Batek child could skip gracefully down a steep slope, I would slide down on my posterior rather than risk a fall.

I did not come easily to my lessons. The Batek are not very helpful. Like most anthropologists, they regard walking as a commonplace. They know that we outsiders do it very badly, and they were most ready to break into smiles and even raucous laughter when I stumbled, tripped, slipped, or slid along their trails. Their lessons

---

8   But Batek friends could be annoying. While they would sometimes carp at my overloaded self, at other times they would ask why I had not brought such-and-such a tool (especially the prized machetes and digging blades that they hoped to wean off me at some point in the future) or picture-book (they especially wanted to see photos of '*batek*' from other parts of the world and their food choices). To appease them, every visit home to Ipoh turned into a loading and unloading exercise, topped up with the ritual weighing of the backpack on bathroom scales (10kg is just right; 15 becomes torturous; and 20 deadly).

were not made any easier by the lofty observation that they knew how to live in the forest and I did not. I became most familiar with the words *goy* (be careful) or *cip goy* (walk carefully/slowly), *pɔp* (to fall), *rɔbah* (to trip), *hadɛp* (to look), *kɔjiŋ* (to hear) and, most curiously, *cip ba-sɛn* (walk in-front [of me]). Translation: Be careful! There you go falling again (stifled giggles). Look over there (stop looking at the ground). Listen to what they're saying (stop asking where we're going). Walk in front (I've got to keep an eye on you). This last, I think, gives us the principal analytical clue.

We anthropologists like to compare ourselves to children: we usually lack basic social skills, linguistic fluency, practical and procedural knowledge, and so on. Many of these are 'teachable'. But in the matter of walking, we are *not* children (however childishly we behave). We arrive pre-designed, as it were. If, as in my case, I had never learnt to handle forest trails, never familiarized myself with this kind of terrain, then what could the Batek do? They could only trust that through trial and error, I would pick up the necessary competences through watching and doing. I detect here a parallel with how the Batek 'train' their children to walk in the forest: to do it on their own and as much as possible, but guided away from mischief (Lye 1997, 352-5). As with their children, they needed to keep me 'under observation' and issue warnings and rebukes any time I threatened to bring the forest down with me.[9] Hence the significance of wanting me at the front of the line.

We disagreed. To me, the front of the line is the place of navigation: how could I lead the group if I didn't know where we were going and how to get there? Later I realized that the front is for the weak – the rearguard is literally that. Giving the lead to the slow and clumsy paces the group and ensures that those who cannot catch up are not left behind. The 'weak' among the Batek, usually the kids, knew how to follow a trail and were comfortable going ahead; I was not. Anthropologically, the front is also a place of weakness: from there it is impossible to hear the muted calls and conversations of those at the back. So I chose the middle. As a participant I could train my body by mimicking the movements of those in front, and as an observer I could monitor moods and concerns aurally.

What lessons should we distil from this outsider's experiences with the Batek? That they are privy to much ecological and navigational knowledge, communicated through shared history along the pathways, is obvious. We can glimpse this knowledge and go some distance into the phenomenology, but only if we like circular movements. As the pathway metaphor reminds us, every move forward takes us back. Fieldwork is supposed to be a rite of passage, a temporary encampment en route to the temple of professional acclaim. Instead, I went out there and returned to childhood! The luggage I took to the field weighed me down literally and metaphorically. I wanted to bring along the 'toys' of my profession in order to collect more sophisticated data. But toys get in the way. Coming to terms with Batek walking practices ultimately owes just as much to leech bites, sore feet, and scarred hands.

---

9   I am not being facetious here. Once while idly standing by, I (like a child) unthinkingly tugged at a suspended vine. Na?Tow shouted at me in horror. Many vines may seem solid but are actually entwined with rotting branches and leaf-debris; I could have released a load of these onto my head.

Fear and loathing

There was an overgrown patch of ground next to the house where I spent my early years. We children were warned never to play inside that field: it bespoke a lot of dangers to my family. It was considered a jungle of secondary growth, a place where malevolence resided. One of my cousins, cutting through the field on his way home from school, was once waylaid and robbed of his necklace there. The unpredictable nature of that environment would reveal itself in other ways; a memorable instance was the sudden appearance of a snake crossing the road. For years that was my view of the jungle. I feared it. My jungle was the product of a collective imagination, and a very different environment than the one I describe here. It was simply a fearsome other-place. Tall grasses, like those growing beside my childhood home, were associated with snakes. Trees were not considered suitable playgrounds by my caregivers, and certainly not for little girls. Water was associated with unseen reeds that might pull a swimmer in. Rocks belonged to the seaside where one went for weekend excursions only. There was no incentive to explore the natural surroundings. Any deviation from this norm, like chasing dragonflies and grasshoppers, would evoke the criticisms of authority. My experience of the 'real' forest had to wait.

Every anthropologist, it seems, has his or her own pantheon of fears. I am often asked about snakes and other bad beasties. Creepy crawlies, especially biting ones, also have their admirers. My honest answer is: I know dangers exist but do not worry when I am with the Batek. Once or twice I have lost my nerve in the forest but these were temporary spells that lifted as soon as I saw a Batek face. Kirk Endicott (who worked with the Batek of Kelantan in the 1970s and 80s) even suggested that: 'The Batek do not fear the forest, nor do they populate it with imaginary evil spirits as many agricultural peoples do' (1979, 8). This is the impression they give, and it is probably a tribute to their confidence in their knowledge and problem-solving skills. They do not fear the forest as an other-place, in the way I did. But that does not mean they have no fear.

The stories they tell and the beliefs and practices they espouse suggest that they do have quite a few, deeply embedded, fears. For example, fear of tigers and strangers is used to deter children from mischief-making (Endicott 1979). There is fear in the collective imagination (of blood flow, violence, floods, treefalls, predators), in the material world (of any social or ecological phenomena that manifest the characteristics of these symbols), and mechanisms to deal with them (avoidance practices). I have discussed the symbols of fear and their avoidances elsewhere (Lye 1994; 1997; 2004; see also Endicott 1979). Less analysed is the relationship between fear and knowledge, and how fear affects walking in the forest.

One evening in June 1996, men at the riverbank rushed in with the news that Telabas, a Batek madman who lived by himself, had been spotted across the river. The camp group was some 60–65 people strong, and included among them two of Telabas' siblings. I was taken aback by what happened next. In less than an hour, we had a leader, a decision, and a route, and the entire group had packed up their belongings and set off on a three-hour journey through the night to a place of safety. We were of one mind; we walked quietly in single file, bodies backed up against each other, kids riding on parental shoulders. No one protested, no one straggled, no child cried; the mood was tense. At one point, there was a break in the forest canopy: in the moonlight Ping and I saw the outlines of people in front of us, spears and blowpipes thrusting at the sky, packs strapped to shoulders. It was an extraordinary scene. As Ping muttered, 'there are a *lot* of people': we were not accustomed to see such a dense knot of Batek in one place. We did not make camp that night, just unrolled mats on a stretch of logging road and slept there. The tension must have been great: one woman went into labour and delivered that same night.

Telabas is a 'real' person; whether he still lives, and if so, how he survives on his own, remain a mystery. But sightings of him – or, rather, his traces – were common that year.[10] Most adults in the group know him and some had witnessed his acts of madness. What he is said to have done is not clear. Accounts differed. That is to be expected. He is a madman who got madder as the stories got wilder. It was prudent to flee from him that night.

To what does this account testify? Firstly, it recalls history. Fear, and the retreat from fear, is historical, present not only among the Batek but also among other Orang Asli ('original people', the official term for the indigenous ethnic minorities in the Peninsula). It can be traced to the history of slavery, specifically the raiding of forest peoples by representatives of lowland polities. The settler-indigene relationship had elements of cooperation and reciprocity in pre-colonial times but became increasingly predatory with the rise of the slave-trade (Dentan 1992; 1997; Endicott 1983). Though slavery has ended, its psychological effects persist. The flight from Telabas represents just the latest cycle in the retreat from fear.

If threats linger, so do the bodily idioms developed to deal with them. *Tala?* (to run from) is one such idiom. You can *tala?* anything: clinging children, falling trees, tigers, menacing people, angry friends. To be effective, one cannot wait for the threat to materialize before springing into action: one must anticipate it. Telabas unites in his persona danger in the abstract (violent behavior from people who do not have control of their senses) and in the concrete (an actual mad person who lives just at the edge of society and may even be tracking people's movements). For all we know, Telabas might be just a harmless old man. That is not the point: nobody wanted to find out. What is remarkable about our flight that night is the confidence with which we followed the trail as well as the absence of the usual rounds of pre-departure argument and discussion. The group did not run randomly through the forest; it was as if they were following some pre-established script. This script is historical, but also borne of deep familiarity with the environment. Elsewhere I have described the Batek's interest in knowledge for its own sake (Lye 1997). Here we see another stimulus for knowledge-gathering: to stave off the threat of danger.

Every escape from something is a flight towards something else. Two things are going on here. On the one hand, the Batek have generally escaped their fears of *gob* (strangers, primarily Malays). They seemed annoyed whenever I asked if this fear still exists. Fear of Malays represents one kind of past to which they do not want to return. But fear itself has not gone away. Rather, it is now projected towards other

---

10 He has counterparts in the collective imagination; there are also illegal Thai traders of aromatic woods, reportedly armed, another Batek madman (considered harmless and accepted as a permanent member of one camp group), and various mad Malay villagers.

kinds of violent exotics, the sighting of which drives people out from some areas, even as they move into others. Lacking the abundant forestlands of former times, their fears may be driving them *out* towards the Malay end of the social-ecological spectrum. The niche for the Batek, though, is not in, but at the *edges* of Malay society; they walk most comfortably there. The larger danger is that they may be unable to maintain that niche, leaving them with no alternative but to assimilate into Malay society.

Conclusion: finding the way back

What is the effect of fear on walking practices? To answer that question I would like to turn to the paradox with which I began: the co-existence, or rather the integration, of fear and confidence. We might think of fear as a sign of weakness, an embarrassment, sometimes even a secret. Not many anthropologists, for example, would admit to fearing the field, yet many do. Evidently, the opposition between fear and confidence is a chimera. Confidence means having trust in the ability to get a job done. It is the result of knowledge and improvisation: trying out variations, experimenting, informed by knowledge of what worked last time. Fear comes from having a realistic appreciation of what doesn't work and is therefore also borne of knowledge. Having confidence does not negate fearfulness; a confident person is one who is sufficiently fearful to be cognizant of potential danger and of what to do should it arise.

But in at least one context this explanation does not quite suffice. An important cultural theme among the Batek is fear of losing the way. Indeed, Batek can get quite perturbed when they lose their way in the forest. I have been along on at least one such occasion. We missed a turning and went a little bit astray before we had to retrace our steps. I would have dismissed the entire episode had it not happened that when we got back to camp this small incident was highlighted as the major event of the day. It became the stuff of myth – exaggerated out of all proportion to its actual gravity.

I think this is also an important characteristic of the phenomenology of walking for the Batek. Walking is about resolving the dilemma between going forward and pulling back – between confidence and fear – but it is essentially about moving on, or having a way. Based on linguistic and symbolic evidence, my tentative idea is that for the Batek 'the way' is life itself. When one dreams of losing the way, the dream is interpreted to mean that one will fall sick. An even more explicit connection lies in the dream symbol of going somewhere, coming back, and going again: the interpretation is that the dreamer will suffer from death throes, dying, recovering, and dying again. Though the evidence is not conclusive I think that there is a sense in which losing the way is tantamount to losing one's life. Becoming lost conjures up the horror of not finding the way back again. This kind of fear, which goes to the heart of being Batek (or being a hunter-gatherer), is probably not something that can be resolved through the acquisition of further knowledge: after all, we know we are going to die – it is just a question of when we will lose the path.

Walking may take us to one place and away from another. I have suggested that for Batek, walking takes us back to where we started from. Every arrival promises a future departure but towards a point whence we can come 'here' again. Movement is inherently circumambulatory. And walking is about knowing how to find one's way through these overlapping pathways. Fear of entities like madmen and tigers, which give rise to endless storytelling, creates landscape markers: places to avoid. The danger is that, in running too fast or too far, people may lose the way completely and thus find themselves unable to return. It is at such a point that the familiar forest of pathways can become a dangerous other-place.

References

Benjamin, G. (1966), 'Temiar Social Groupings', *Federation Museums Journal* (N.S.) 11, 1-25.

Botkin, D. (1990), *Discordant Harmonies: A New Ecology for the Twenty-First Century* (New York: Oxford University Press).

Cronon, W. (1996), 'The Trouble with Wilderness; or, Getting Back to the Wrong Nature', in Cronon, W. (ed.) (1996), *Uncommon Ground: Rethinking the Human Place in Nature* (New York: Norton).

Dentan, R. (1992), 'The Rise, Maintenance and Destruction of a Peaceable Polity: A Preliminary Essay in Political Ecology', in Silverberg, J. and Gray, J. (eds) (1992), *Aggression and Peacefulness in Humans and Other Primates* (New York: Oxford University Press).

—— (1997), 'The Persistence of Received Truth: How Ruling Class Malays Construct Orang Asli Identity', in Winzeler, R. (ed.) (1997), 'Indigenous Peoples and the State: Politics, Land, and Ethnicity in the Malayan Peninsula and Borneo', *Yale Southeast Asia Studies* 46 (New Haven, CT: Yale University Press).

—— (2002), 'Disreputable Magicians, the Dark Destroyer, and the Trickster Lord: Reflections on Semai Religion and a Possible Common Religious Base in South and Southeast Asia', *Asian Anthropology* 1, 153-94.

Dove, M., Sajise, P. and Doolittle, A. (eds) (2005), *Conserving Nature in Culture: Case Studies from Southeast Asia* (New Haven: Yale Southeast Asia Council Press).

Ellen, R. (1998), 'Indigenous Knowledge of the Rainforest: Perception, Extraction and Conservation', in Moloney, B. (ed.) (1998), *Human Activities and the Tropical Rainforest* (Dordrecht: Kluwer Academic Publishers).

Ellen, R. and Fukui, K. (eds) (1996), *Redefining Nature: Ecology, Culture and Domestication* (Oxford: Berg).

Endicott, K. (1974), *Batek Negrito Sex Roles* (Unpublished MA thesis, Australian National University).

—— (1979), *Batek Negrito Religion: The World-View and Rituals of a Hunting and Gathering People of Peninsular Malaysia* (Oxford: Clarendon Press).

—— (1983), 'The Effects of Slave Raiding on the Aborigines of the Malay Peninsula', in Reid, A. and Brewster, J. (eds) (1983), *Slavery, Bondage, and Dependency in Southeast Asia* (Brisbane, Australia: University of Queensland Press).

Fairhead, J. and Leach, M. (1996), *Misreading the African Landscape: Society and Ecology in a Forest-Savanna Mosaic* (Cambridge: Cambridge University Press).

Gell, A. (1999), *The Art of Anthropology: Essays and Diagrams* (London: Athlone Press).

Harris, D. and Hillman, G. (eds) (1989), *Foraging and Farming: The Evolution of Plant Exploitation* (London: Unwin Hyman).

Ichikawa, M. (1998), 'The Birds as Indicators of the Invisible World: Ethno-Ornithology of the Mbuti Hunter Gatherers', *African Study Monographs* Suppl. 25, 105-21.

Latinis, K. (1999), *Subsistence System Diversification in Southeast Asia and the Pacific: Where Does Maluku Fit?* (Unpublished doctoral dissertation, University of Hawaii at Manoa).

Lye, T.-P. (1994), *Batek Hep: Culture, Nature, and the Folklore of a Malaysian Forest People* (Unpublished MA thesis, University of Hawaii at Manoa).

—— (1997), *Knowledge, Forest, and Hunter-gatherer Movement: The Batek of Pahang, Malaysia* (Unpublished doctoral dissertation, University of Hawaii at Manoa).

—— (2004), *Changing Pathways: Forest Degradation and the Batek of Pahang, Malaysia* (Lanham, MD: Lexington Books).

—— (2005), 'The Road to Equality? Landscape Transformation and the Batek of Pahang, Malaysia', in Widlok and Tadesse (eds).

Miklucho-Maclay, N. (1878), 'Ethnological Excursions in the Malay Peninsula', *Journal of the Straits Branch of the Royal Asiatic Society* 2, 205-21.

Rambo, A. (1979), 'Primitive Man's Impact on Genetic Resources of the Malaysian Tropical Rain Forest', *Malaysian Applied Biology* 8, 59-65.

Rosaldo, R. (1993), *Culture and Truth: The Remaking of Social Analysis* (2nd edition) (Boston: Beacon).

Tilley, C. (1994), *A Phenomenology of Landscape: Places, Paths and Monuments* (Oxford: Berg).

Widlok, T. (1997), 'Orientation in the Wild: The Shared Cognition of Hai//om Bushpeople', *Journal of the Royal Anthropological Institute* (N.S.) 3, 317-32.

Widlok, T. and Tadesse, W. (eds) (2003), *Property and Equality. Volume 2: Encapsulation, Commercialisation, Discrimination* (Oxford: Berghahn).

Yen, D. (1989), 'The Domestication of Environment', in Harris, D.R. and Hillman, G.C. (eds), *Foraging and Farming: The Evolution of Plant Exploitation* (London: Unwin Hyman).

Chapter 3

Walking Stories; Leaving Footprints

Allice Legat

Between 1993 and 2001, I worked with the Dogrib[1] Regional Elders' Committee on three separate multi-year research projects to document the Tłı̨chǫ people's knowledge of governance, caribou and places. The Tłı̨chǫ[2] are among the Dene (or Athapaskan language speaking people) of northwestern Canada, and continue to occupy and use the area between Great Slave and Great Bear Lakes in the Canadian Northwest Territories.[3] While working on these projects a constant theme for discussion and action among the elders and their leadership was the importance of telling stories, travelling trails and walking the locations where past events occurred. Although the projects were to document Tłı̨chǫ knowledge for the purposes of resource management and self-government, it became increasingly clear that both elders and the leadership were primarily concerned with the significance of becoming knowledgeable and using stories to 'think with'. Since 2002, I have been trying to come to grips with this process; to understand what it means to become knowledgeable to a Tłı̨chǫ person. In this chapter, I will consider becoming knowledgeable from the perspective of walking stories and leaving footprints. More specifically, I will consider walking as the experience that binds narrative to the acquisition of personal knowledge. Walking, then, validates the reality of the past in the present and in so doing, continually re-establishes the relation between place, story and all the beings who use the locale. When walking a person can become intimate with a locale, creating situations in which one can grow intellectually while travelling trails under the guidance of predecessors who have both followed and left footprints.

Many scholars have considered the relations between oral narratives, experience and place. Anthropologists working with Dene people, including the Tłı̨chǫ, generally accept that northern Dene narratives contain knowledge of considerable

---

1   Prior to August 2005, the Tłı̨chǫ referred to themselves in English as Dogrib. They now refer to themselves as Tłı̨chǫ in all situations.

2   Tłı̨chǫ is a high tone language with some vowel falling – *à, ì, è, ò*, as in the case of the place names Ɂek'atì, Ɂezhogǫghǫ̀, Kǫk'èetì and Gots'ǫkàtì, used in this chapter. Other sounds are the glottalized stop Ɂ as if saying a voiceless haa; the ' after some consonants such as *k'* and *ts'* gives the consonant a click; vowels are pronounced as follows: *a* is as in father; *e* as in set; and *i* as in ski; the nasalization of *į* as in means; *ǫ* as in don't; and Tł' is pronounced as in settle (Dogrib Divisional Board of Education 1996: ii-v). An approximation of the word Tłı̨chǫ into English orthography would be Klinchon.

3   Further ethnographic and ethno-historical research has been carried out by Helm (1972, 1981, 1994, 2000), Helm and Gillespie (1981) and Helm and Lurie (1961).

time depth (Cruikshank 1981; 2001; Hanks 1996) and that being knowledgeable is based on experience (Cruikshank 1998; 2001, 390; Goulet 1998) gained by working and listening to those with more skill (Jarvenpa 1998). The Dene themselves accept that those who travel widely are respected, because travel is key to learning and understanding Dene cosmology (Andrews et al. 1998, 312; Brody 1981; Ridington 1990). Furthermore, Dene people respect those who have the ability to learn by themselves through dreams and visions, among other means (Goulet 1998; Watson and Goulet 1992).

Learning by oneself, however, does not take place in isolation; rather one learns during activities with, and in the presence of, others. Goulet (1998) shows how learning is anchored within the Dene community. Of Saami people in Lapland, Ingold and Kurttila (2000, 192) argue that it involves the 'generation and regeneration [of knowledge] within the contexts of people's practical engagement with significant components of the environment'. For the Tłicho significant components include human as well as non-human beings, implying that learning is always situated and guided, even if there are no other humans around. What I call 'guided learning', for the Tłicho, entails a combination of receiving information – through hearing stories – and travelling trails while carrying out tasks at particular locales. Information, then, is not to be extracted as the *content* of the story, but *is the story itself*, namely the happenings and occurrences as they are related and fit together. The stories tell of places as they are associated with political and social endeavours. An example of such a place is Gots'okàtì, the place where the Akaitcho, whose descendants are Yellowknife-Chipewyan Dene, and Edzo, whose descendants are the Tłicho Dene, agreed in 1829 to live in peace (Helm 1981, 296).[4]

Places, then, are not simply spaces where people feel good when they visit them. Rather, relations with places are initiated as soon as children first hear the narratives. Most stories have been heard many times before travelling to the sites named and experiencing them directly. Through visiting, walking and performing tasks at a locale individuals both take something of the place with them and leave a bit of themselves. In so doing, individuals add their narrative to that of others while refining the deepest levels of their perception (Casey 1996, 18). Basso (1984) emphasizes that places are used by the Western Apache as indices to access stories, histories and knowledge of the land. Place names may convey meaning to those who know the locales and the stories connected to them (Cruikshank 1990), however such names can only reflect what any given person can comprehend, which is based on experience and interaction with other members of the community (Hallowell 1967, 193).

Andrews and Zoe (1997, 172) explain that, for the Tłicho, stories reside in places along trails, and that place names serve as memory 'hooks' for the stories that contain knowledge. Further, 'places represent the physical embodiment of cultural process, which is realized through the combination of travel and story-telling' (Andrews et al. 1998, 312). Building on their discussion, I consider several situations where Tłicho of various ages follow the footprints left by their predecessors. In unravelling the

---

4   See Helm and Gillespie (1981) for an explanation of the fighting between these two Dene groups.

relation between the story and personal knowledge gained through experience at the place, I aim to show that the period between listening to stories and walking them marks an in-between phase of learning during which people who have heard 'talk' do not yet know the 'truth' or reality of a narrative.

Sharing narratives

In rituals associated with respecting the land, it is common to compare the land to one's parents 'as it provides everything', including the ability to 'know something'. The land, then, is a living entity with powers that should be shown respect if harmony is to be maintained. One way of showing respect is by 'paying the land', which usually entails leaving an item that one considers useful. This is done when travellers enter new bodies of water (Andrews et al. 1998, 307). They also pay locales where supernatural power resides. I have never known any Tłıchǫ travellers to pass these places without stopping and showing respect. This often entails walking around the location to determine if all is as it was, and tidying burials if any are in the vicinity. Individuals who have visited the place before tell the stories that dwell in the location to those who are travelling with them, and a 'picnic' – which usually includes feeding predecessors by putting favoured food in the fire – is enjoyed before continuing the journey. The process allows everyone to know the place and the story a little better. These actions validate the story in the present while maintaining relations with predecessors who continue to be attached to Tłıchǫ places. I have seen Tłıchǫ elders pay the land as they walked towards a Chipewyan sacred site where the spirit of a woman willing to help those who require healing resides in the waterfall. Although people leave sharp tools such as awls, needles and knives at the falls, the Tłıchǫ elders I observed paid the trail leading to the falls with spruce boughs.

Upon returning from trips such as these and when visiting burials and other sacred sites each individual shares their experience through stories. Elders often respond by telling stories that clarify, enhance or add to them. Listeners grow and change as they are drawn to the places, walking the footprints of others through their minds as they are drawn down the trails once again. As Basso (1996, 31) explains, many footprints or tracks come in the form of place names, stories and songs telling of where past events occurred. Similarly, Cruikshank (1998) and Sarris (1993) note the importance of the relationship between the manner in which the storyteller relates the narration and the audiences' ability to listen and understand. This is key to how people learn to think.

For the Tłıchǫ, predecessors' footprints are embedded in places and trails that continue to be used and travelled. Thus the stories they think with are steeped with detailed and accurate accounts of trails and locales. These stories form the basis for building one's perception of reality.

Adults constantly tell stories, including to young children, so that they can grow from the place they call home, eventually travelling trails and walking locales where they can experience the stories for themselves. Ridington (2002, 117) has similarly noted that for the Dane (Dene)-zaa, children are prepared for their experience through the shared narrative tradition. Tłıchǫ individuals, then, are forever listening to stories whose truth is subsequently validated through experience. Retelling the story in light of this experience, the teller builds on the original by incorporating her or his own occurrences and happenings. Once one has gained personal knowledge, one tells one's own stories and eventually leaves one's own footprints for the future. As Ridington says of the Dane-zaa, 'each telling is an interpretive recreation rather than a recitation' (2002, 113). It is important to note, however, that Tłįchǫ consider bragging about what one knows to be a demonstration of ignorance. Therefore the stories they tell of their experiences usually focus on what one observed and encountered and with whom one was travelling. It is for others to comment on whether or not someone is knowledgeable. This is usually based on a person's skill in narration, but also on their productive capacity: say, for example, success in caribou hunting, the ability to sway the attitude of government bureaucrats, appearance of fish on drying racks, skill in sewing beautiful clothing and the capacity to secure funding from territorial and federal governments.

Tłįchǫ elders encourage individuals to learn from places and to use 'stories to think with' as they are confronted with new situations. They use stories to structure the contexts within which their juniors perceive their experiences. As Romie Wetrade, a Tłįchǫ elder in his late seventies, said:

> As for myself, I do not understand English. None at all. I do not know how to read. None at all. I do not know how to read the white man's words. ... Even so, my elderly parents raised me and I have lived a good life because I heard their stories. My predecessors' talk is like keeping a book. I remember it. ... I have reached this age by living on the knowledge from my predecessors. Their knowledge comes from beyond books ... The knowledge my predecessors possessed that has brought me thus far makes me feel as if I were sitting next to them. If I were to think about it, I am sitting under all their knowledge (Romie Wetrade, TGP-93/03/30-1/1).[5]

Likewise Andrew Gon, an elder in his mid-eighties, explained how his predecessors had walked the land using knowledge from the past to survive. They had to know three distinct physical environments as they followed the caribou from the boreal forest to the barren ground. Furthermore, they had to know where to camp to ensure good fishing in case the caribou migrated elsewhere and, during years when resources were limited, they had to know where their relatives may be camped – including those that lived in other regions. At the very least this meant knowing narratives that allowed them to find trails through the complicated river systems, and how to travel in the barren ground where large lakes and tracts of land have to be crossed while the wind constantly blows. As Andrew said: 'Our predecessors went through hard times, and to this day we are still following their footprints and using their knowledge in order to survive' (Andrew Gon, TGP-94/02/17-1/1).

In this and other statements, 'their footprints' and 'their knowledge' are interchangeable. 'To know something' is to be able to take some form of action. Both Romie and Andrew were explaining the importance of listening to stories for the

---

5   Celine Football and Madeline Chocolate translated the passage quoted in this chapter. The letters and numbers following the name of the person speaking represent the tape number, including the date of the recording.

future, not only by recognizing their predecessors' knowledge but also by validating the truth of it and then using that knowledge to perform a task. The importance of maintaining and enhancing one's knowledge through action can be heard again in Madeline Judas's statement:

> I am a woman. Thinking it would be good for whoever lived after me, I did not toss away the words of my parents … I left my footprints. […] When a relative killed a caribou, I would help; I would drive the dog team to help get the meat […]. That is how I worked for the future generations (Madeline Judas, CHP-95/10/27).

Madeline took action, allowing herself to experience the 'words' of her elders, which maintained the continuity of the footprints and their visibility for future generations. Being visible through her action allowed her to become increasingly knowledgeable and visible in the stories she would tell, allowing others to follow.

Listening to stories and following the footprints of those who are more knowledgeable allows one to think by drawing on philosophical understanding and practical knowledge that originated in the past. This is a perspective that encourages everyone to acknowledge that there is much to learn. It also provides people with an understanding of the importance of walking and observing – watching for the unexpected – while thinking about all that dwells within the land. Children are taught to watch as they grow to adulthood. As they walk, they are to think about what they smell, see, feel, always looking behind them to see how the trail will look on their return trip. Madeline Chocolate remembers:

> As a child, walking through the bush with my parents, I was taught to walk slowly and observe everything that was around me – including behind me. Then I went to residential school where the teachers taught me to hurry when I moved. I was then encouraged to run in races and enter in the cross-country ski races to win, and sometimes I did win. We were encouraged to go fast. It was harder to observe, understand and remember (November 27, 2005).

Madeline was encouraged to remember through being aware and through maintaining a relationship with her surroundings, and was taught not to disconnect, which can happen if one moves too fast. This creates flexible people who carefully consider situations as they draw on all they have learned while acknowledging that there is much more to know. They acknowledge that humans can only know a little (Ridington 1990) and are constantly learning. Being aware while walking and thinking with stories provides a context that allows for the acquisition of new knowledge. Tłı̨chǫ people talk about John B. Zoe, a man in his forties who learned the stories, travelled trails, visited and walked places. They tell of how he was offered the task of chief negotiator for Tłı̨chǫ land claims. Before he accepted, he 'walked around' several southern cities. People talk approvingly about how he walked the streets, familiarizing himself with the 'white character' before accepting the position, which entailed sitting across from several 'whites' whose homes are in southern Canada. What community members mean by this is that he learned a little bit about white people and their habits by walking the places were they reside. Similarly, Grand Chief Joe Rabesca never flies to a destination. If he cannot drive, canoe or walk, and thereby experience the land, he does not go. These two men are respected for knowing stories, for walking the land and for following the footprints of their predecessors.

The importance of the relationship between story, walking the land, experiencing places and knowledge is a continual topic of discussion. Tłįchǫ of all ages spend a lot of time and energy finding ways to share stories with those younger or less aware than themselves. Every autumn the Tłįchǫ Divisional Board of Education provides opportunities for teenagers and 'white' teachers to travel to the barrenland by canoe. I have been told that when they stop at places, the story of the place is told and they are encouraged to walk around with those who know the place. The Regional Elders' Committee with whom I worked requested that stories be recorded 'so that future generations can listen to them when they need them'. They also requested that their recordings should not be translated or written, so that future generations would have to listen with those who understand the 'old Tłįchǫ language' and the ideas and concepts the elders wish to convey through it. The elders also encourage listeners to walk the place from which every story grows – where its core dwells and whence it spread out through being told and re-told.

These formalized storytelling sessions and trips are simply extensions of what is taking place in people's homes on a daily basis. Adults are constantly telling 'old time stories' as well as stories of what they have seen and experienced. They also tell of when, where and how they experienced the stories that came from ancient times, or 'when the world was new'. Adults continually encourage those younger or less experienced than themselves to walk the land, to experience the truth of the stories for themselves, and to share what they experience – including what they saw, heard and felt, and with whom (including non-human beings) they shared the experience. Telling a series of stories is, inevitably, the most appropriate way to proceed.

Walking the story

Observing while walking in their predecessors' footprints provides individuals with an understanding of a world that has both continuity and change. In 2001, one of the autumn hunting camps was located on a sand bar on Ɂewanı̨tı̨ı̨tı̀, a lake in the barren grounds. It was selected because caribou are known to cross the lake at this location, if they are in the area. Before leaving for the barrens, elders who were not accompanying us told stories of this area. The stories told of hunters being lost in blizzards – some found, others never found but whose remains are still being sought. They also tell of graves that have not been visited and need to be attended to, and of an old time burial that is suppose to be near Ts'iedaa, the last stand of trees before entering the barren land. The sand bar is also known to the women as a good place to find 'stones that are just right for softening hides'. Younger women were asked to find stones and bring them back.

Figure 3.1 Dora Nitsiza and Liza Jerameka finding stones for softening hides

A few days after we arrived, I was walking with Liza Jerameka, Georgina Chocolate and Dora Nitsiza. None of us had been to ʔewanɪtɪɪtì but we had heard stories of the importance of the sand bar and where to find stones for softening hides. As we walked, Dora had found three of these perfectly shaped stones, when she turned to Georgina and said, 'It's true, what our elders have told us. It is good to follow their footprints'. We were walking on a gravelly sandbar so that no trail was actually visible from the past. But her predecessors had walked on the sandbar before her and shared their knowledge through narratives so that we too could benefit from the resources to be found there.

A few days later, several of us boated to Ts'iedaa, an area that continues to be important for the Tłįchǫ people, particularly in the communities of Behchokǫ̀ and Wekweètì. All the oral narratives of Ts'iedaa emphasize how safe it is to leave families there. The stories tell of the people who have camped there, of wood, of fish in the lake, and of hare and other small animals that can be snared by women, children and older people while the trappers walked to the barren land to trap white fox in the winter. We walked around Ts'iedaa. We looked at the old cabins. Some of us walked among the spruce trees. No-one talked much, which surprised me as Elizabeth Michel, Jimmy Martin and Joe Suzi Mackenzie had all lived at Ts'iedaa. Usually when camped at or visiting a place these elders were happy to spend hours telling us about it. They usually walk us around, explaining where to set snares, where to fish, where to find medicine. However, they were quiet. I thought it might have been because Joe Suzi had been urging everyone to set up an autumn camp at Ts'iedaa for a decade and was thoughtful about being there. Before leaving, we walked a kilometre or so to visit Georgina and Jimmy's relatives who were buried on one of the eskers,[6] but here they were not quiet. They talked of their relationship to Georgina, 'talked' to the ancestor through prayer and left gifts.

Just before leaving, we sat in the boats and motored slowly past the numerous oil barrels lying in the water around Ts'iedaa. Again, no one was talking. I was struck by the fact that I did not hear anyone say 'It's true', as so often happened when people affirmed a story when visiting a place. I had heard stories of Ts'iedaa and the trails leading to it for several years, so I knew that everyone else had heard these stories. Why was it that only those who had heard the stories, but not visited before, were saying 'It's true'?

Although everyone was conscious of the wind, and wanted to return to camp before the waves on the lake became dangerous, the silence had to do with more than a concern for the weather. On returning to our camp on the sand bar, we sat long into the night as the elders talked about what they had observed as they walked around looking at the place. The rest of us listened. I learned that evening that the place had changed. Elizabeth Michel, Jimmy Martin and Joe Suzi Mackenzie, all of whom had walked with us at Ts'iedaa, talked of the number of trees that had disappeared. They talked about why these things may have happened, but here I want to explore the broader context of the story and the trail.

Within the oral tradition of the Tłıchǫ, a story comprises events and occurrences as they fit together. Any story can be part of a longer version or can lead into other occurrences. While sitting and listening to the elders, the story trail eventually turned to Mowhi, who had stayed at Ts'iedaa and extensively travelled the trails through there. The stories of Mowhi himself inevitably led to talk of the Mowhi Trail, on which Ts'iedaa is located, and of whether the Federal Government would agree to protect the Mowhi Trail under the Federal and Territorial Protected Area Strategy. Tłıchǫ elders and leaders want the Mowhi Trail protected for several reasons, three of which are relevant here. Firstly, they want the young people to remember the person Mowhi, after whom the trail acquired its name, not only because he signed Treaty 11 in 1921,[7] but also because he knew the extent of Tłıchǫ country (*nek'è*). Mowhi is remembered as having gained his deep understanding through travelling trails and walking where stories originated and continue to reside. He was therefore able to tell the Treaty Commissioner the extent of the land needed for the Tłıchǫ to survive.

---

6   Most burials are located in high areas with good drainage. In the barrenland, eskers are ideal as they consist of gravel left by retreating glaciers. Furthermore, both human beings and caribou use the eskers to walk on as they are higher and dryer than the surrounding muskeg, and provide relief from mosquitoes as well as a long range view.

7   Treaty 11 is the last of the numbered treaties to be signed between the Government of Canada and First Nations people. According to oral narratives I heard, Mowhi was selected and to him was delegated the authority to speak for them. In his speech, Mowhi outlined the extent of Tłıchǫ land. There are discrepancies between the oral record and that of the Federal Government. In 1973 Judge Morrow, who oversaw the *Re Paulette Case*, ruled that the Dene had established a *prima facie* case for their continuing Aboriginal title in Denendeh.

Secondly, they want Mowhi to be remembered for his commitment to providing young people with experience – helping them to walk the stories and follow the footprints of their predecessors while becoming knowledgeable and leaving their own footprints for others to follow. Stories would give them the ability to think and therefore to survive in what they knew would be a changing world. Most of the young people who travelled with and learned from Mowhi are now elders who continue to be socially and politically active even though they do not read or write, or speak English. Two such people are Alexis Arrowmaker, Mowhi's nephew, and Jimmy Martin, Mowhi's grandson. Both are considered to be knowledgeable, and people continue to refer to them as following in the footprints of Mowhi. Alexis Arrowmaker advised the Tłįchǫ leadership – particularly the land negotiators – until his death in autumn 2005, and Jimmy Martin continued to lead the student canoe trips from Behchokǫ̀ to the barrenland each September until prevented by an injury sustained in 2003.

Thirdly, they want Mowhi to be remembered as a person who continually extended his knowledge past the limits of the oral narratives he had heard as a young man, and past his own political and kinship affiliations into the stories of others from neighbouring groups with whom he sought to establish relations. He pushed past his own knowledge to experience and know the places of others. He was the first Tłįchǫ to be chosen by people from all Tłįchǫ regions to speak for them all; he was the first to be given the task of standing up to the Canadian Federal Commission because he knew through travelling trails and walking stories where the Tłįchǫ belong. The story of Mowhi resides on the Mowhi Trail – a place incorporating locales, stories and trails where the footprints of Mowhi, his predecessors and descendants continue to dwell, including Ts'iedaa. Each year, students follow knowledgeable elders, being guided as they walk the stories that dwell along the trail.

It was during our time in the autumn hunting camp at ʔewanıtıìtì that I realized that when Tłįchǫ people use the term 'place', they can mean a variety of things. Place can refer to a locale or site along a trail or to the trail itself including all the locales on it. Place also refers to the entire region including the trails and locales in it, and the total extent of Tłįchǫ territory including all regions, trails and locales where you expect to find Tłįchǫ stories. People know the stories because their predecessors have walked and left footprints in these places.

A narrative told by Robert Mackenzie addresses the multi-faceted concept of place. It shows the importance of knowing the places of your predecessors by knowing the stories which make it possible for their footprints to be followed. It also illustrates how walking and accomplishing tasks in a place can be understood as leaving a portion of oneself in that place while taking a bit of it away. Robert Mackenzie's story, which was told to him by his grandfather, comes from the time when the Yellowknife Dene were raiding Tłįchǫ camps. He said:

> Once the people were camped at Kǫ̀k`èetì [where they were hunting caribou and musk-ox] when they realized some of Akaitcho's band were travelling close to them. They packed and left quickly. They were able to travel a trail they knew Akaitcho's band would not know – their parents and grandparents had not left their footprints around Kǫ̀k`èetì. My grandfather said our predecessors followed the footprints of their elders and crossed

the water where it was shallow enough to walk across. They were fortunate. One man, travelling with them, had a special relationship with Fox, and he asked Fox to help them. Although Yellowknife Dene followed them, they were unable to cross the water. They did not know the trail and did not have a story for the trail. They tried to turn back, but Fox caused them to travel in circles so they could not go back the way they came. Our predecessors were safe because they knew. Those that tried to harm them eventually starved.

Robert added:

How can some people say a place is their land when their predecessors have not left their footprints, and have not walked with their parents in these places? They did not know that area; they had no stories to guide them …

Remember the first time John B. led the students to Wekweètì without Jimmy Martin. John B. was travelling a trail that he had never travelled before but Jimmy gave him a story for the trail. When John B. realized he was lost, he turned back, travelling to the place he knew was right with the story. Then he started again, paying attention to Jimmy's words. He had the story to think with. He got all those students to Wekweètì (pers. comm. January 16, 2002).

Robert emphasizes that holders of their predecessors' oral narratives do, in fact, use a kind of mental mapping as they travel the land. The Tłı̨chǫ people with whom I have travelled are well aware of when they are using oral narratives to 'think with'. And, although peoples' personal knowledge is continually being formed as they move about in the environment (Ingold 2000, 230-31), they know that they are also thinking with the narratives that they have heard numerous times before.

Leaving footprints

Just as Robert Mackenzie pointed out in his narrative, the Yellowknife Dene did not have a relationship with the area because even in his grandfather's time they did not know it. They literally did not have stories with which to follow their predecessors' footprints. But the Tłı̨chǫ people of his grandfather's generation did have stories, including those from the time when the world was new, some of which are attached to place and others not – stories that English speakers would refer to as myths. People experience the information in stories through everyday relations with each other and with other beings, and so the elders encourage their juniors to use these very old stories to think with. Most Dene elders stress the importance of understanding the difference between those who claim to know something – including places – and those who have the experience that leads to their actually knowing something. Only through having taken action, usually in the form of tasks such as hunting, trapping, tidying burial sites or building an ice road, are predecessors considered to have left their footprints for others to follow. This point became particularly clear when discussing the environmental management plans presented by Broken Hills Property Co. Ltd, which wanted to develop a diamond mine. In reference both to this plan and to the massive mineral staking that had often taken place in communities, close by or adjacent to Tłįchǫ homes, Romie Wetrade said:

> Our predecessors' footprints show on the ground. What about these people from down south? There are no footprints of theirs, but still they talk. They don't have any trails; they haven't left their footprints, but that's what they are assuming; they are assuming that they have worked on the land. They are telling the people "this is how I worked on the land and this is how the land looks". It is the Tłįchǫ people who have travelled way beyond the map – it seems as if they are prowling though our homes (Romie Wetrade, 95/03/04).

Romie's use of the term 'footprints' describes an action taken, an action that depends on knowing how to live and leave information for others to follow, thus emphasizing the continual use of both the trails that are visible and the story in which the footprints bind person to place. The narrative provides details of the events as they originally occurred and describes the land, including other beings – animals, plants, land forms – that also inhabit and use the place. The narrative, then, both recounts ongoing relations with those who walked before, and circumscribes the walking of the story for oneself. It tells the life history of places. Without oneself walking and leaving footprints, one can only listen to and repeat the narratives of others who have walked the story.

Following the story that comes from those who left footprints is often not enough; it depends on whom one walks with. Ideally, when following the footprints of one's predecessors, one walks with someone who has already walked there before, and is considered to know something about the events and the place.[8] This is part of becoming ever more knowledgeable. I can best explain this by briefly describing a discussion with 24 Tłįchǫ people who continued to obtain most of their resources, directly or indirectly, from the land. Their discussion was in response to the request from the Federal Government that traditional knowledge be used along with scientific knowledge in an environmental monitoring programme. The programme was to be associated with the ʔek'atì area,[9] where the mining company Broken Hill Property was operating and Kennicott was in the process of construction. Hunters, fishers, trappers and gatherers were concerned that decisions were being made based on data collected from plane-based surveys and satellite tracking of several animals including caribou. The Tłįchǫ discussants thought these surveying and tracking systems provided only limited understanding of the place. They were particularly concerned about the 'fine yellow substance' that lay on the plants, which they knew would not be observed unless one was walking the land – as many of them had done while hunting near the mines.

---

8   See also Akan (1999), who in her article on 'walking and talking' among the Saulteaux, discusses the importance of not leaving young people alone with their thoughts. Saulteaux elders consider it their responsibility to live in a way that reflects the discourse they share with young people.

9   ʔek'atì is known as a place that always has lots of fish, and the caribou, more often than not, travel through the area in the spring and autumn. ʔek'atì has been used by people from all regional bands as discussed by Helm (1981, 295-97; 2000, 1-20), especially when resources were scarce in other areas – it is said to be 'like a freezer'.

They devised a monitoring programme based on walking and learning from those with more experience, while drawing on the skills of everyone. Three generations would be involved. The middle-aged would both learn from the elders and walk with and tell stories of the place to those still in high school, walking the land with those who knew and following their predecessors' footprints. Younger people could use the knowledge from the past so they would know what was changing and what was staying the same. Charlie Tailbone, a hunter and trapper said,

> I know places from my father; other men my age know places I have only heard stories about. If we are to go to other regions to monitor the land, the elders and hunters, who know the place, will have to walk with us – so we can know – so we can pass the knowledge on to those of the next generation (personal notebook, May 2002).

These men and women are acutely aware that it is their responsibility to pass on their predecessors' knowledge, so that Tłįchǫ in the future can monitor and make decisions on areas where their predecessors dwell and continue to walk. Those still involved with land-based procurement would guide the learning of high school students by sharing their knowledge through oral narratives and by walking the area of ?ek`atì with them: discussing the taste, look, and smell of fish and plants, and the condition of caribou, to mention just a few considerations. The students, too, would have a task. They would actively contribute by writing reports for the bureaucrats. Knowledge would be continually passed through generations in narrative form while walking, so that each successive generation could become knowledgeable of the intricate details of the place known as ?ek`atì.

Although this plan has yet to materialize, it shows the continuing importance of sharing skills between all generations, while guiding the learning of others through sharing stories and walking places where predecessors have left their footprints. It also demonstrates the importance to the Tłįchǫ of continually updating occurrences and happenings through experience – by walking the story.

Travelling trails – experiencing place

Stories may reside in locales but they grow out from where the original event occurred just as individuals grow out from their home – the place where they began. Storytellers usually incorporate the events leading up to a situation and those occurring after. Although many trails are well worn, footprints are not always visible on the ground nor can material remains from human activity always be seen (Andrews et al. 1998, 306). Many footprints and trails are only accessible through stories that tell of what has gone before, so that one can grow into the present and think about what is the same and what has changed.

I have shown that Tłįchǫ individuals are encouraged to 'walk the land' so that they can experience and validate information in the stories that reside in and grow from places. Through listening to narratives and walking with one's predecessors, the process of guided learning is continous. It provides individuals with the information and knowledge necessary to keep life going, and to maintain harmonious relations by showing respect to all entities that dwell within the land. Furthermore, the Tłįchǫ understand that one always has more to learn, more stories to experience and, therefore, more places to walk. Individuals learn that the world is in constant change and that they must remain flexible and willing to think about new and unexpected situations. Although some trails are well worn, one's predecessors' footprints are not always visible on the bedrock and the muskeg where snow cover lasts at least seven months, or on the ice which gives way in summer to a labyrinth of waterways. By footprints, then, is not necessarily meant the actual impressions of a track or trail made by the movement of human feet. It is rather that the wayfarer's movement should be at once knowledgeable, task-oriented and attentive to relations with other beings in the environment through which it passes.

Walking is an activity in which one is not cut off, as one is in an aeroplane or when too busy or going too fast or not paying attention to one's surroundings. To walk is to pay close and careful attention to one's surroundings while thinking with the multitude of stories one has heard. Similarly, following footprints is about gaining knowledge through action and the ability to use that knowledge. Individuals who walk the land are respected because they have experience, the interpretation of which is based on continual social interaction.

Personal knowledge comes when the story and one's experience converge in a narration. Although the focus of the story remains the same, it grows in ways that depend on whom the story is shared with and in what context. In the telling, the stories reach out to other individuals, drawing them back down the trail, back to the places where individuals can experience the stories for themselves. Thus, individuals grow outward at the same time as they become rooted within the several locales of Tłįchǫ country. All Tłįchǫ people are encouraged to grow through the knowledge their parents and grandparents (and others) have offered them. In other words, being knowledgeable is the culmination of listening to stories and following footprints. This provides the foundation for leaving one's own footprints for future generations.

References

Akan, L. (1999), 'Pimosatamowin Sikaw Kakeequaywin: Walking and Talking', *Canadian Journal of Native Education* 23:1, 16-39.

Andrews, T. and Zoe, J. (1997), 'The *Idaà* Trail: Archaeology and the Dogrib Cultural Landscape, Northwest Territories, Canada', in Nicholas, G. and Andrews, T. (eds) (1997), *At a Crossroads: Archaeology and First Peoples in Canada* (Burnaby: Archaeology Press, Simon Fraser University).

Andrews, T., Zoe, J. and Herter, A. (1998), 'On *Yamòzhah*'s Trail: Dogrib Sacred Sites and the Anthropology of Travel', in Oakes, J., Riewe, R., Kinew, K. and Maloney, E. (eds) (1998), *Sacred Lands: Aboriginal Worldviews, Claims, and Conflicts* (Edmonton: Canadian Circumpolar Institute).

Basso, K. (1984), '"Stalking with Stories": Names, Places, and Moral Narratives among the Western Apache', in Bruner, E. (ed.) (1984), *Text, Play, and Story: The Construction and Reconstruction of Self and Society* (Washington: American Ethnological Society).

—— (1996), *Wisdom Sits in Places: Landscape and Language Among the Western Apache* (Albuquerque: University of New Mexico Press).

Brody, H. (1981), *Maps and Dreams* (Vancouver: Douglas & McIntyre Ltd).

Casey, E. (1996), 'How to get from Space to Place in a Fairly Short Stretch of Time: Phenomenological Prolegomena', in Feld, S. and Basso, K. (eds) (1996), *Senses of Place* (Santa Fe: School of American Research Press).

Cruikshank, J. (1981), 'Legend and Landscape: Convergence of Oral and Scientific Tradition in the Yukon Territory', *Arctic Anthropology* 18:2, 67-93.

—— (1990), 'Getting the Words Right: Perspectives on Naming and Places in Athapaskan Oral History', *Arctic Anthropology* 27:1, 52-65.

—— (1998), *The Social Life of Stories: Narrative and Knowledge in the Yukon Territory* (Vancouver: UBC Press).

—— (2001), 'Glaciers and Climate Change: Perspectives from Oral Tradition', *Arctic* 54:4, 377-93.

Goulet, J.-G. (1998), 'An Experiential Approach to Knowledge', in Goulet, J.-G. (ed.) (1998), *Ways of Knowing: Experience, Knowledge, and Power Among the Dene Tha* (Vancouver: UBC Press).

Hallowell, A. (1967), *Culture and Experience* (New York: Schocken Brooks).

Hanks, C. (1996), *Narrative and Landscape: Grizzly Bear Mountain and Scented Grass Hills as Repositories of Sahtu Dene Culture* (Ottawa: Historic Sites and Monuments Board of Canada).

Helm, J. (1972), 'The Dogrib Indians', Bicchieri, M. (ed.) (1972), *Hunters and Gatherers Today: A Socioeconomic Study of Eleven Such Cultures in the Twentieth Century* (New York: Holt, Rinehart and Winston).

—— (1981), 'Dogrib', in Helm (ed.) *Subarctic* (Washington: Smithsonian Institution).

—— (1994), *Prophecy and Power Among the Dogrib Indians* (Lincoln: University of Nebraska Press).

—— (2000), *The People of Denendeh: Ethnohistory of the Indians of Canada's Northwest Territories* (Montreal & Kingston: McGill-Queen's University Press).

Helm, J. and Gillespie, B. (1981), 'Dogrib Oral Tradition as History: War and Peace in the 1820s', *Journal of Anthropological Research* 37:1, 8-27.

Helm, J. and Lurie N. (1961), *The Subsistence Economy of the Dogrib Indians of Lac La Martre in the Mackenzie District of the Northwest Territories* (Ottawa: Department of Northern Affairs and National Resources, NCRC).

Ingold, T. (2000), *The Perception of the Environment* (London: Routledge).

Ingold, T. and Kurttila T. (2000), 'Perceiving the Environment in Finnish Lapland', *Body & Society* 6:3/4, 183-96.

Jarvenpa, R. (1998), *Northern Passage: Ethnography and Apprenticeship Among the Subarctic Dene* (Prospect Heights, Illinois: Waveland Press).

Ridington, R. (1990), *Little Bit Know Something: Stories in a Language of Anthropology* (Iowa City: University of Iowa Press).

Ridington, R. (2002), 'When You Sing It Now, Just Like New: Re-creation in Native American Narrative Tradition', in Steward, H., Barnard, A. and Omura, K. (eds) (2002), *Self- and Other Images of Hunter-Gatherers* (Osaka: National Museum of Ethnology).

Sarris, G. (1993), *Keeping Slug Woman Alive* (Berkeley: University of California Press).

Watson, G. and Goulet, J.-G. (1992), 'Gold In; Gold Out: The Objectification of Dene Tha Accounts of Dreams and Visions', *Journal of Anthropological Research* 48, 215-30.

Chapter 4

The Dilemmas of Walking: A Comparative View

Thomas Widlok

Introduction

Walking has been a prominent topic of philosophical reflection both throughout the history of Western thought and, more recently, in the field of cultural history. Recent cultural historical studies of walking have ranged from discussions of the connection between walking and specific genres of writing, across military history, fashion, art and architecture, to the consideration of walking as a protest movement (see Amato 2004; Jarvis 1997; König 1996; Solnit 2000; Wallace 1993). With so much ground to cover, cultural historians have tended to concentrate their attention on the Western world, leaving it to anthropologists to document the non-Western cases they have set aside (Amato 2004, 15). Yet with its focus on cultural difference, the discipline of social anthropology has up to now had rather little to say about what is perceived to be a universal attribute of human nature – namely, the ability to walk upright (for example, Keesing 1981, 13-14). Only with the contemporary rise of interest in the evolution and history of bodily skills has walking been returned to the anthropological agenda (Ingold 2000; 2004), adding to the demand not only for genuinely comparative studies of walking practices in both Western and non-Western societies, but also for reflection on the role of walking in anthropological enquiry itself. This chapter seeks to advance both these aims by comparing two modes of walking – one Western, the other non-Western, but both practised in the same environment – that I have studied ethnographically.

The modes I want to consider may initially seem to have much in common, since both involve bush walkers. Practitioners of the first mode are quite well-known to anthropologists. They used to be known by a name given to them on the basis of their walking in the bush: the 'Bushmen' of southern Africa.[1] More has to be said by way of introduction about practitioners of the second mode. Their cultural background is unequivocally Western, but within that context their peculiar preoccupation marks them out not just as members of a subculture, but perhaps of a subculture within a subculture. They are walkers, users of GPS technology and an internet community at

---

1   I have discussed the issues concerning this name elsewhere (see Widlok 1999, 15-17, see also Barnard 1988), pointing out that the people concerned are now officially and collectively named 'San' in Namibia and that there is wide agreement among anthropologists to use their own autonyms when referring to specific groups.

the same time. For want of a better word I will call them 'confluencers'. A confluence is the name given to any point on the globe where full degrees of longitude and latitude intersect. The ambition of the confluencer, equipped with a hand-held GPS, is to visit and document such points. The history of the confluence movement is recorded on the internet homepage of its American founder, Alex Jarrett, who began these visits in 1996, put their documentation onto the world wide web and created www.confluence.org, an internet community with growing popularity and numbers. On its homepage the mission of the Degree Confluence Project is summarized as follows:

> The goal of the project is to visit each of the latitude and longitude integer degree intersections in the world, and to take pictures at each location. The pictures, along with a narrative describing the adventures it took to get there, are then posted on this web site. This creates an organized sampling of the world (FAQ on www.confluence.org, August 3, 2005).

My study of confluencers was based on itinerant participant observation. I registered as a member on www.confluence.org, read about other members' visits to confluences, downloaded the instructions for a 'successful' visit and for submitting a report, made visits to three confluences in Namibia, documented and submitted, 'uploaded' the photos and the story. We, myself and a linguist colleague, became confluencers. We were excited to have found a 'useful' use for the GPS, an excuse for driving offroad and then walking into the bush in order to reach the confluence. This seemed to be a fairly straightforward case of men playing with technology (GPS and offroad vehicles) and exploring the wild (see Figure 4.1). This impression is supported by the all-male voices in the project description that speak of 'confluence hunting', the thrill of preparing a confluence visit, the technical precision and the ethos of collection. Neither our female colleague in the team nor a female colleague of mine who, due to her research permit in the Etosha Park, would have had an exclusive opportunity to visit the confluences there, could see the point of these confluence visits. The majority of members registered at www.confluence.org are men, as are all but one of the regional coordinators who check the confluence submissions in a region before they go online. Is this predominantly male pursuit, then, also based on a chauvinist subcurrent, a continuation of the imperialist and colonial project of the early explorers? With no more blank spaces on the world map, the confluence movement provides opportunities for enjoying the experience of 'being first', of 'making it despite considerable obstacles' and for demonstrating this feat to the world (wide web). The Degree Confluence Project homepage (www.confluence.org) is headed by a montage of ecological images, exotic people on foot in front of a 4x4 vehicle and a confluencer in explorer pose next to the American flag.

However, there are caveats. Firstly, confluence.org's mission statement promises not only first visits but regular revisits to confluences in order to gain an ecologically informative record of environmental change:

> Another goal is to document the changes at these locations over time. Although we initially want to visit as many different locations as possible, don't hesitate to revisit a confluence if you're in the area (FAQ on www.confluence.org, August 3, 2005).

It is true that there are many more first visits than second visits on record and more than one would expect, given the remoteness of many confluences and the more ready opportunities for revisits. The stories that go with the visits are usually exploratory tales with a focus on the difficulties of getting to the place, especially where there are no roads and when one has to resort to walking. Thus the dominant motive seems to be one of personal challenge and satisfaction, as in other 'sporting' activities.[2] Secondly, the appropriation of these places is not permanent. Just as shooting wild animals with a gun is being replaced by shooting photos (at least for the majority of visitors to faraway places), so has taking the land been replaced by taking GPS readings (as well as photos) – and drawing a limited amount of glory from having been there first.[3] In our particular case we added another reflexive (and in a sense subversive) element by taking a local person to the confluence. As we were involved in a language documentation project, our idea was to elicit some linguistic description of the landscape to be found at various confluences, to reveal the indigenous way of perceiving the land as an alternative to the grid-based European approach, and to publicize the claim of colonially dispossessed local people to this land by putting the information on the web. These aims were only partially realized, as we shall see. Confronting local 'Bushmen' with the confluences project led to a much more comprehensive comparison than was initially envisaged.

Despite the different cultural backgrounds of confluencers and local inhabitants, there are analogies between their respective practices that point to a more general underlying dynamic. One element of this dynamic lies in the dilemma that to turn towards one place or person entails turning away from another. Another is what I call the path-dilemma. This refers more specifically to walking in the wild, and inheres in the way that one person's opening of a path may, for others, effect a closure. These dilemmas, I argue, are apparent in both the cases explored here as well as more widely, and have implications, too, for the journeys undertaken by anthropologists as they enter and leave the field. Tangentially to this comparative argument, I will argue that the distinction between walking and riding (or driving) is less important than that, on the one hand, between coming and going, and on the other between opening and closing a path, both of which apply not only to walking but also to other modes of movement.

---

2 A related GPS-based sport is 'geocaching' (see www.geocaching.com) where 'caches' are hidden, the instructions to find them published on the web, together with reports by those who have set out to find the caches, who replaced the objects hidden in them, and so on. This regionalized and popular version of electronic paper-chase has interesting parallels with confluencing. The arbitrarily set places are 'refreshed' regularly as visitors leave new objects and it has the added 'thrill' of preventing so-called 'mugglers' from observing the visit and destroying the placed cache.

3 As in the age of exploration this 'being there first' is in any case largely an illusion because local people have been living in the region all along with a likelihood of having been even to the very spot of the confluence, albeit unwittingly.

Coming is going away

The so-called 'Bushmen' of southern Africa and their mobility patterns have been well documented in anthropology (for instance, Barnard 1991) so that a short resumé of the ethnography will be sufficient. My own field research was carried out primarily with Akhoe Hai//om people in the north of Namibia.[4] Like many of the other 'San' groups they move more or less regularly within a land that they consider to be theirs but which has been appropriated by other groups (Barnard and Widlok 1996). Today most Akhoe Hai//om have a semi-permanent residence from which they undertake visits to other places that can range from day trips and short stays to those which, in effect, move the home base (usually with an option to return or move on).

The first point to note in this pattern is that visits and moves are not only intended to get to a certain place, with a certain resource or a certain relative living there, but also and at least as often, are a means to get away. Social disruption and conflict of any kind, including the attempt to avoid conflict, are common motives for trying to leave. Mobility studies informed by an ecological paradigm have tended to identify resource depletion, dirt, disease or the occurrence of a death as factors which make people want to move away (Kelly 1995). My own research, however, indicates that social causes frequently lie behind ostensibly ecological ones. In discussing the reasons for actual or possible moves, people commonly refer to such matters as dirt or resource depletion in order to avoid having to draw attention to more sensitive issues of interpersonal relations.

Moreover today, possibly more clearly than in the past, conflicting pull and push factors have to be considered. Going away to enjoy a certain resource to be found elsewhere (be it a wild fruit in season or a government service such as schooling or food distribution) may entail separating from people with whom one would otherwise want to stay and leaving a place that one likes for its social harmony or for a variety of other reasons, both economic and social. What is true of moving one's residence or occupancy between settlements also applies to moving a hut within a settlement and even to the micro-level changes of bodily positioning and posture in conversation. And it involves non-human as well as human partners, for instance when – in the context of hunting – a decision has to be made to follow the track of one animal instead of another. The dilemma that going or turning *towards* somewhere implies going or turning *away from* somewhere else is found in a variety of contexts on a continuum from micro- to macro-settings.

This casts doubt on the conclusion put forward by many historians of European culture, that walking (like hunting or fishing) has changed from being a matter of necessity to being one of choice (Amato 2004, 255). Even where riding was not available as an alternative to walking, staying put or non-walking frequently remained as at least a temporary option. It is not however one that escapes the underlying dilemma that arriving presupposes leaving. The first corrective to be made to the predominantly Eurocentric perspective of historical studies is thus that walking in a hunter-gatherer society (and, I suggest, in most other contexts) has never been

---

4   For a positioning of the Akhoe Hai//om in the classification of hunter-gatherer and other groups in the area see Widlok (1999).

merely a matter of necessity. People choose to walk or not to walk, often as a way of maintaining or restoring peace of mind. Because it contrasts with the option of staying, the act of walking is significant in itself. The physical cost of walking differs only in degree from that of merely attending to or turning towards someone or someplace – an act that is no less physical. Moreover, *not* going somewhere can also have its costs in terms of missed opportunities, and there is also a certain threshold when walking away is a result of prior opportunities. In my ethnographic work I found that mobility often increases after 'returnees' had arrived and been taken in. Prior opportunities for returning include the arrival of other persons, or of a seasonal fruit, or rain.

Returning now to the 'confluencers': the prominence they attach to the difficulties of finding a place and getting to it is in marked contrast to the apparent ease with which hunter-gatherers orient themselves and move around in their home region. The 'Bushmen' seem to side more with working class people living a constrained life in their own quarters (Rose 2001), and with other folks who know their habitual ways (Ingold 2000, 219), than with map-users and others who set out to explore new routes (Gell 1985). Where hunter-gatherers move away from conflictual relations and towards harmonious ones, so also do explorers walk 'to meet friendly and to escape hostile populations' (Amato 2004, 135). Unlike local people, however, explorers aim to make their way from familiar to unfamiliar places. And in this, confluencers are no exception. As I hinted above, confluencers share with explorers some of the colonial and imperial ambitions of occupying space, of 'getting there first' and of taming wilderness.[5]

One could even argue that confluencers, despite their expressed aims, pursue the ultimate appropriation of space that goes beyond colonial projects. Colonial explorers and settlers were seeking resources such as minerals, ivory or good pasture. In northern Namibia they exploited Hai//om hunting skills as well as their knowledge of iron ore deposits. They co-opted local leaders into deals, offering them gifts, and ultimately took over their land (see Gordon 1992; Widlok 1999). Confluencers, however, invent their own resource (the confluence) about which locals know little and care less. Their intentions are not as commercial and exploitative as those of mining corporations but they nevertheless subordinate local concerns to the homogenizing grid of longitude and latitude, taking the shortest route with little regard for local conditions. There is an interesting twist here as confluencers naturalize their own cultural inventions. In the words of a confluencer:

> Confluences are interesting to me because they represent randomness that emerges from strict order. It goes far beyond a silly quest for invisible man-made boundaries. The confluence latticework is an open defiance of the order our culture imposes on us, which frowns on tourists who abandon the travelled roads, the sanitized vistas, and the

---

5 If wilderness is defined as 'a place in which humans never set foot' (Amato 2004, 83; see Mitchell 2001), then going to places as the confluencers do effectively reduces wilderness and the unknown.

stops designed to conjure up dollars for empty memories (Tim Vasques quoted on www. confluence.org, August 3, 2005).[6]

Confluencers share this naturalization of their approach with natural scientists. Botanists, for instance, who seek to establish the 'natural' distribution of species, commonly resort to statistical analysis of samples found on the ground onto which they have superimposed a map-like grid. Zoologists and other natural scientists use the same strategy.[7]

The confluence project, with its aim to document natural change, uses this strategy in resorting to the global grid of full degrees. The cultural specificity of the ideas of 'arbitrariness' and the 'random sample' is eclipsed in the process of naturalization. In reality, confluencers make their own salient places, and the reaction of the local people who followed us to these places testifies to the artificiality of this salience as they shake their heads about those who undertake great effort to arrive at a spot that to them, in most cases, has no significance whatsoever. However, in selecting their own places confluencers are caught in the same trade-off described above for mobile hunter-gatherers. Focusing their attention on confluence points, it is diverted from the salient places that locals may identify but which happen to fall in between confluences. This came back to us forcefully when we were trying to appropriate the confluence idea for publicizing the fate of Akhoe Hai//om people. There is a place called Sanab which has gained salience in the Akhoe Hai//om struggle over land-encroachment (see Widlok 2003). A grove of mangetti trees nearby yields a traditional staple fruit; today it has a water-pump established by the government, it has been subject to illegal fencing and to resettlement by agropastoralists, and it was here that negotiations took place between the National Minister of Lands and local headmen and NGO representatives. A salient point indeed, it would have been perfect for a confluence report by locals telling the story of their connections to the land. Unfortunately, the place is not a confluence, in fact it is in between two confluences and therefore could not even be considered a place in the vicinity.

Salient places like Sanab, which have an interesting and relevant local story, literally fall through the global grid of confluences. At least the confluence project allows confluencers to take photos and notes of salient features in the vicinity of confluences. Having visited three confluences in northern Namibia, all of which were outside settlements, I found it remarkable that in the vicinity of all these places the triad of fences, livestock and people was to be found. I think this is ubiquitous in

---

6   The passage continues: 'Confluences are in curious places that embrace you in their history, character, and ecology, surrounded by people who are locals in every sense of the word. You simply haven't experienced a region unless you've tried seeking out its confluences.' In other words, the claim is that local meanings are best (naturally) captured through a strategy of randomness (see below).

7   Zoologists put up pit-traps to count the animals caught in them (see Widlok forthcoming); environmental biologists take samples from the 'arbitrary' points in a grid to assess ecological changes caused, for instance, by animals grazing. Somewhat different is the strategy of geomorphologists who seek to establish a culturally neutral conceptual grid for describing landscape types onto which ethnomorphologies can then be mapped. They do not rely on randomness but still have to face the fact that many of the distinctions that their categorization produces are non-salient for locals and vice versa.

Namibia today, characterized as it is by the enclosure and privatization of communal land, by overstocking, and at least in some parts of the country by overpopulation relative to the capacity of the land. To document this triad in the confluence project is possible but depends on the background of the confluencer, in particular the amount of time he or she has spent in the region. A 'confluence visit', therefore, not only selects some places and disregards others, it also selects a certain time (a 'visit') and disregards others (above all time spent 'living there'). Although confluencers are encouraged to undertake revisits during other seasons they will never reach the temporal depth that a place or an area carries for local people. Again, this became clear to us when involving local people in confluence visits (Figure 4.1). They would attach very different temporal saliencies to a place, ranging from stories about the past when they had passed through the area, to expectations about the future (wondering when the owner of the place would show up) or about potential points in time (wondering what they would do if they were given this land to live on). The point here is not to discredit confluencers but simply to show that by selecting a place and a time for their visit they turn away from other places, not only from the place outside the wilderness from which they started their journey but also from other, alternative places and times that matter to people living in the area. The trade-off is inevitable, and the anthropologically interesting question is how it is resolved by the two groups concerned.

Figure 4.1 Christian Rapold, Abakub //Gam//gaeb and Thomas Widlok at the 18/18 confluence, recording local stories about the land

The Akhoe Hai//om, like any other people in a similar situation, have a number of means of dealing with the 'coming is going' dilemma outlined above. For instance, they may leave a hut or some parts of their possessions as a material place-holder which promises their return to the place they are about to leave. They can thereby underline any verbal promise of return that may be given or sent through others. Similarly, the frequency of moves back and forth testifies to a commitment to more than one place and neutralizes the dilemma to some degree. Conversational analysis has shown how, with words, gestures or gaze, things may be put on hold as one turns away momentarily, ready to turn back to a conversational partner or keeping up attention to more than one person or situation. By these means the dilemma may be resolved by stretching it over time, making co-presence in two places and movement in two directions possible.

The confluencers, by contrast, seem to resolve the trade-off in what appears to be the opposite manner, converting it to a matter of chance and non-commitment. If the confluence happens to be a featureless place in the scrub so be it: it is not the responsibility of the confluencer but has been 'decided' by those who established the grid a long time ago. If the time of the visit happens to be just after a devastating fire, so be it: others will have the chance to re-visit at another point in time. This leads us to another dimension of comparison. 'San' stress their autonomy when moving (or not moving) from one place to another. However, as shown above, they make use of messengers and place holders to express their commitment to places and they build on the memory of their interlocutors to whom they have promised their visit (or return) or whom they have threatened with their departure. Confluencers, too, emphasize their individual feat of having reached a place. They also register their plans to visit a confluence on the webpage and mark the liminal period between the visit and submitting the documentation online. They therefore rely critically on others. They depend on others to maintain the homepage, and thereby the public memory of their visit. They also rely on others to respect the rules of the game and to visit other confluences (and to revisit theirs) in order to make the random-selection strategy of time and place worthwhile. In other words, the dilemma that turning to a place means turning away from another not only concerns the isolated agent in a situation of individual decision making, it also involves other people, in particular those who made their own movements earlier and who will make more movements at a later stage partly in response to the agent's act. The underlying dilemma is thus extended to a third party, creating a dilemma of its own, namely, the path dilemma.

Opening a path is closing a path

Consulting a map of northern Namibia, as in other parts of Africa, one soon realizes that the cartographic grid of longitude and latitude is not an abstract and 'innocent' convention but has informed how colonial forces organized space, delimited the land and divided it. Local boundaries were either not known or understood, or were deliberately disregarded in the colonial ordering of space. A good part of the northern boundary of Namibia with Angola divides the settlement area of the Kwanyama Owambo in parallel to the 17th degree southern latitude. When South Africa administered Namibia before its independence and sought to introduce an apartheid homeland policy the 18th degree eastern longitude was taken to be the boundary between the Owambo and the Kavango 'tribes', leaving no space to the Hai//om and other 'San' who actually occupied the land between these two groups. Today there is still a road (and a fence) that marks this degree, just as the grid is still visible on the ground as it separates 'communal' land from 'private' land as well as boundaries between farms, national parks, etc. Once markers such as roads and fences are constructed on the mapped ground they gain a force of their own, spawning new divisions oriented with regard to these 'given' features. For instance, the South African army, which used 'Owamboland' as a buffer zone to prevent the infiltration by the armed independence movement SWAPO into the land occupied by White settlers, created a grid of 'cutlines' which served not only as a system of roads for the rapid movement of troops but also as carefully guarded linear clearings that would show if anyone had moved across the sand leaving tracks behind. Anyone found walking in the bush was suspicious and could be shot. The army used a strategy that has a long tradition, at least as far back as the enclosure of the commons in Britain, by which the establishment of roads was a means not only to bring people forward but also to keep them out – out of the land in between roads. In their use, these roads continue to open up land and close it off at the same time.

Just after Namibian independence the Australian UN troops deployed to this part of Namibia introduced heavy machinery to cut a grid of trails through the forest of north-eastern 'Owamboland', opening the land to new settlers, to resettlement and 'development', and making it more difficult for anyone to hide and to escape the fencing and 'valorization' of the land. In Namibia, farmers today put a high emphasis on the maintenance of roads, not only for their own convenience of movement but also to make sure that farm workers use these roads instead of crossing the land using footpaths or short cuts. Anyone found crossing a privately owned farm is suspected of slaughtering or stealing livestock, of introducing diseases and of making unlawful use of the land. A young Akhoe Hai//om man recently replied to my question as to why he wanted to attend literacy classes, by saying that it was important to be able to read because one would otherwise easily get shot for failure to observe the 'no trespass' signs. Road makers not only want to keep people from their land, they also want to control access to places more generally. If a road leads to a place – a farm homestead for instance – anyone using that road had better be invited or welcome by the owner of the place. Being the first to make a road is not necessarily tantamount to opening up space, it may also be a means to close it. Confluencers are no exception in this regard. Their detailed descriptions of how to get to a confluence, published on the internet, can open up the place for future visits. At the same time they decrease its attraction as a place for others to visit, removing the incentive for those who want to be the first at a confluence – which is after all one of the strongest motives driving the confluence movement.

How does this compare to the Akhoe Hai//om who have neither the opportunity to restrict the movement of fellow people nor the interest to compete in the way that confluencers do? Their main concerns are potential conflicts and dilemmas arising from the restrictive behaviour of farmers. Often they have to ask themselves whether they should take the road or a short cut with the possible danger of being shot at. However, they are also caught in the path dilemma as described above. Foraging nearly always entails some degree of trail blazing in that, since food sources are quickly depleted next to a path, it usually pays to venture a little further, for example to mangetti trees from which others have not yet harvested nuts. On the other hand established paths not only make walking easier and save the trouble of constantly having to orient oneself, they also lead to resources with seasonal reliability such as water sources, termite mounds or groves of trees. These paths are not deliberately cut but rather emerge as a consequence of regular use. Moreover, at least in some cases, the regular movement also generates the reason for using these paths, through a process that involves the unwitting cooperation of humans, animals and plants. At several places the rich mangetti trees not only grow in groves but also along lines, mostly but not always connecting water pans (Widlok, forthcoming). It is likely that both animals and humans have created these lines of trees not only by chewing nuts, but also by dropping them or spitting out the hard kernels, from which new trees can grow. Mangetti trees have a fairly short lifespan but once a line or path of trees is established it 'invites' future use through providing shade for walking, food in the way of nuts, or water resources as rain water can be found in hollow tree-trunks. Individual decisions to walk to a certain place using a certain route have lasting implications for third parties (those who may use the path in the future), since each decision has itself been informed by the previous walks of others.

It is common for modern roads to follow existing paths which in turn – as in North America – were often based on animal tracks (Jackson 1994, see also Hulbert 1902). Geographers and historians have had great difficulty in distinguishing 'roads' from 'trails' or 'paths', partly because of this developmental link, and partly because the physical state of roads may differ greatly according to time and season, depending on how they are used. The same applies to paths (Amato 2004). Roads follow the intention to regulate movement, to open up access for those following the road, and at the same time to close it to others and to bar other areas next to the road from trespass. However, particularly in a walking environment, there is a limit to the degree of control that road-makers can exert over people's movements. The presence of roads (or well-trodden paths more generally) is both an attraction and a disincentive, not only for confluencers and committed outdoor enthusiasts but also for 'San' and others who walk the land in daily routines of making a living and of getting around. Both groups have to face the fact that simply by using a route they cannot help but establish some sort of path or trail that others can then follow, or deliberately choose not to follow. The outdoor slogan 'leave nothing behind but your trail' can be inverted to confirm that it is not possible to move around the land without leaving trails which can then inform the movement of third parties (and of course, one's own future movements as well). Again, we can ask how the two groups under consideration here deal with this inherent feature of walking.

For the Akhoe Hai//om at least part of the answer is to be found in foraging as their erstwhile dominant mode of subsistence. With no livestock to steal and no fields that could be destroyed, Akhoe Hai//om have been fairly relaxed about anyone crossing their land or leaving a path (Widlok 1999, 80). In hunting animals that move, gathering plants that provide edible roots and collecting nuts and berries, it pays both to roam widely and to leave well-trodden paths. To interpret the tracks of game animals, hunters need always to keep open a number of hypotheses which can be tested as more information becomes available (Liebenberg 1990). Every path is a potential source of information that can contribute to hunting success. Thus, leaving paths is not just permitted but encouraged. Unlike farmers who guard their enclosed fields and herds against outsiders, among hunter-gatherers everyone is free to go whatever way they will, whether this means following in the footsteps of others or striking out in unorthodox directions. So long as population densities remained fairly low, forager groups were open to seasonal or other visits by neighbouring groups who wanted or needed to make use of local resources and who might also bring other resources and trade items from neighbouring regions. In sum, with a fairly abundant resource base and social relations based on mutual assistance and equal rights of access, the path-dilemma of walking lost its relevance in practice, except perhaps in times of severe food shortage.

But things changed dramatically with the arrival of powerful groups seeking exclusive access rights to land. In the early colonial context, for instance, when 'wild Bushmen' could be shot or chased away as 'vermin' (see Gordon 1992), leaving a trail would allow the colonizers – supported by indigenous trackers – to find and kill whole families. Although the situation is not so severe today, groups of 'San' who lack land rights are potentially at risk of being suspected of cattle theft and disruption and are therefore subject to expulsion. Frequent clashes between 'San' and landowners testify that the dilemma is far from resolved and that various degrees of force are being used to compel 'San' to use official roads and resettlement sites.

In a certain sense the situation of confluencers in the early years of the confluence project is similar to that of foragers living undisturbed by encroaching powers. As long as there is a relative abundance of confluences that have not been visited[8] the path-dilemma does not lead to negative results. In fact, it lends an in-built tension to the project that probably adds to its attractiveness. The chance to be the first at a confluence, to blaze a trail and to depart from established paths in order to get to a confluence, is no doubt attractive to confluencers. At the same time, documenting one's achievement in reaching a particular confluence adds the extra attraction of making one not only an explorer but also a map-maker of sorts, doing something not just for one's own pleasure but for the common good – if only for that of a specific internet community. However vaguely defined, documenting a confluence visit is said to be beneficial for potential future visitors (who need to know the way) and to the project at large, which needs this information to establish its relevance (as furnishing an inventory of the current state of global ecology). It remains to be seen whether and how this situation changes once most confluences have been visited. There may be scope to stave of imminent saturation by adding complicating factors such as being the first to visit the confluence at a certain season or after a long drought. Since the more precise the visit, as measured by GPS (Figure 4.2), the higher its ranking on the Degree Confluence Project's homepage, there is always room for topping an existing visit. In the long run it is likely that confluences that can readily be reached will lose their attractiveness in the way that mountain peaks do that can be comfortably reached at any time of the year, such as by cable-car.

---

8   At present about 11,000 of the over 16,000 relevant confluences have not yet been visited and recorded in the Degree Confluence Project (www.confluence.org, October 12, 2007).

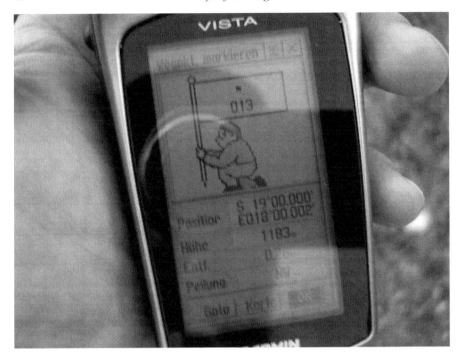

**Figure 4.2 GPS reading at a degree intersection, known among confluencers
as 'the confluence dance', whereby the visitor makes steps in
various directions in order to have full figures on the GPS display
(see also http://www.confluence.org/confluence.php?visitid=8170)**

The ways of anthropology

After having compared the two kinds of 'bush-walkers', namely confluencers and
'Bushmen' of southern Africa, we may ask what insights this comparison may hold
for what anthropologists do when they 'go to the field'. Anthropology is, in origin, a
European project. It is therefore not surprising that the ethnographer has a firm place
in the European history of walking. Reacting to a long history of denigrating walking
as something primitive and inferior, the era of romanticism and enlightenment began
to give intrinsic worth to walking as 'a unique way of experiencing and knowing
the world' (Amato 2004, 103). The countryside ramblers of the nineteenth century
also went out to encounter diverse people, a practice that subsequently became
the hallmark of folk studies and ethnography. Turning away from the developing
industrial society, they found not only a way 'back to nature' and an entry to hitherto
unknown places but also a means to make contact with the 'forgotten people' who
dwelled in or used to inhabit these places (Amato 2004, 123).

   As I have suggested above, this is connected to the imperialist and colonial
projects, but not in the way that is commonly perceived. Although ethnographers
benefited from the colonial control that allowed them to enter faraway regions in
relative safety, it is worthwhile to distinguish the motives of ethnographers from

those of colonialists. The ethnographers' escapism, along with the widespread sentiment that non-European ways of life offered a critique of Western civilization, contrast with the typical colonial idea of implementing European rule and European standards in the colonies. Early explorers and the colonial administrators of later years imported to the non-Western setting the distinction between riding and walking, which was a strong marker of class difference in Europe's hierarchical societies. Typically the White man would be carried or would ride (first a horse or ox-drawn wagon, later a car), while the locals would walk and carry the loads (see Amato 2004, 206). Not only was the distinction reinvigorated by its transfer to the colonial setting; ultimately it also justified the maintenance of the hierarchical system at home. Thus, it is worth considering not only the direct effect of colonization on the colonized, but also the indirect effect of justifying the established order in the society of the colonizers that came to dominate the world. In this respect it is instructive to look at anthropology.

Ethnographers have long reflected on the issues of culture shock and cultural relativity that emerge when, in their fieldwork, they turn towards their host society and inevitably, if only temporarily, away from their home society. To the degree that they engage with another social order they tend to become critical of the social rules they learned in their first socialization. With regard to the 'third parties' involved, however, a somewhat different picture emerges. An ethnographer's identification with 'his tribe' or 'her village' is a well-known theme in anthropology. For long it was the accepted view that once the ethnographer had made his or her way into a field, this field was then 'taken' and no longer available to others. Making an inroad into a particular community or society was considered tantamount to blocking the way for any other ethnographer who wanted to enter. This kind of territoriality has often been attributed to the early ethnographers. However, with traditional field sites becoming increasingly 'scarce', as a result of social change as well as the greater say that research subjects now have in regulating access to their communities, the phenomenon has not disappeared. Most anthropologists identify their professional profile in the first place in terms of regional expertise and the location of their field research, while the particular questions and problems they seek to address usually come second. This 'colonial' behaviour does not necessarily affect research subjects directly but – as with the feedback processes described above – it continues to shape the discipline and the hierarchical relations within it. Ethnographers are mobile and, rather like the confluencers, take pride in opening up new ways and vistas. But the celebration of this ethnographic trail-blazing often eclipses the fact that it may be part of a process of closure whereby other ethnographers (or indeed other non-locals entering the field such as travellers, missionaries and academics of other disciplines without a tradition of long-term field research) are kept at bay or excluded altogether. Today the value of restudies is often recognized, as are the limitations of even 'long-term' field research by comparison with the *truly* long-term (that is, transgenerational) and regional dynamics that no single researcher would have the capacity to encompass.

This makes it even more striking that, when faced with the underlying path-dilemma, many ethnographers choose to resolve it by siding with closure as they clearly mark their trail and continue to be defensive towards others trying to take advantage of the paths they have made. One of the reasons for this strategy is that in contrast to hunter-gatherers, and the early confluencers for that matter, the situation is not one of abundance but of scarcity, or at least of perceived scarcity. Opportunities for doing field research with indigenous people who form the traditional subject of ethnography are scarce, even more so because of the widespread perception that social change is 'destroying' field sites. Despite changes in the way 'the ethnographic field' is defined, in terms of both the expansion of its regional scope and the removal of its limitation to a single site, research funding, publication opportunities and job recruitment are still organized largely along lines of regional specialization, with a clear bias towards 'exotic field sites' that are, by definition, low in number.

Does that leave anthropologists with no alternatives in dealing with the dilemmas described above? I think there are alternatives and that they are best described as a continuation of the discussion of walking with which this chapter began. Only under certain conditions does walking towards a place unequivocally imply walking away from another. The conditions are that the movement should follow a direct course from A to B, such that a return to A would imply a 180-degree shift and a retracing of one's own steps. Confluencers may choose to travel in this way, but it is not characteristic of the movements of hunter-gatherers, nor in all probability of most people in their everyday lives. When foraging for a day people move in a roundabout fashion, as do window-shoppers and strollers, so that they are moving away and back again at the same time. As they advance from their point of origin they are simultaneously approaching it. Though they may have changed in the process (lost energy, gained food) there is no point that demarcates 'going out' from 'coming back'. The path-dilemma, too, loses much of its import when we shift from paths *between* two places to paths *around* a multitude of places. The more numerous the places, the less likely it is that the links between them will be well-trodden or worn out.

For the anthropological enterprise this mode of movement *around* would translate into a pattern that breaks with the conventional, bidirectional movement 'into the field' and back again. This is fairly easily achieved through a combination of multi-sited ethnography, comparative work and the recognition that 'home' is also a worthy field of research. The last point refers not just to the idea, already well established, that anthropological fieldwork may be carried out in nominally Western societies. More fundamentally, it entails a rethinking of the subject matter of anthropological research. Anthropological linguists, for instance, have suggested that the narrow definition of a language as comprising of grammar and lexicon prevents us from understanding language differences on the basis of the processes of extension that characterize the pragmatics of everyday speech (Agar 2002; Hanks 1996). Similarly, instead of looking at different modes of movement (walking and riding for instance) as completely separate 'fields', they may more profitably be researched on the grounds of the everyday phenomenology of movement (Ingold 2000). For ethnography more generally this would mean a convergence of experiences in 'other cultures' with the daily experiences of living in a cultural world. This would help to open up new views while breaking down the present tendency towards academic closure.

References

Agar, M. (2002), *Language Shock: Understanding the Culture of Conversation* (New York: Harper Collins).

Amato, J. (2004), *On Foot: A History of Walking* (New York: New York University Press).

Barnard, A. (1988), 'Cultural Identity, Ethnicity and Marginalization Among the Bushmen of Southern Africa', in Vossen, R. (ed.) (1998), *New Perspectives on Khoisan. Quellen zur Khoisan-Forschung 7* (Hamburg: Buske).

—— (1991), 'Social and Spatial Boundary Maintenance Among Southern African Hunter-Gatherers', in Casimir, M. and Rao, A. (eds) (1991), *Mobility and Territoriality: Social and Spatial Boundaries Among Foragers, Fishers, Pastoralists and Peripatetics* (New York: Berg).

Barnard, A. and Widlok, T. (1996), 'Nharo and Hai//om Settlement Patterns in Comparative Perspective', in Kent, S. (ed.) (1996), *Cultural Diversity Among Twentieth Century Foragers: An African Perspective* (Cambridge: Cambridge University Press).

Gell, A. (1995), 'How to Read a Map: Remarks on the Practical Logic of Navigation', *Man* (N.S.) 20, 271-86.

Gordon, R. (1992), *The Bushman Myth: The Making of a Namibian Underclass* (Boulder: Westview Press).

Hanks, W. (1996), *Language and Communicative Practices* (Boulder: Westview Press).

Hulbert, A.B. (1902), *History of Indian Thoroughfares* (Cleveland: A.H. Clark).

Ingold, T. (2000), *The Perception of the Environment* (London: Routledge).

—— (2004), 'Culture on the Ground: The World Perceived Through the Feet', *Journal of Material Culture* 9:3, 315-340.

Jackson, J. (1994), *A Sense of Place, a Sense of Time* (New Haven: Yale University Press).

Jarvis, R. (1997), *Romantic Writing and Pedestrian Travel* (New York: St Martin's Press).

Keesing, R. (1981), *Cultural Anthropology: A Contemporary Perspective* (2nd edition) (Fort Worth: Holt, Rinehart and Winston).

Kelly, R. (1995), *The Foraging Spectrum: Diversity in Hunter-Gatherer Lifeways* (Washington: Smithsonian Institution Press).

König, G. (1996), *Eine Kulturgeschichte des Spazierganges: Spuren einer bürgerlichen Praktik, 1780-1850* (Vienna: Böhlau).

Liebenberg, L. (1990), *The Art of Tracking: The Origin of Science* (Claremont: David Philip).

Mitchell, J. (2001), *The Wildest Place on Earth: Italian Gardens and the Invention of Wlderness* (Washington: Counterpoint).

Rose, J. (2001), *The Intellectual Life of the British Working Classes* (New Haven: Yale University Press).

Solnit, R. (2000), *Wanderlust: A History of Walking* (New York: Viking).

Wallace, A. (1993), *Walking, Literature, and English Culture: The Origins and Uses of the Peripatetic in the Nineteenth Century* (Oxford: Clarendon Press).

Widlok, T. (1999), *Living on Mangetti: 'Bushman' Autonomy and Namibian Independence* (Oxford: Oxford University Press).

—— (2003), 'The Needy, the Greedy and the State: Dividing Hai//om Land in the Oshikoto Region', in Hohmann, T. (ed.) (2003), *San and the State: Contesting Land, Development, Identity and Representation* (Cologne: Köppe).

—— (forthcoming), 'Where Settlements and the Landscape Merge: Towards an Integrated Approach to the Spatial Dimension of Social Relations', in Bollig, M. (ed.) (forthcoming), *Anthropological Approaches to Landscape* (Berlin: Springer).

Chapter 5

Feet Following Hooves

Pernille Gooch

The Gujjars are calling
mountains and forests that now
we are leaving for different pastures
and no-one knows whether we will meet again.[1]

Introduction

The Himalayas give rise to many forms of walking. For some people walking in the mountains is part of everyday lives, while others walk them for leisure during their spare time. Amongst the different kinds of mountain wanderers are the pastoralists who traverse the whole region as part of their livelihood and for whom walking is the main technique of subsistence. The *Van* (forest) *Gujjars* are one of many pastoral communities who, throughout history, have walked the altitudes of the Himalayas with their herds in accordance with the changing seasons. While for most of the Himalayan pastoral communities the walk of transhumance has stopped – if not for the animals then at least for the majority of the people – for the Van Gujjars, who are specialized pastoralists, the walk continues, involving men, women and children moving with their herds of milk buffaloes. The walk goes through a terrain intimately known and consisting of movements and places apprehended through an embodied knowledge possessed by people as well as animals. This is – to quote Merleau-Ponty – 'the simultaneous patterning of body and world in emotion' (1966, 189). It is a use of the body brought into being through a common history where movement has always been undertaken on foot at the rear of the herd as part of the great pastoral migrations through the region.

But this bodily movement – feet following hooves – is now everywhere hindered by barriers in the landscape, physical and discursive, showing that the region through which they walk is not just a life-world for local communities. It is also a highly politicized landscape, where the power over movement and the apprehension of space in the landscape is, to a great extent, dictated by policies originating in other places. The Himalayas hold a special grip over the human imagination and give rise to rich narrative traditions. As such they are symbolically constructed, poetically imagined, and heavily contested. In one sense, of course, they are very real, in rising out of the Gangetic plains to meet Tibet and China, while in another sense they

---

1   Song by Noor Ahmed, Van Gujjar singer and poet. Translated from Punjabi by Praween Kaushal (known here as Manto).

stretch out of this world and into the sky to meet a world of myth and fantasy. The Himalayas are a place where the sublime meets the everyday struggle for existence, where snow-covered summits towering above green valleys constitute the natural framework for yogis and pilgrims in deep contemplation, for graziers with their herds in the alpine pastures and for peasants toiling in their terraced fields. Lately, though, this idyllic picture has started to crack and through the ruptures another grimmer picture emerges. This is the image of a devastated mountain landscape drifting rapidly towards irreversible destruction.

So we have two competing narrative representations of the Himalayas: one is of the Himalayas shaped by Nature (and the gods) where man dwells in harmony, and the other is of the Himalayas destroyed and misused by man and therefore in need of protection (Gooch 1998a, 326; Ives and Messerli 1989). Suddenly the pastoralists moving through the terrain are no longer peaceful figures naturally blending into the landscape; instead they take on a sinister connotation as a threat to the very world through which they walk. As with the changing patterns of a kaleidoscope the Himalayas are many things to many people, but for the people on the ground – those surviving on the resources they find there – they constitute a life-world that is intimately known by bodily being-in-it and moving-through-it, swinging the arms, and putting one foot in front of the other. But as the Van Gujjars walk through mountains that are also encircled by myth, considered environmentally fragile, contested and politicized, they are confronted with a 'world of discourse' that now threatens to put a final stop to the walk of transhumance. And while this is a result of discussions in faraway places, the threat to the Van Gujjars and their buffaloes, slowly moving through their mountain environment on their seasonal migration, is real and ingrained in the very texture of their walking.

On the path of migration

I will start with a narrative of an episode that took place on a narrow road in the higher ranges of the Central Indian Himalayas in 1992. That summer Manto, my research assistant, and I had joined a group of Van Gujjars in their summer camps close to the tree line, in order to participate in the downward trail of transhumance. Prior to leaving we had had to promise to participate fully in the migration. Kaseem, who had the biggest herd and therefore acted as an informal leader, explained to us that when they stayed in one place in winter or summer they could care for guests in the proper way but on the *rastha* (path of migration) life would be hard and precarious, the journey full of hazards, and anybody joining would have to help in getting the herds back safely to the lowlands. We were now following the milk buffaloes and the bullocks and horses, used as pack animals, on the walk back to the forests of the foothills and the winter camps; a slow walk that would take almost a month and which seldom covered more than 10 to 15 kilometres a day.

On the fourth day of the migration we started moving already at 2am. Walking through the night was a long winding line of animals and people in ordered sections, each herd of buffaloes followed by their herders. Still left sleeping in the camp at the *parao* (halting place) were the women with the children and youngsters who would follow later in the morning with the pack animals. Manto and I walked with Sain Bibi, the only woman among the buffalo herders that morning. As we moved through the night we talked and Sain Bibi, whose herd was at the rear, told stories about places that we passed and about the precariousness of pastoral life: there a buffalo had once fallen; behind that hill relatives of Sakeena, her sister-in-law, had been settled by the government. They had lost all their buffaloes and now they were very poor; and here in this village on the border[2] the forest guards would put up barriers as checkpoints for the herds, demanding money, milk and butter to let them through. This gave rise to several stories about threats from the guards and about avoidance and resistance. But this night the strategy had been to move early and we slipped quietly under the barrier and through the sleeping border village without incident. Everything was peaceful until just before dawn, when the youngest and newest member of the herd, a male calf, disturbed the calm. Sain Bibi had bought him from a farmer up in the hills as a future beast of burden and named him *Baccheru*. He was now making the journey down for the first time and, terrified of the strong light and noise from a passing truck, disappeared back *up* the road in the direction that for him meant home. Sain Bibi and Manto chased after him while I ran after the disappearing buffaloes that had maintained their direction *down* towards the lowland. I now suddenly found myself alone in the night with the responsibility for seven buffaloes, the sole livelihood of a family. Noor Jamal had disappeared around a bend in the road and Kaseem and the others were far ahead. As I could not make the buffaloes stop and wait I had to follow, waving frantically with the stick which is always in the hand of the herder, wanting them to move faster so they would catch up with Noor Jamal. I had no idea which route we were to take and I was worried that I might miss some track leaving the road. On one side of the road the hills rose and on the other there was a steep slope down to the river running swiftly far below. It was cloudy and quite dark in spite of an almost full moon. There were no lights and no houses. After about 15 minutes of utter disorientation I caught up with the rear of Noor Jamal's herd and could resume the slow, casual gait of the migration. Five minutes later I was relieved to see Sain Bibi and Manto returning with the calf. Sain Bibi had slipped on some dung and hurt herself and that was why it had taken them so long (Gooch 1998a, 239).

Weaving the fabric of transhumance

While I was anxious and feeling lost, stepping impatiently along that dark mountain road behind the buffaloes, Sain Bibi's tale was about tripping and getting hurt while chasing the calf. This was an incident that had for a moment disrupted the rhythm of the migration while still being completely embedded within the everyday situation of the walk. The tale was one that could be remembered and retold next time that particular part of the road was passed (Vergunst, this volume). Sain Bibi was not worried about her herd. My experience was to her a non-event, unconnected to the

---

2   Between the Indian states of Himachal Pradesh and Uttaranchal (part of Uttar Pradesh in 1992).

flow of migration, and she did not understand it. How can one be lost behind the buffaloes on the way down? According to her the old buffalo cows *know* the way down. *They* walk at the front and the people follow. The Van Gujjars thus see their buffaloes as agents in the walk and not as objects to be moved. When it is time to return back to the lowlands in autumn, Sain Bibi said, the buffaloes get restless. They start moving downwards and have to be herded back until the people are ready to follow them. According to her, the old buffalo cows sense a change in the air and know it is time to go back. Behind they will leave a landscape of spruce forest and alpine pastures, which will soon become cold and covered in snow, while at the other end of the walk waits the forest of the foothills covered in new green leaves after the monsoon. But it was my first time taking part in the Van Gujjar migration. So even if I could move my feet along the mountain road at the tail of the herd, apart from knowing that I was heading in the general direction 'down', *I* was completely lost while, had I trusted the buffaloes, I should have known that they were not.

The perspective that I brought with me, though, as I tried to find my footing at the rear of the herd, was not only that of an anthropologist but also a practical understanding of pastoralism. But this was with another breed of animals and in a different mountain setting as I had made a living for some years in the 1970s as a goat pastoralist in the hills of Northern Sweden. In summer I used to pasture our flock of about thirty goats in the woods around our farmhouse. Goats are browsers and not grazers and after eating for a while would become restless, whereupon – sensing this mood in the flock – I would take the initiative, call them, and move to a new place with them catching up and following me. In this way we moved, twisting and turning through the landscape, never staying long at one spot and never leaving much of a trail behind us. Being used to the swift and intelligent yet rather anarchistic and whimsical goat, I had great difficulties with what I felt to be the extreme s-l-o-w-n-e-s-s of the buffalo. Buffaloes move and the Van Gujjars follow, and, as I followed the Van Gujjars, I experienced the difference between steering swift goats from the front, feet-leading-hooves, and following slow buffaloes from the rear, feet-following-hooves. It gives rise to very dissimilar perceptions of moving through a landscape as well as different ways of finding routes, leaving trails, and making places.

Left alone with the buffaloes, worried and disoriented, I tried to treat them as goats, taking the command and making them move faster. But I soon realized that it was no use. Van Gujjar buffaloes cannot be hurried; they walk at their own speed. They can be turned in a new direction if trespassing into a farmer's field for a tempting bite, but they cannot be steered and they will not follow. You can take a goat for a walk but it is the buffalo that will take you along. Pastoralists moving with goats and sheep, such as the neighbouring Gaddis or Bhotiya, are much more mobile during migration and can evade dangerous situations and threatening people using alternative routes. But the Van Gujjars, on their walk through the mountains, are stuck at the tail of their heavy buffaloes. They have to follow the main and well-known routes along roads that have changed from horse paths during colonial times to dangerous motor roads today. This makes them feel vulnerable and exposed while out in open landscape. The slowness as well as the existential anxiety of buffalo herding is passionately expressed in this short song by the Van Gujjar poet Noor Ahmed:

Oh buffalo you walk slowly and slowly
while climbing so high.
It is easy to cry
if we lose you.[3]

The Van Gujjars only begin to feel secure when they can at last slip back under cover of the forest at the end of the journey, either in the foothills or close to the tree line.

The spatial extension of Van Gujjar pastoralism stretches over a whole region, but for individual groups it comprises a thin line traversed through land inhabited by agriculturalists during migration, at each end of which are areas of forest inhabited by the Van Gujjars and their buffaloes. Below are *desh*, the forested foothills in the lowlands where they live during winter. This is the place with the strongest connotation of 'home' as they stay there for the longest period. Above are *parhar*, the mountains, where they go during summer to pasture their herds in the *bukiyals*, the alpine pastures, and to escape the scorching heat of the lowlands. This is a time of relative leisure as it is the only phase in the pastoral cycle when the animals can find their own grazing. Connecting the foothills and the mountains are *rastha*, or paths of migration, edged by a number of halting places (*parao*). The Van Gujjars make patterns in their environment by walking through it at the tail of their buffaloes. Their world of hills, mountains, forests and pastures can be seen as a region connected by a 'matrix of paths' in which places are brought into being 'as nodes within a wider network of coming and going' (Ingold 2000, 227). Within this region the Van Gujjars are known as *ana-jana lok*, which can be directly translated as 'coming-going people', the people who come to places and leave them again. We could imagine a textile woven by Van Gujjar walks following the buffaloes as consisting of two clusters hanging at either end of a single knotted line. As the pattern of transhumance is the same from year to year this forms a forwards and backwards movement of coming-and-going that follows the change of seasons and is punctuated by long pauses during summer and winter. This resembles the rhythmic up-and-down beat of a shuttle on a loom. There are many small Van Gujjar groups, like the one described here, each of them weaving their own particular thread, and together they fill the whole region with the texture of pastoralism. Whenever a group stops migrating a thread in this fabric will break. We could say that for each of these groups, everyday walks of path and placemaking in forest and meadows, undertaken during winter and summer respectively, constitute tightly woven webs of capillary theads that are bridged by the arterial walk of transhumance.

Today this bridge is a shaky structure spanning troubled water and when the Van Gujjars stop walking along it the direct link between *desh* with *bukiyals* will cease to exist. Whenever transhumance comes to a halt, as happened to Sakeena's relatives mentioned above, the Van Gujjars use the expression *beithna*, to sit down, while settled people are seen to be like 'stones that cannot easily be moved' (Gooch 1998a,

---

3   Translated from Punjabi by Manto (Praween Kaushal).

220). To sedentarize, for a pastoralist, is to stop walking and sit down. For the Van Gujjars this is a threat more than a promise of rest. Saying goodbye to movement is also saying goodbye to the buffaloes, companions in the walk, and with them to the whole Van Gujjar life-world.

The fabric of Van Gujjar pastoralism is historically constructed by a combination of pastoral needs and administrative rules. Schlee (1992, 110; Croll and Parkin 1992, 21) sees the movements of Gabbra camel herders of the Kenya-Ethiopia borderlands as giving rise to a patterning in space whereby the various landmarks along a route are connected to each other as if by lines. He claims that as pastoralists, the way Gabbra appropriate space is more like that of hunters and gatherers than that of farmers or nation states. While the latter divide up the land into delimited surface areas within territorial boundaries, pastoralists move from one relevant feature of the landscape to another, turning and following an alternative route if necessary, depending on available pasture. In previous times the Van Gujjars also had more freedom to move between relevant features of the landscape, such as good pastures, and along routes most suitable for the seasons' movements. During the colonial period, however, such freedom was severely curtailed by the state in its effort to control buffalo nomadism. The result was that the forest areas, both in the summer and winter pastures, were divided up between individual heads of households as permits to keep a specified number of animals within a delimited area. After independence the Indian forest department continued with this policy. Van Gujjar movements are thus now restricted to particular migration routes during specified periods and their winter and summer grazing is tied to delimited areas of the forest constituting the clusters at either end. But although the choices of the Van Gujjars have been curbed and the alternatives available to them very much limited, they still make full use of what freedom of movement is left to them (Gooch 1998a, 113).

Moving with animals

Van Gujjar buffaloes, as we have seen, are agents and companions in the walk, not objects to be moved. 'Our buffaloes are of a different kind', the Van Gujjars say. They belong to an indigenous breed of hardy animals that have shared their life-world with people for generations. They are efficient in converting forest roughage into milk and they can walk for long hours in rugged terrain. Van Gujjars do not use bulls from outside, of other breeds, because they think such bulls will produce calves that are soft and useless and unable to walk. Crucial to Van Gujjar pastoralism are the strong, personal relationships that develop between particular animals and their human guardians, and which are evident from the ways the animals are treated. It should also be noted that Van Gujjars are vegetarians and that buffaloes are left to die of old age and not slaughtered.[4]

The skills of the Van Gujjars in moving with their animals are critical to their ability to make a living in their world. For a farmer controlling his cattle behind

---

4   At least this was the case during the main part of my fieldwork. There are indications that this is slowly changing as the Van Gujjars come more into contact with mainstream Muslims.

a fence moving with animals is not a great problem, but for a pastoralist walking through open country with a herd of unfettered animals it is crucial. In Sweden I could move with my goats and simultaneously steer them because I assumed a role in the flock as leader, pushing to second-in-command the she-goat that would otherwise have taken the lead. To do that, and to make them trust me as leader, I had to perceive the world through the eyes of a goat, as it were, while moving with them. It was a question of understanding their rhythm of movement in eating-and-walking, looking out for good places to stop as you move along, and anticipating changes in mood just seconds before they would have grown impatient and moved of their own accord and in their own direction. Imagine a hypothetical scenario in which Sain Bibi turned up at my doorstep in Sweden only to find herself alone in an alien forest with a flock of goats she did not know. She might have treated my goats as buffaloes,[5] walking after them and prodding them with a stick. In that situation the goats would have simply scattered, she would not have known which goat to follow and she may have cursed such silly animals that could not move straight ahead in ordered formations and that did not seem to know where they were going.[6] Walking along with a herd of animals thus demands practical mastery of navigating in a world shared by humans and animals.

As this example shows, such mastery is situated *within* a life-world. I found it very hard to perceive the world through the eyes of a buffalo moving through the Himalayas, but this is precisely the perception that guided Sain Bibi and the other Van Gujjars on their walk of transhumance. Successful pastoralism demands a strong feeling of understanding between herders and the animals they herd, tantamount to a shared world-view, whereby the world can be perceived through the senses of the animals in question. When passing through a particular landscape on the downward migration, Lal San defined what he saw as the perfect place for Gujjars: 'This is Gujjar land, good grass, trees, water close by and the fields of the *zamindars* [landowners] far away.' So when it comes to assessing the landscape and its inherent possibilities, the pastoralist may be seen as a kind of 'centaur', simultaneously wo/man and beast, moving along and noticing features relevant to such a being. What is entailed here is a relationship of direct involvement of beings sharing the same world (Ingold 1994, 19). The Van Gujjars become buffalo-people (*baas-lok*). After centuries of moving together, people and animals are united in a shared ontology (Gooch 1998a, 216).

This is reflected in styles of walking, in the technique of human bodies moving with the animals. While I tried to change the rhythm of walking by shortening my steps, in order not to run my nose into the rear of the buffalo in front of me, the Van Gujjars did the opposite. When moving without buffaloes they walked with long strides and it was difficult to keep up with them. While herding the buffaloes they kept the long strides but did so in ultra-slow motion. They also broke the walk frequently, taking pauses by the roadside for a smoke or a chat, letting the buffaloes

---

5   Although of course she would never really do this because her knowledge of goats is much greater than mine of buffaloes.

6   Of course, the goats would also know their way through the woods and, if left on their own, would return to the safety of their stable before nightfall after a busy day of eating and moving and possibly creating havoc in a neighbour's garden.

walk ahead and then catching up with them. A frequent sight on the roads we walked were women agriculturalists from the hills, bending double under heavy loads of grass, straw or firewood as they moved along their trails. Contrasting with them, the Van Gujjars of both sexes walk at ease during migration, using their bodies for moving and their animals for carrying their loads. One strategy for settling the Van Gujjars suggested by the state administration was to offer cheap loans for buying heavy consumer items such as sewing machines. The thought behind this was that the ownership of such cumbersome burdens would wean them away from nomadism. A nomad travelling on foot must travel light through life.

While I enjoyed walking through the forest with the goats and felt impatient with the buffaloes, it was the opposite for Sain Bibi. Although some Van Gujjar families kept small herds of goats, she did not, considering that controlling them was too much work. When she, as the only woman, walked with the family herd of buffaloes during migration, this was a conscious choice of hers. She actually preferred the slow walk following the buffaloes in the coolness of the early mornings to the faster speed of the pack animals later when the day was getting hotter. As she did not have any small children that needed the extra sleep in the morning she could leave the bullocks to her husband, Lal San, who, according to her, 'liked them so much that he would rather carry most of the load himself than put it on the animals'. This also demonstrates the flexible nature of work sharing among Van Gujjars. When I asked 'who does what?' the answer was usually: 'it depends'. When Sain Bibi fell back with her herd and walked last, as in the incident discussed above, it was not because as a female herder she was not respected but rather because she wanted to speak to us without being disturbed. At other times she walked in the middle, talking and laughing with the other herders.

While the buffaloes, born into the circle of pastoralism, know the way and are followed, this is not the case with the bullocks and ponies. Van Gujjar bullocks, used as pack animals, are mainly surplus animals that the agriculturalists in the hills do not want to keep over the winter.[7] The bullocks eventually acquire the skill of transhumance and close friendships may evolve between them and people during the walks. But at first they have to be led in order to move in the right direction. As they learn what is expected of them it becomes more a case of animal and person walking side by side than of one following the other. The same is true for the ponies, which are never ridden. Horses and people walk together. The caravan with loaded pack animals is called the *maal* and distinguished from the other part of the migration, the *baas*, buffaloes. The person walking at the front of the *maal* is usually an older, experienced woman who can find the way down and handle any dangerous situation that might arise on the way. She has a pack animal on a leash beside her and can set the speed and rhythm of walking. As the whole household from the eldest grandmother to the smallest child takes part in the walk of migration the speed has to be adjusted to that of the slowest mover.

---

7   As this is India surplus cattle cannot be slaughtered. An alternative to sending them down with the Van Gujjars is to 'give them to God', that is, closing the stable door to them and letting them fend for themselves.

That women and men walk separately, with each gender having its responsibilities to ensure a safe migration, has resulted in a relatively strong position for women within the Van Gujjar community. The *maal* moves much faster than the *baas*, allowing women and children to sleep longer in the mornings before packing up the camp and moving at ease to the next halt, talking and laughing on the way through uninhabited landscape but with more tension as they pass through villages. The buffaloes start early while the night is still dark so that they can reach the next halt (and food) in mid-morning before the heat of the day becomes too intense. The grown men, assisted by elder boys and sometimes also by girls, walk with the buffaloes. During the night they have to be prepared to hurry off at any time because the buffaloes might get restless and hungry and start moving on their own. Through physically taking part in the walk of transhumance, first with the *maal* and later with the buffaloes, Van Gujjar children grow to embody the cultural and technical skills needed for their life as pastoralists *from the ground* and *through their feet*. And so, the Van Gujjars would argue, do the buffalo calves.

The *dera* (camp), comprising an individual household, is the basic unit of Van Gujjar society. During transhumance a small group of *deras* migrate together. The structure of such groups might vary from year to year as they are kept together by ties of personal friendship as well as by kinship. The groups have to be relatively small so as not to restrict mobility and still large enough for mutual security against robbers and other dangers that might be encountered on the way. Kaseem emerged as the leader for the small migration group described above, although everyone insisted that they had no leaders and did not need any. As one woman, Shammi, said, 'We do not need a leader when going to the market. So why should we need a leader when going to the mountains?' Kaseem was the eldest man and he and his wife Rosni had the largest herd, amounting to almost thirty buffaloes. Kaseem's old buffalo cows led the migration, followed by Kaseem himself. After him came his younger sons with groups of younger animals that were more difficult to manage. What we saw during the days of the migration was that the men wanted to move during the night and early morning and then again in late afternoon after a break for food and rest while the women preferred to make camp early and only move in the mornings. As it turned out the women usually won. The only times we did move in the afternoon were out of dire necessity when there was not enough fodder for the animals in the *parao*.

We have met Van Gujjars and buffaloes walking together through the mountains. Obviously, spending two months of each year on the move places a tremendous strain on both people and animals. The Indian administration has put up more and more hindrances to pastoral nomadism, both as actual barriers on the routes of transhumance and as laws and regulations, the latter often physically manifested in the former. The traditional campsites in state forest are now encroached upon by other people, making it difficult to find fodder. Often the Van Gujjars have to buy it from local farmers at exorbitant prices. Tents made from a sheet of black plastic give little shelter from the rain or during nights of freezing cold. The walk goes through what the Van Gujjars often perceive as a hostile landscape. On one of the first days of the journey down in 1992 we were standing high up on a mountain slope and watching the landscape stretching out to the horizon far below us. Kaseem pointed out the route we were to take and said: 'They are all waiting for us down there, all the way back down to *desh*, just waiting to squeeze as much out of the Gujjars as they can.' The drive behind transhumance is obviously survival, and the buffaloes move according to the availability of green fodder and the people following them. The Van Gujjars consider walking to the mountains as a must for their specific breed of buffaloes. If the buffaloes were forced to spend summers in the dried-out forests of the lowlands, then they would not survive, and nor would the forest, which would be very quickly over-exploited.

A strong motivation for migration given by all is spending the summer away from the heat of the lowlands and giving the forest time to recuperate. As Feroz, one of the men, said: 'The *rastha* is very hard, especially for the children and the old people, but it is very good and cold for both people and animals in the mountains at the end of the journey'. Athru is an old woman of about seventy who still headed the caravan of loaded ponies and bullocks followed by her grandchildren and daughters-in-law. When I asked her if she wanted to settle down, she answered: 'It is good to migrate to Ganga [the place at an altitude of 3,500 metres to which she goes in summer]. Up there is grass in summer. Here in the lowlands there is nothing for us in summer'. Lal San expressed it by simply saying: 'Hindustan is a very good country. When it is cold you can go to the plains and when it is hot you may be in the mountains.' Similar sentiments motivated the British during the colonial era to move to the hill stations in summer riding their horses. The Indian tourists of today do the same, driving their cars; and so do the mountain leisure walkers with their fancy gear. All follow the same tracks as the Van Gujjars and their buffaloes and the roads are getting increasingly crowded.

Movement and placemaking behind the veil of forest

While feeling anxious and exposed when moving through the open mountain landscape of transhumance, safety for the Van Gujjars lies in the forest, especially in the *sal* forests of the Shiwalik foothills where they stay from October to April. The Van Gujjars say, 'We live behind the veil of forest' (Gooch 1998a). The main routes providing entry to the forest behind the veil are the seasonal streams and rivers (*raos*) that receive the torrents of the monsoon during summer but are dry during the rest of the year. The major *raos* run through the foothills from east to west, taking the monsoon water from the Himalayas and down towards the Gangetic plains. They comprise a mesh of broad river tracks with branch tributaries, which form the only entries into an otherwise impenetrable interior. Their bottoms are made up of a thick layer of shingle and boulders that increases with each year. This creates an uneven texture that makes walking with ordinary hard-soled shoes difficult. I used to measure fieldwork periods in numbers of running shoes; a pair was worn out in about a month. Still, one of the reasons why the Van Gujjars accepted me was because I came walking up the *rao*, carrying my own rucksack. Dangerous people do not walk; they come by jeep. Van Gujjars wear soft, thin rubber shoes that take their shape from the texture of the ground beneath them so that wearing them is more like walking barefoot. Although the *raos* make heavy marks in human footwear – at least for an anthropologist – the movements of human and animal feet along them leave little imprint. So while all walking for the Van Gujjars during winter spreads out from these pathways, the movement leaves no visible paths in the beds of stone.

The main *raos* along with the forest surrounding them on either side are known as *khols*. The *khols* play very important roles in the formation of identity and in placemaking for the Van Gujjars. Individual households are identified with the *khols* to which they return each winter. The group that we followed above were *Timli Gujjars* on their way back to their winter land in Timli *khol*. The forest (or *jangal* as the Van Gujjars say) of the *khols* is divided up into permit lands for individual households, a legacy from the British colonial forest administration.

Walking up the *raos* in winter, one passes the *deras* of the Van Gujjars dispersed as dots along their banks and placed in such a way that their inhabitants have a good view of whatever moves on the *rao* beneath. Each *dera* is surrounded by an area of forest from which the household living there is allowed to take fodder for its buffaloes. While the *raos* themselves, the routes into the forests of the Van Gujjars, show little sign of the movements along them, we find the complete opposite in the *jangal* surrounding the *dera*. Here human and buffalo feet have created intricate webs of paths and tracks, all spreading out like many-branched trees from the location of the *dera*. We thus have two systems of tracks. The first, the *raos*, act as social pathways for human-human interaction connecting the camps along their banks. They also open up the forest to interaction with the outside world. The second system, of paths in the forest, is created in the course of animal-human practice within their shared life-world. During winter the buffaloes are fed with leaves lopped from trees and the Van Gujjars have a vast knowledge of the fodder qualities of the trees within their area. Forests are seen through the eyes of the buffalo. A good forest is one that has a large proportion of 'trees-good-for-buffaloes-to-eat', with species such as *bakli, sain, papri, sannan, panchara,* and *maljan.* In daytime the leaves are brought to the animals in the compound of the *dera* at the *rao*, but during the night the buffaloes are fed underneath the trees on the slopes of the hills in the interior of the forest. After the midday rest youngsters of both sexes walk to the area selected for the night, climb up fodder trees that are often very tall, lop the trees and spread out the leaves beneath them ready for eating. The buffaloes then leave the *dera* at dusk, followed by one or two members of the household. They criss-cross through the forest, past ravines, up and down slopes, always selecting the correct turn of the path, and end up ultimately at the place where food is waiting.

As I followed the Van Gujjars following the buffaloes, I was intrigued as to how the animals managed to find the right route. The answer is that the buffaloes follow sounds associated with food and their human caretakers. While sitting up in the trees and lopping the leaves, people sing. And when the time comes that they know the buffaloes must have started walking, they call them with high voices: 'ooh, ooh'. They might also call out the names of individual animals. The buffaloes move in the direction of the sound, and if they seem confused the person following will call out and get an answer from the right bearing. During the night the buffaloes stay in the forest beneath the trees while the people walk back. Buffaloes are strong and can be ferocious, and are well able to defend themselves against the tigers, panthers and leopards of the Himalayan foothills. In the morning the people go to the trees and fetch back the buffaloes for milking.

All this coming and going of buffalo hooves and human feet branches out from every Van Gujjar *dera* to each and every fodder tree of the Shiwalik forest, and weaves a distinctive fabric of human and animal interaction. What outsiders perceive as 'wild' nature is of course a landscape formed by generations of people and buffaloes moving through it, and where deer also feed with the buffaloes beneath the trees. The fabric created by feet and hooves is to a great extent the same from year to year as fodder trees are lopped in a certain sequence. One pattern follows the shedding of foliage, always cutting leaves before the particular species of tree would have lost them naturally. The other pattern starts with the trees furthest away from the *dera* after returning to the forest in autumn and then moves back towards the *dera*. The last tree to be lopped is the one just next to the *dera*. When that has been cut it is again time to leave the dried-out forest behind and start the walk through the *rao* and back up into the mountains.

In winter the *deras* are manifested in huts built along the *raos*. The *dera* symbolises belonging and home and when stationary the *dera* of this or that person is where you go to visit. All the time during my first fieldwork period in winter I thought the *dera* was the hut, because people would tell me to go to the *dera* of this or that person and what I saw was a hut on the bank of a *rao*. But I realized I was wrong when the *dera* moved and the hut was left behind as an empty shell. I then learned that the hut, or *chhan* as it is called, is the outside structure while the *dera* is the inside: all the people, all the belongings, and all the animals. Because the *dera* is the home of a nomad it migrates with him or her and as such it includes everything that moves. The Van Gujjars put down deep roots in specific places, the deepest being where the *dera* is *placed* in the forest of the foothills. As this location is the same from year to year each return up the *rao* to the site of the *chhan* is a homecoming. Or at least it should be. What actually happens is that after the migrating households leave in spring the forest guards in their *beat* (forest area) auction off the materials of the huts, which are then demolished. On returning the Gujjars have to gather new material from the forest and built a completely new *chhan* to house the returning *dera*. It is after such 'homecomings', camped under the open air with the animals, that I have heard Gujjars talk about giving up. At such times they feel alienated from the forest, as it is taken over by powers before which they feel helpless. It is to these that I now turn.

Barriers open – barriers closed: navigating through a landscape of ambiguity

Above we have followed the Van Gujjars on their walks of subsistence. I have stressed the pattern and rhythm of movement and placemaking embedded in their day-to-day life-world of pastoralism. But while they navigate the mountain paths and walk through the forest a strong sense of anxiety creeps in, hampers the step and interrupts the rhythm. The Himalayan landscape is simultaneously a home, an embodied life-world, *and* hostile and alienating. For the Van Gujjars the terrain traversed becomes a landscape of ambiguity as they are caught between their own narratives, ingrained in the practical use of the landscape, and the discourses of power that come to regulate that usage. Pastoral practice moves according to the needs of the buffalo but is everywhere hampered by barriers set up by the discourses of power. As the state sees 'moving as a way of life' as an abnormality and 'staying in one place' as the norm, all efforts by the authorities ever since colonial times have been concentrated on limiting or putting an end to nomadism (Rao and Casimir 2003). There is thus a political dimension to the continuance of the walk, *a resistance by moving feet and hooves.* But being forced to live in a constant state of revolt against the norm of sedentism is exhausting for people whose understanding of the world is grounded in moving through forests and hills on the yearly rounds of transhumance. For the Van Gujjars walking is an intricate part of a life-world shaped by 'the simultaneous patterning of body and world in emotion', to recall Merleau-Ponty's phrase. It is perhaps symptomatic that the authorities use the word *weaning* when describing their policies towards nomads. People such as the Van Gujjars must be weaned away from their nomadic way of life as a child (or a calf) from its mother's milk.

I have followed the Van Gujjars on and off now for two decades (since 1987). The main part of my fieldwork took place in the early 1990s, and since then I have become an *ana-jana-wallah* (person coming and going) in the Van Gujjar world. In 1992 I experienced how many of the Van Gujjars, returning with their herds to the foothills, literally ran their bodies into one of the main discourses on the Himalayan environment: a discourse that tells of the overexploitation by migratory herders of natural resources and the consequent need to protect them. The natural resource in this case was the Van Gujjars' *jangal*, the forests of the foothills. Returning to the lowlands that year the barriers were closed and they were denied entrance to their winter camps. This gave rise to a mobilization by the Van Gujjars that I have described in detail elsewhere (Gooch, 1997; 1998a; 1998b; 2004). Here I want to draw a connection with Widlok's discussion in this volume on the 'ways' of anthropology and its openings and closures. In this case, anthropological fieldwork opened the way for a new discourse regarding the Van Gujjars, but like all ways, it was partial, and privileged some directions over others.

Walking up the *raos* to the *deras* of the Van Gujjars for the first time in 1987 I encountered a largely unknown ethnographic site. I was 'first'. In 1992 I undertook what I thought would be my last period of fieldwork. But then the situation changed. The whole life-world that I had studied was endangered. I had made a trail into that world but so far only Manto and I had used it; now there was not much choice but to use that opening to get help. There were no others. The Van Gujjars used us as a bridge to reach the outside world. Having gained entrance we could move out with the Van Gujjar message: *We are not the ones who destroy the forest, we are part of forest.* The opening was used by a local NGO of a friend of mine. The NGO had very good contacts with journalists and within a short while the whole story of the 'hidden people living in harmony with the forest' filled glossy Sunday magazines. I lost control of my research results as I found my texts living their own lives and popping up in the 'controversy over nature conservation leaving out local people'. This played its part in creating a new discourse: 'Local people live in harmony with nature'. When that gained precedence for a while, the barriers were opened and Van Gujjars came close to gaining management of the forest (RLEK 1997). After some time however the NGO lost interest in the Van Gujjars. Now the barriers are closing again and some groups of Van Gujjars are being settled by the Forest Department (Gooch 2004). So we see the changing discourses manifested in the landscape as barriers close or open and the Van Gujjars are caught between them, not knowing if they can move forward or if they will have to become like 'stones that cannot be moved'. The group of Van Gujjars described in this chapter are still in the forest in winter and still walk to the mountains in summer, but without Sain Bibi who passed away suddenly in autumn 2005. While I come and go, Manto (Praween Kaushal) stayed and still works with the Van Gujjars on issues such as domicile rights, livelihood, land rights, and education in the forest through the NGO, SOPHIA. The *rao* is now wide open.

References

Croll, E. and Parkin, D. (1992), 'Cultural Understanding of the Environment', in Croll, E. and Parkin, D. (eds) (1992), *Bush Base: Forest Farm: Culture, Environment and Development* (London: Routledge).

Gooch, P. (1997), 'Conservation for Whom?' in Lindberg, S. and Sverisson, A. (eds) (1997), *Social Movements in the South: Dilemmas of Globalization and Democratization* (London: Macmillan).

—— (1998a), *At the Tail of the Buffalo: Van Gujjar Pastoralists Between the Forest and the World Arena* (Lund: Lund Monographs in Social Anthropology).

—— (1998b), 'Community Management Plan: The Van Gujjars and the Rajaji National Park', in Toft Madsen, S. (ed.) (1998), *State Society and the Environment in South Asia* (London: Curzon Press).

—— (2004), 'Van Gujjars: The Persistent Forest Pastoralists', *Nomadic Peoples* 8:2 125-35.

Ingold, T. (1994), 'From Trust to Domination: An Alternative History of Human-Animal Relations', in Manning, A. and Serpell, J. (eds) (1994), *Animals and Human Society: Changing Perspectives* (London: Routledge).

Ingold, T. (2000), *The Perception of the Environment* (London: Routledge).

Ives, J. and Messerli, B. (1989), *The Himalayan Dilemma: Reconciling Development and Conservation* (London: Routledge).

Merleau-Ponty, M. (1966), *Phenomenology of Perception* (London: Routledge and Kegan Paul).

Rao, A. and Casimir, M. (2003), 'Nomadism in South Asia: An Introduction', in Rao, A. and Casimir, M. (eds) (2003), *Nomadism in South Asia* (New Delhi: Oxford University Press).

RLEK (1997), *We Will Turn This Forest Into A Diamond: Community Forest Management of Protected Areas. A Van Gujjar Proposal.* RLEK (Dehra Dun: Natraj).

Schlee, G. (1992), 'Ritual Topography and Ecological Use: The Gabbra of the Kenyan Borderlands', in Croll, E. and Parkin, D. (eds) (1992), *Bush Base: Forest Farm: Culture, Environment and Development* (London: Routledge).

Chapter 6

Performing on the Landscape versus Doing Landscape: Perambulatory Practice, Sight and the Sense of Belonging

Kenneth R. Olwig

Throughout history, whether as hunters and gatherers, farmers or herders of livestock, people have drawn a living from the *land*, not from space. Farmers plant their crops in the *earth*, not in space, and harvest them from *fields*, not from space. Their animals graze *pastures*, not space. Travelers make their way through the *country*, not through space, and as they walk or stand they plant their feet on the *ground*, not in space. Painters set up their easels in the *landscape*, not in space.

Tim Ingold

Thus writes Tim Ingold in the first paragraph of an article entitled 'Against Space: Place, Movement, Knowledge' (Ingold forthcoming). Two different senses of landscape, I will argue, can be linked to this passage. The first is concerned with the landscape of *earth, fields, pastures, country* and *ground*, and the second is the landscape of space. These two different senses of landscape are linked to two different ways of seeing. The first involves binocular vision, movement and knowledge gained from a coordinated use of the senses in carrying out various tasks (Ingold 1993). The second derives primarily from a monocular perspective that is fixed and distant from the body. The first modality engenders a sense of belonging that generates landscape as the place of dwelling and doing in the body politic of a community, whereas the second constructs a feeling of possession and staged performance in a hierarchical social space.

Two different senses of landscape are delineated in Doctor Johnson's famous dictionary, where he gives the definitions:

1. A region; the prospect of a country
2. A picture, representing an extent of space, with the various objects in it
   (Johnson 1755 [1968]: landscape).

In the first instance the *land* in *landscape* has the meaning of the place, region or country of the people of a body politic, in the sense that Scot*land* is the *land* of the Scots or Jut*land* the land of the Jutes. It is also the prospect of such a place. It is the place of a culture, as defined by common customs and language, rather than the space of a state, defined by maps, rules and statutes – though the two can overlap (Olwig 2002a; 2005a).[1] This is the land 'scaped', 'shaped' or created as place and polity by people through their practices of dwelling – their 'doing' of landscape. The suffix *–scape* embodies this sense of creative shaping and carving (Olwig 1993).[2] *–Scape* is also, however, cognate with the suffix *–ship*, which gives the concrete a more abstract quality in the sense of a condition or quality as in: 'friendship', 'scholarship', or as 'something showing, exhibiting, or embodying a quality or state', as with the case of 'township' or 'fellowship' (Merriam-Webster 2000: –ship; see also Olwig 2004).[3] One might have a number of concrete friends, or scholars, or fellows, but the relation between them is cemented by something more abstract and qualitative: friendship, scholarship and fellowship. The farmers in the passage from Ingold quoted above thus have their various croplands, pasturelands, and so on, but the painter, as an artist, is trying to capture the more abstract condition or quality of these lands as they make up the landscape prospect before the easel. In his painting, as the art historian Michael Rosenthal points out, Brueghel 'emphasizes not only the logic of the terrain', but also 'the logic of the activity' that is depicted. It contains 'an element of explanation, sometimes … near-diagrammatic' (Rosenthal 1982, 12). A Brueghel painting thus represents not just a prospect of landscape, but the shaping up of the landscape's prospects.

It is possible, as the art historian Arthur Wheelock explains, for a painter such as Jan Vermeer to create depth through the depiction of 'overlapping forms rather than by orthogonal projections'. The end result was that 'in the subtle balance and internal logic of his best compositions, [Vermeer] managed to create a sense of space for his figures without forcing the observer to view them from a single vantage point or at a single instant' (Wheelock 1977, 274, 282, 327). Something different happens, however, if the painter seeks to capture the nature or character of the landscape by depicting it within the gridded and orthogonal spatial framework of central point perspective, which does force the observer to view the scene from a single vantage point in abstract space and at a particular instant in abstract time (Olwig 2005b). Then we get the second sense of landscape listed by Doctor Johnson: 'A picture, representing an extent of space, with the various objects in it'. In this sense land is reduced to the scenic surface of the painting (a superficial study of the earth), and the suffix –scape to a 'view: pictorial representation of a (specified) type of view

---

1   This first sense is also found in other languages, as with the prefix *pays* in *paysage*, the French equivalent of landscape, which can also mean region.

2   Merriam-Webster's *Third New International Dictionary* lists 'nature, condition and quality' as synonyms of the Germanic etymological roots of *–ship*, stating that these are etymologically akin to Old English *sceppan, scyppan*, meaning 'to shape', referring the reader to 'SHAPE' for more information. Under the body of the definition of *–ship* it lists meanings such as 'state, condition, quality, art and skill'. It also refers the reader to *–ship* for the meaning of the suffix *–scape* in *landscape* (Merriam-Webster 2000: landscape, –ship).

3   Merriam-Webster's *Third New International Dictionary* gives the following etymology of 'land' and '-scape' in landscape: 'Dutch *landschap*, from Middle Dutch *landscape*, region, tract of land (akin to Old English *landscape* region, Old High German *lantscaf*, Old Norse *landskapr*), from land + *–scap*, *–ship*; akin to Old High German *lant* land, and to Old High German *–scap* –ship, – more at LAND, –SHIP' (Merriam-Webster 2000: landscape).

"cityscape", "waterscape"' (Merriam-Webster 2000: –scape). In relation to the first sense of landscape, this second sense represents, I would argue, a version of what Ingold has called 'the logic of inversion', by which 'the pathways along which life is lived' are turned into 'boundaries within which it is enclosed'. 'Life', he adds, 'is reduced to an internal property of things that *occupy* the world but do not, strictly speaking, *inhabit* it' (Ingold forthcoming). This is a rather abstract statement, but this inversion can in my view be concretized by showing how it is tied to two very different senses of belonging, depending on whether one is *performing* upon, or *doing*, landscape.

Performing upon landscape versus doing the landscape

The scenic landscape – landscape in the second sense – perceived pictorially as 'an extent of space, with the various objects in it', is literally that of the map. The techniques of perspective drawing were derived, in large measure, from techniques of cartography (Edgerton 1975; Cosgrove 1988), and hence also from the techniques of the cadastral property map. Whereas maps tend to have a perpendicular projection, focusing directly downward, a change in the angle of projection creates the basis for a scenic view. The term 'scene' should similarly be taken literally, for it derives from the perspective scenery of the stage, with its 'blocked out' space upon which the action is performed.[4] The space of the map, like that of the landscape scene, is an extent, with various objects plotted in terms of its coordinates. On the quadratic space of such a map life is enclosed within property boundaries. The land demarcated on the map belongs to the landowner, who commands a view of the land from the perspective of the map, the landscape painting or the world viewed as if in a landscape painting or on a stage. It is upon this stage that the landowner creates his landscape garden and his 'improved' agricultural fields, and upon this landscape labour and recreation are performed, as in a theatre. As Yi-Fu Tuan explains:

Scenery and landscape are now nearly synonymous. The slight differences in meaning they retain reflect their dissimilar origin. Scenery has traditionally been associated with the world of illusion which is the theater. The expression "behind the scenes" reveals the unreality of scenes. We are not bidden to look "behind the landscape", although a landscaped garden can be as contrived as a stage scene, and as little enmeshed with the life of the owner as the stage paraphernalia with the life of the actor. The difference is that landscape, in its original sense, referred to the real world, not to the world of art and make-believe. In its native Dutch, "landschap" designated such commonplaces as "a collection of farms or fenced fields, sometimes a small domain or administrative unit". Only when it was transplanted to England toward the end of the sixteenth century did the word shed its earthbound roots and acquire the precious meaning of art. Landscape came to mean a prospect seen from a specific standpoint. Then it was the artistic representation

---

4   The transitive verb 'block', in this context, means: 'to work out (as the principal positions and movements) for the performers (as of a play); also: to work out the players' positions and movements for (as a scene or a play)' on the gridded surface of the stage (Merriam-Webster 2000).

of that prospect. Landscape was also the background of an official portrait; the "scene" of a "pose". As such it became fully integrated with the world of make-believe (Tuan 1974, 133).

Tuan identifies landscape, in the sense of region or place, with the Dutch, who are famous for their landscape paintings, but as the quotation from Doctor Johnson's dictionary suggests, this meaning of landscape is also native to English, and it can actually be found throughout the Germanic languages (Olwig 2002a). This 'platial' landscape of farms, fenced fields and regional polities (Mels 2005) is not so much a scenic surface as a woven material created through the merging of body and senses that occurs in dwelling.

Sensing landscape and the sense of belonging

One of the most revealing ways to approach the differing senses of belonging identifiable with the two forms of landscape delineated above is to examine the role of the eyes in shaping each form. In the first sense, the landscape is shaped in large measure through doing, and apprehended through the use of two eyes. Nowhere is this mode of apprehension more evident than in the practice of walking. The walker experiences the material depth of the proximate environment through binocular vision and through the effect of motion parallax created by the blurring of near objects in contrast to those further away. The touched, smelled and heard proximate material world is thereby woven into the walker's sensory field, leading him or her to experience the landscape as a topological realm of contiguous places. From the stationary central point perspective of the painter, by contrast, the walker is an object occupying a fixed location frozen in abstract Newtonian space (Olwig 2005a). Apprehending the landscape in this second sense, the viewer is positioned at a given location and uses only the singular perspective of one eye. Thus the landscape is rendered, in terms of one dictionary definition, as 'a portion of land that the eye can comprehend in a single view' (Merriam-Webster 2000: landscape). The eye, moreover, is fixed in space and time, as can be seen from another dictionary definition according to which landscape is 'a portion of territory that can be viewed at one time from one place' (Merriam-Webster 1996: landscape). These definitions invoke the scenic conception of landscape as 'a picture representing a view of natural scenery (as fields, hills, forests, water) [landscape painting]' and 'the art of depicting such scenery'(Merriam-Webster 2000: landscape). When painting with one eye closed, squinting over your thumb, you flatten out the world so that you can better block it onto your canvas, while simultaneously distancing yourself from the proximate environment in which depth perception depends upon binocular vision. Once the landscape has been thus flattened and distanced, it can be disaggregated into objects located within the geometries of a one-eyed perspectival framework, thereby recreating an illusion of the depth that was lost when you closed one of your eyes.

These two very different modes of perception create the basis for contrasting *senses* of belonging in regard to the 'land', and hence of what it means to say that Scotland is the land of the Scots, or Jutland the land of the Jutes. One can belong to the land, or the land can belong to you. In the former sense, a feeling of belonging is fostered by movement with both eyes wide open; whereas the latter sense is fostered by the possessive one-eyed gaze of the surveyor, the perspective painter, or the tourist with a single-lens camera. It has its roots, however, in the space of the map, overlain upon the surface of the earth and punched into the soil with boundary posts. When you buy a piece of property, this bounded, usually quadratic piece of real estate becomes a personal possession. Ingold's statement that 'the pathways along which life is lived', through the process of inversion, are turned into 'the boundaries within which it is enclosed', applies literally to the historical process by which the commons were enclosed through surveying and map-making (Neeson 1993). The surveyor and mapmaker were the agents of this inversion, which served the interests of the enclosers – often the state in collusion with estate owners, with their exclusive scenic landscape gardens. Today, property ownership has become endemic, and mass communications and mass tourism have taught the world to appreciate landscape scenery as a good that becomes yours when you purchase a charter tour, a guidebook and a one-eyed camera (Urry 1990). Landscape has become largely synonymous with scenery, but the older, pre-inversion meaning of landscape still lurks in dictionaries, in the guise of definitions such as: '**c** : a particular area of activity' (Merriam-Webster 1996: landscape), where what counts is not what you see or how you are seen to *perform*, but what you *do*.

Herd animals and the doing of the pedestrian landscape

Historically, I suggest, the feeling of belonging to the land through movement is as old as the activity of hunters and gatherers in tracking game and finding edible materials along habitual paths woven by the inhabitants of a familiar habitat, or in the exploration of a new one. There is a fine line between tracking a herd of animals on a hunt, and herding the same animal, such as a reindeer, as a pastoralist. People have been following various herd animals for a long time, and it is through this activity, I would venture, that many of our earliest senses of belonging in relation to landscape have their origin. My own speculation on this subject comes from delving into the meaning of the word *fee*. Here is a brief etymology:

> Middle English, from Old English *feoh* cattle, property, money; akin to Old High German *fihu* cattle, Old Norse fe cattle, sheep, money, Gothic *faihu* money, wealth, Latin *pecus* cattle, *pecunia* money, *pectere* to comb, Greek *pekein* to comb, *pokos* fleece, Sanskrit *paKu* cattle; basic meaning: to fleece, pluck (wool); obsolete: personal property: GOODS, LIVESTOCK, MONEY (Merriam-Webster 2000: fee).

To judge from this, it would appear that in earlier times it was not so much the pastureland as the herd animals grazing the land that belonged to people. This, of course, fits well with the fact that much grazing land, to this day, is used on the basis of rights of common use rather than individual property.

The process by which people became attached to the land through their herding of various quadrupeds has been documented ethnographically by anthropologist John Gray, who studied the practices of shepherding in the Scottish borders. The shepherd's pattern of movement is largely directed by the movement of the sheep from pasture to pasture. Shepherds say the sheep *heft on* or bond themselves to various places in the land (Gray 1999, 451). They become attached to particular grazing places through familiarity, so that the shepherd can expect them to follow a cyclical course as they move from meadow to meadow. The term *heft* is applied, however, not only to the process by which sheep bond to the land but also to the bonding of these sheep into a social unit also called a *heft*. It is moreover applied to the hill pastures attached to the farm. Thus in use, the term is extended from the animals' bonding to the land, through their bonding with one another, to the attachment of the farm, as a human social institution, to the land (Gray 1999, 451). So it is that *heft* comes to refer to people's feelings of belonging. It means both (of animals) 'to become accustomed to a new pasture' and (of people) 'to become domiciled, settled or established in a place or occupation, to dwell' (S.N.D. 1960: heft). Spelled *haft*, the word is also found elsewhere in Britain. The etymologically primary sense of *haft* is 'to accustom (sheep) to a different pasture', but it also has a later sense, applicable to people, 'to settle or establish especially in a place of residence' as in 'we are now nicely hafted here' (Merriam-Webster 2000: haft; see also O.E.D. 1971: haft). What we see, then, is a transferal of meaning from the processes through which sheep become bonded to a place and to each other, to the figurative understanding of human bonding to place and the community dwelling there.

Etymologists believe that both *heft* and *haft* have their origins in Old Norse (S.N.D. 1960: heft; Merriam-Webster 2000: haft). This is interesting in part because it indicates the age of the terms in Britain. It is also interesting because it suggests that the notion of *hefting/hafting* may be tied to ancient principles of customary law. *Haft* is thus 'probably of Scandinavian origin; akin to Old Norse heftha to gain (land) by right of occupation, *hefth* possession, act of gaining by occupation, Old Norse hafa to have – more at HAVE' (Merriam-Webster 2000: haft). *Heft* and *haft*, it appears, are related to a constellation of Old Norse words that, despite possibly different etymological origins, have become associated in meaning through context and similarity of pronunciation. The Old Norse word *hæfð* (in which the *ð* is a combination of d and t) is derived from a common Germanic word meaning 'have' and is linked to words meaning 'bind', 'grab' and 'hold', as well as to phrases such as to 'holde i *hævd*' (to use the modern Danish spelling). *Hævd* means 'to keep up', as with the holding of an 'old custom', but also in the sense of the 'maintenance' by which one keeps up, for example, a meadow (or one's lawn) through mowing, or a path through walking. The maintenance of such use is, in turn, connected with the meaning of *hævd/hæfð* as a prescriptive use right (O.D.S. 1931: hæft; Vinterberg and Bodelsen 1966: hævd; Falk and Torp 1996: Hævd, Hæve, Hefte).

Doing landscape

The transferal of meaning from observations made concerning the place and social bonding of sheep (and other herd animals) to human behavior is 'figurative', as the dictionary says, but it is at the same time a figure that derives from actual bodily engagement with the perambulatory process of herding sheep and, no doubt, of sharing through empathy the sheep's feeling of attachment to a pasture and to its flock. By the same token, there is a strong visceral element to customary law. When you continually walk and wear a path, and thereby maintain its appearance and structure as a path, you simultaneously maintain your prescriptive right to use that path. Legal systems rooted in customary law, like that of the English, accept worn paths and maintained hedges as evidence of use rights upheld through precedent of 'time immemorial'. Through this process the various croplands and grazing lands of a given area are woven together and shaped into what I have termed a 'substantive' landscape (Olwig 1996). This landscape is a creature of inhabitants' daily tasks and habits (Ingold 1993), but habit becomes custom and morality as people's interests both meet in agreement, and clash in dissention (Thompson 1993).

One way of reinforcing the commonwealth of interests of the community is through customary rituals, such as beating the bounds, or fetching wood for a communal bonfire or maypole. In this case the weaving of the material existence of the landscape takes on a textual dimension through the repetition of passages walked, and passages recited, both having their origins in religion and folklore. These rituals also involve doing the landscape with feet, body and both eyes, to the extent that the sense of place was even reinforced through bodily pain. The perambulation of the village during the annual beating of the bounds thus involved various rituals in which pains were taken, for example, to assure that boys' heads were knocked on a boundary marker and that their bodies otherwise experienced the pain of strong physical contact with important places, such as a ditch or wall, so that they would remember them later in life should a dispute arise (Houseman 1998).[5] One should not, however, be too alarmed by what might appear to be child abuse. The games and merriment of centuries past were often quite rough and painful by modern standards (Malcolmson 1973). Beating the bounds was a seasonal event characterized by much carnivalesque holidaymaking, involving bodily sport and humour, thereby reinforcing the sense that the village literally formed a community body (Bakhtin 1984). These festive occasions were nevertheless also of legal importance as proof of the community's use right to walk upon, or utilize, a common resource (Thompson 1993). This is illustrated by the following excerpt from the records of an English court quoted by the historian, E.P. Thompson:

> Gervas Knight ... aged sixty seven yeares and upwards Maketh Oath that ever since he can remember ... he has known Farming Woods Walk within the Forest of Rockingham ... and says that ever since he was big enough ... viz. from about the yeare 1664 until about the yeare 1720 he yearly or every two yeares ... went with the Vicar and Parishioners of Brigstock to perambulate publickly for the same Parish and thereby make clayme of the Lands thereto belonging and to set forth their bounds (Thompson 1993, 98).

When disputes over the interpretation of custom are taken to the courts, custom becomes the basis for common law, and when formalized by churches, it becomes the basis for morality and ethics (both words deriving from words meaning custom).

---

5   I would like to thank Paul Basu for alerting me to the existence of this article.

Doing custom versus performing tradition

When discussing custom, it can be useful to distinguish it from tradition, even if the two words are often treated as synonyms. In my view tradition, along with scenic landscape, is an invention of modernism and a corollary of its idea of progress (Olwig 2002b). This is yet another example of the logic of inversion, of turning pathways along which life is lived into boundaries within which it is enclosed (Ingold, forthcoming). Eric Hobsbawm offers the following clarification of the difference:

> The object and characteristic of "traditions", including invented ones, is invariance. […]
> "Custom" cannot afford to be invariant, because even in "traditional" societies life is not
> so. Customary or common law still shows this combination of flexibility in substance
> and formal adherence to precedent. The difference between "tradition" and "custom" in
> our sense is indeed well illustrated here. "Custom" is what judges do; "tradition" (in this
> instance invented tradition) is the wig, robe and other formal paraphernalia and ritualized
> practices surrounding their substantial action. […] Inventing traditions, it is assumed here,
> is essentially a process of formalization and ritualization, characterized by reference to the
> past, if only by imposing repetition (Hobsbawm 1983, 2-3).

Custom, then, is something one does as part of an ongoing process of dwelling through which a lived landscape and its ways are continually shaped. Tradition, on the other hand, is generated when custom is enacted on the stage of a landscape transformed into the frozen geometrical space of scenery, whereupon custom becomes costume.

In times past, the beating of the bounds was both a religiously sanctioned ritual and a manifestation of customary law. Today, it is largely a nostalgic tradition, intended to establish a sentimental form of identity with location (Houseman 1998). There are however other ways in which pedestrian movement continues to reinforce both customary rights and the sense of belonging that comes with *hefting* to the land. When, in 1932, members of the Manchester Area committee of the British Workers' Sports Federation staged a mass trespass on the open grouse-hunting moorlands of Kinder Scout, they were engaging in an ancient practice by which first sheep and then people *hefted* both to each other and to the land. The mere doing of the landscape in this way would probably have been enough to cause a dispossessed and propertyless factory worker, who may have remembered walks on the commons from childhood (Barrell 1972), to feel a sense of belonging. The leaders of mass trespass, such as Benny Rothman, were highly conscious, however, of what they saw as 'the history of the injustice of enclosures, which had stolen Common Land from the people' (Rothman 1982, 28). After the trespass Rothman was arrested. The court, it turned out, did not share his beliefs concerning 'the rights of ordinary people to walk on land stolen from them in earlier times', and he was sentenced to four months in jail (Rothman 1982, 36, 44). The leaders of the movement also understood, however, that society had changed, creating a huge urban proletariat, which meant that it was now necessary to work for a national rather than a village commons. This is why mass trespasses are considered to have been a significant factor in paving the way for Britain's national parks.

People today *heft* with their feet in different ways, ranging from villagers religiously walking the paths that join village to village, so as to maintain the right to use them, to hikers in national parks perambulating the mountains and vales of their nation. Not only do they thereby maintain a right to the land, and the sense of belonging that goes with it, but because they often go in a group, they also help to generate a sense of belonging to a community, in relation to both the group of hikers and the larger community imaginatively identified with the nation (Darby 2000).

'All we like sheep…'

Living in our cities, barricaded behind our computer screens, we readily lose touch with the quadrupeds that once taught us to *heft* to the land as landscape and to one another as a community or fellowship. We pay our college fees in the hope, perhaps, of one day becoming a fellow of the college with the right to walk across its carefully manicured commons. Under these circumstances it is easy to forget that the prefix in fellow derives from an ancient word for such herd animals as cattle or sheep:

> Middle English *felawe*, from Old English *feolaga*, from Old Norse *felagi*, from *fe* cattle, sheep, money + -lagi (akin to Old Norse leggja to lay).

To *lay* sheep together means to pool them, and thereby to form a working community, or *lag* in the Nordic tongue, regulated by its own laws (law also derives from *leggja*) (Merriam-Webster 2000: law). And, of course, these jolly good fellows share between them the abstract quality of fellow*ship*, which hefts them together within the landscape they share.

The words 'All we like sheep…' are taken from the libretto to Handel's *Messiah* (Part 2, No. 26) by Charles Jennens, who, in turn, took it from Isaiah 53:6. It means, of course, that we are as sheep – though we may like them too. It is remarkable how many references to sheep are to be found in the Bible, in Christian art and in Christian iconography, but also even in such pagan sources as Plato's Statesman (Plato 1961). Sheep are perhaps our most vital symbol of community, and that is why sheep that have gone astray, 'turned everyone to his own way', are a symbol of iniquity. Perhaps, in some sense, we are like sheep, *hefting* to the land and to each other, doing landscapes to which we belong both bodily and socially, with all our senses; both eyes wide open.

References

Bakhtin, M. (1984), *Rabelais and His World* (Bloomington: Indiana University Press).

Barrell, J. (1972), *The Idea of Landscape and the Sense of Place, 1730-1840: An Approach to the Poetry of John Clare* (Cambridge: Cambridge University Press).

Cosgrove, D. (1988), 'The Geometry of Landscape: Practical and Speculative Arts in Sixteenth-Century Venetian Land Territories', in Cosgrove, D. and Daniels, S. (eds) (1988), *The Iconography of Landscape* (Cambridge: Cambridge University Press).

Darby, W. (2000), *Landscape and Identity: Geographies of Nation and Class in England* (Oxford: Berg).

Edgerton, S. (1975), *The Renaissance Rediscovery of Linear Perspective* (New York: Basic Books).

Falk, H. and Torp, A. (1996 [1903-06]), *Etymologisk Ordbog over det Norske og det Danske Sprog* (Oslo: Bjørn Ringstrøms Antikvariat).

Gray, J. (1999), 'Open Space and Dwelling Places: Being at Home on Hill Farms in the Scottish Borders', *American Ethnologist* 26:2, 440-60.

Hamilton, H. and Cairns, E. (eds) (1961), *The Collected Dialogues of Plato* (New York: Pantheon).

Hobsbawm, E. (1983), 'Introduction', in Ranger, T. and Hobsbawm, E. (eds) (1983), *The Invention of Tradition* (Cambridge: Cambridge University Press).

Houseman, M. (1998), 'Painful Places: Ritual Encounters With One's Homelands', *Journal of the Royal Anthropological Institute* (N.S.) 4:3, 447-67.

Ingold, T. (1993), 'The Temporality of the Landscape', *World Archaeology* 25:2, 152-72.

—— (forthcoming), 'Against Space: Place, Movement, Knowledge', in Kirby, P. (ed.) (forthcoming), *Boundless Worlds: An Anthropological Approach to Movement* (Oxford: Berghahn).

Johnson, S. (1755 [1968]), *A Dictionary of the English Language* (London: W. Strahan).

Malcolmson, R. (1973), *Popular Recreations in English Society 1700-1850* (Cambridge: Cambridge University Press).

Mels, T. (2005), 'Between Platial Imaginations and Spatial Rationalities: Navigating Justice and Law in the Low Countries', *Landscape Research* 30:3, 321-55.

Merriam-Webster (1996), *Collegiate Dictionary* (Springfield, MA: Merriam-Webster).

—— (2000), *Webster's Third New International Dictionary of the English Language*, Unabridged, electronic edition (Springfield, MA: Merriam-Webster).

Neeson, J. (1993), *Commoners: Common Right, Enclosure and Social Change in England, 1700-1820* (Cambridge: Cambridge University Press).

O.D.S. (1931), *Ordbog over det Danske Sprog* (Copenhagen: Gyldendal).

O.E.D. (1971), *Oxford English Dictionary* (Oxford: Oxford University Press).

Olwig, K. (1993), 'Sexual Cosmology: Nation and Landscape at the Conceptual Interstices of Nature and Culture, or: What does Landscape Really Mean?' in Bender, B. (ed.) (1993), *Landscape: Politics and Perspectives* (Oxford: Berg).

—— (1996), 'Recovering the Substantive Nature of Landscape', *Annals of the Association of American Geographers* 86:4, 630-53.

—— (2002a), *Landscape, Nature and the Body Politic: From Britain's Renaissance to America's New World* (Madison: University of Wisconsin Press).

—— (2002b), 'Landscape, Place and the State of Progress' in Sack, R. (ed.) (2002), *Progress: Geographical Essays* (Baltimore: Johns Hopkins University Press).

—— (2004), 'The Landscape of State Justice contra that of Custom', *Diedut* 3, 39-63.

—— (2005a). 'The Landscape of "Customary" Law versus that of "Natural' Law", *Landscape Research* 30:3, 299-320.

—— (2005b) 'Liminality, Seasonality and Landscape', *Landscape Research* 30:2, 259-71.

Plato (1961), 'Statesman', in Hamilton, H. and Cairns, E. (eds), *The Collected Dialogues of Plato* (New York Pantheon), 1018-85.

Rosenthal, M. (1982), *British Landscape Painting* (Oxford: Phaidon).

Rothman, B. (1982), *The 1932 Kinder Trespass* (Timperley, Cheshire: Willow Publishing).

S.N.D. (1960), *Scottish National Dictionary* (Edinburgh: The Scottish National Dictionary Association).

Thompson, E. (1993), *Customs in Common* (London: Penguin).

Tuan, Y.-F. (1974), *Topophilia: A Study of Environmental Perception, Attitudes, and Values* (Englewood Cliffs, NJ: Prentice-Hall).

Urry, J. (1990), *The Tourist Gaze* (London: Sage).

Vinterberg, H. and Bodelsen, C. (1966), *Dansk-engelsk Ordbog* (Copenhagen: Gyldendal).

Wheelock, A. Jr. (1977), *Perspective, Optics, and Delft Artists Around 1650* (New York: Garland).

Chapter 7

Listen to the Sound of Time: Walking with Saints in an Andalusian Village

Katrín Lund

Introduction

During my fieldwork in Bubión, an Andalusian village located in the mountains of the Alpujarra region in southern Spain, I was frequently told a story that I not only found amusing but also provoked my curiosity.[1] The reason I found it amusing was partly because of the content and partly because it was always told with such delight. The reason I found it curious was that, although fictitious or even mythical in nature, it was supposed to have happened within the living memory of at least the older generations of the village inhabitants. The story is about San Sebastian, the patron saint of Bubión, and it goes something like this. During the Spanish Civil War, Bubión and the surrounding villages were under the control of the Spanish Nationalists. This meant that all icons and statues related to practices of 'popular Catholicism' had to be kept hidden from the authorities. Because of the panic prevailing when removing the items out of sight, the people were not able to recall where each of them was hidden after the tension of the civil war ceased. The story tells how, after the civil war, the inhabitants of the villages started recovering their icons and statues and the people from Capileira, the neighbouring village of Bubión, found the statue of San Sebastian in the basement of their church. Because several years had passed, they assumed that San Sebastian was their patron saint and took the statue on a procession through the village's streets. But the statue felt a great deal heavier than expected, to the point that the men could barely carry it. They nevertheless carried on walking with the procession in the direction of the central square, where the road out of the village and down the mountain slope, in the direction of Bubión, commences. As the procession moved towards the square, the statue started to feel lighter and, as a result, the procession continued to walk down the road towards Bubión. The closer they moved towards Bubión the lighter San Sebastian became and when they came to the boundaries that divide the land of Capileira and Bubión, his weight felt normal. It was at this point that the inhabitants of Capileira realized that San

---

1   I want to thank Jo Vergunst and Tim Ingold and the participants in the walking seminar for their feedback. My colleagues at the School of Anthropology, Queens University Belfast, where I also delivered a version of this chapter, provided lively and helpful discussion. Jonathan Macintosh and Karl Benediktsson read it over at different stages and offered some useful comments.

Sebastian really belonged to Bubión. They had only mistaken him as their patron saint because his statue had been found in the basement of their church. They handed San Sebastian over to the inhabitants of Bubión, who continued the walk with their saint through the streets of their village and to the church. San Sebastian remains the patron saint of Bubión and his day is celebrated twice a year when the people from Bubión carry his statue out of the church and form a procession through the village during the fiesta.

Although the event described in this story only dates back to the end of the Civil War, an air of timeless mystique was often added to the tale by the fact that I was most often told it by younger people who were not born at that time. When, on the other hand, I asked Pepe, one of my older informants, to tell me about the story, he responded: 'There is no story.' I did not understand how a story I had frequently been told suddenly did not exist. 'There is no story', I said, 'but people tell me … !' Pepe looked at me and asked: 'You mean the story about San Sebastian?' He recited it to make sure that we were talking about the same story. Then he added: 'This is no story, this is just something that people say.' Still, by reciting the story Pepe not only allowed the anthropologist to get it on tape but also verified that it existed. He said it is 'just something that people say' and that is precisely what is important to this chapter. As Bruner has argued, 'narration recognizes that no story is "a" story or "the" story but rather a dialogic process of many historically situated particular tellings' (1984, 57). When narratives are examined one should emphasize the process involved over the end product (Jackson 2002, 18). The process of storytelling moves on with the telling. It is about sharing one's own experiences with those who listen and turning the story into a part of the listeners' own experiences (Benjamin 1970, 87). The narration is a constant process. Furthermore, as Stewart states, 'narrative is first and foremost a mediating form through which "meaning" must pass. Stories, in other words, are productive' (1996, 29). Indeed, to understand the meaning and the productivity of a narrative one has to follow how it is told, passed on, re-told and, most importantly, shared. In the case at hand, the story is about when the statue of San Sebastian was carried by the people of Capileira to Bubión on foot. It is however not only *about* how the statue of San Sebastian was carried; it is also a story that unfolds in the very activity of walking, in the striding of many feet, echoing de Certeau's claim that the story 'begins on ground level, with footsteps' (1984, 97). In this chapter I examine how perambulatory narratives are shared during the course of the procession of San Sebastian, and reflect on their productivity and meaning.

The story as it is told ends when the statue of San Sebastian is brought to its rightful place. For the story as it is walked, on the other hand, that ending provides a beginning. The walk is about how San Sebastian entered Bubión after a period of forced absence. It provides an entrance into a place made by narratives. Furthermore, as the inhabitants of Bubión continue to process with their patron saint, the narrative goes on and the place remains in production. But of course, the procession provides a particular kind of narrative and a particular framework for the place. Michael Jackson writes: 'stories are a kind of theatre where we collaborate in reinventing ourselves and authorising notions, both individual and collective, of who we are' (2002, 16). That the story takes place during the aftermath of the Spanish Civil War is important. It tells about how order is shaped after a period of oppression, and emphasizes the unity and harmony embodied in the figure of San Sebastian. As they walk in unison through the village, carrying their saint, participants in the procession join together in reproducing and authorizing a sense of who they are, and of their belonging to the same place. In the synchronization or bringing-into-phase of perambulatory movements which, on more everyday occasions, have no common direction, rhythm or pace, they bind into a single narrative the numerous stories they would otherwise have to tell about their own lives, and the different ways of being and belonging these entail.

To illustrate how the narrative works I start by introducing the place in question and the role of the patron saint in its production. I then describe the many ways in which people participate in the procession, providing an insight into how place and belonging are narrated through synchronized walking.

The place in context

In his writing about shrines and pilgrimages in Spain, William Christian (1972) describes how images of saints are symbols that stand for social collectivities. They hold a fixed point in the landscape, a shrine, which is usually the local church or a chapel of the surrounding community. He describes the shrine as a 'transaction point in the landscape between the human group, the land, and the powers that influence the success of the group's enterprises' (Christian 1972, 44). The common commitment to the patron saint of a particular place, in his view, reinforces the solidarity of the group for whom that place is a shared space. Thus each group, by setting itself up in opposition to other groups, affirms its existence 'as the moral centre of the universe' (Crain 1992). Christian's analysis is central to understanding religious activities and sacred spaces in the Mediterranean, and his discussion has provided a spatial emphasis that has remained at the forefront of studies of festivals in this region. More recently, studies of Mediterranean rituals have been much influenced by the work of Jeremy Boissevain (1992). Boissevain focused on how 'tradition' has undergone a combination of decline and revitalization brought about by economic changes during the latter half of the twentieth century, which he claims are indicated in the Mediterranean by the shift from a pre-industrial to an industrial economy. His observations bear much relevance to Spain, but they also call for some qualification.

The main period of Spanish industrialization was in the late 1950s and early 1960s when General Franco lifted restrictions on the boundaries between Spain and other countries in Europe. Spain had been experiencing serious economic difficulties in the aftermath of the Second World War and its isolation became an increasing hindrance. As well as opening the doors in and out of Europe, General Franco also started building up industry in the northern regions of Spain. People from southern Spain, and particularly Andalusia, who still relied on unstable agriculture and farming, started migrating north to the industrial centres of Barcelona and Madrid and further afield to Germany and France. This migration initiated what Boissevain has called the phase of decline for 'tradition', during which rural areas and villages were deserted by young and able people who had left to look for a better way of life. People in Bubión, however, told me that such was the importance of the patron saint that his day continued to be celebrated even in these difficult times, although more quietly than today. The procession itself is the most important part of the celebration.

Then, in the 1970s a period of revitalization of 'traditional' festivities commenced, characterized by a general awareness and revaluation of authenticity. This movement was, according to Boissevain, brought from the urban areas into what he calls the 'traditional' landscape and, as a result, local festivals were reinvented according to new interests. The conditions for revitalization, he suggested, were established by tourists, expatriates and those who had emigrated to urban areas but come back to celebrate the saint's day with their relatives. These people are included in what Boissevain calls 'a category of outsiders, an audience of Others, in previously homogeneous communities' (1992, 9). His emphasis is on how spatial borders between insiders and outsiders are reinforced in a changing social and economic environment.

I do not dispute that studies such as those in Boissevain's collection provide a valuable insight into rapidly changing Mediterranean societies. But I agree, with Barbara Bender, that this type of spatial emphasis tends 'to create an opposition between a rooted sense of belonging and the alienating forces of modernity' (2001, 8). In order to look at life as it is lived, rather than concentrating merely on how people become subjects of political and economic forces introduced from outside, we need to introduce an element of time. Once this element is brought in, and by looking at narratives and how they are shared, the categorization of insiders vis-à-vis different kinds of outsiders becomes much more complex and obscure.

Although the inhabitants of Bubión have without doubt experienced the economic transformations described by Boissevain, it was not until the late 1970s and even the early 1980s that the period of revitalization started in the region of Alpujarra. This delayed onset may be due to the region's isolation, located as it is at the foot of the mountains of the Sierra Nevada range. At this time people from northern Europe had for almost two decades been visiting the coastline of Andalusia *en masse*, and many had been induced to settle there. With tourism booming, the coastline came to be seen as an undesirable place of rapidly rising hotels and expanding services that increasingly resembled the places from which the expatriates had escaped. This was especially so for those who had been seeking a life of authenticity and simplicity in 'backward' Spain in contrast to the overwhelmingly 'modern' rest of Europe. They started heading to inland Andalusia and encountered rustic and thinly populated mountain villages. Gradually this movement progressed higher up the mountains (see Lund 1998; 2005) and reached the Alpujarra during the mid to late 1970s. The settling foreigners brought with them curious guests and visitors, and prospects for developing tourism in the area. As a result, many of those who had migrated from the Alpujarra started to return since there were now opportunities to make a living in the place they had left. Others were also attracted to the region, including younger people from urban Spain who were looking for an authentic past to which they saw themselves as belonging.

During my first fieldwork in 1994 and 1995, Bubión had just over two hundred inhabitants, about a quarter of whom had moved from outside of Alpujarra. During the San Sebastian festivities, however, many people who emigrated in the 1960s and 1970s return with their families to visit relatives in the village. Despite the diverse backgrounds of the people present at the festivities, they share a strong sense of belonging to the place. This is because their 'histories and relations are embedded in the place through their presence' (Lund 2008, 7). What it means to belong and how one belongs is, however, contested, especially when it comes to what constitutes a place of belonging. Sarah Green writes: 'identity and place are continually contested domains, and ... both are constituted through processes of exclusion and othering, of generating differences' (2005, 90). Consequently, it is important to bear in mind that 'one does not only locate oneself in a place but is also located by other people which can bring shifting dynamics into the ways in which one belongs' (Lund 2008, 7). A person may be made to feel, by others, either an outsider or an insider.

Still, the complexity of these categories is such that one is never totally inside or totally outside, and belonging can be about creating a personal space on the margins between these two. This allows movement in different directions between the inside and the outside depending on the context. Furthermore, this process of inclusion, exclusion and othering does not simply define insiders and outsiders. Rather, it creates situations in which people reflect consciously or unconsciously on the ways they belong and relate to other part-insiders and part-outsiders. Individual biographies are put into contact with the present – biographies in which are embedded the history of transformation and change, decline and revitalization documented by Boissevain. This history does not diminish the authenticity of the performance; instead it is an integral part of the ritual itself. As Dirks points out: 'the authenticity of the event [is] inscribed in its performance, not in some time- and custom-sanctioned version of the ritual' (1994, 499). Thus in order to understand what is produced through and meant by the activity of walking with the patron saint, one needs to locate oneself within the ritual by taking part in the walking. For participants in the performance, authenticity cannot be seen, but is imprinted in the sonic rhythm of synchronized movements. A story is a form of telling to which one listens.

Synchronized walking

Recent studies of commemorative ceremonies and pilgrimages (Connerton 1989; Coleman and Eade 2004; Solnit 2000) have discussed the significance of co-ordinated movement in the same direction as a metaphor for the journey through life, a kinetic experience that 'knits together time and place ... into a vital whole' (Solnit 2000, 216). As several authors have shown (Solnit 2000; Ingold 2000; 2004; 2007, 90-91; Jackson 1983; 1998), paths and routes 'unfold in time as one moves along them, just as a story does as one listens' (Solnit 2000, 72). Walking can be seen as a narrative process that weaves together time and space because at the same time that stories connect the past and the future they also 'articulate peoples' notions of who they are and where they belong' (Jackson 1998, 177).

In the case of the procession, the synchronized movement of walking with the patron saint in the same direction and at the same pace articulates notions not only of who belongs where but also of how they come to be there, uniting people in a sense of belonging to the same place. The procession binds an assortment of otherwise disparate narratives into a manifestation of unison and harmony through which the participants, at least momentarily, 'become what they display' (Myerhoff 1982, 106). It is, however, evident that although the movement performed in the procession is one in pace, rhythm and direction, particular narratives still make themselves apparent through the various ways in which people take part. To be able to tell the story that authorizes the notion of belonging, participants need at the same time to be able to negotiate their personal narratives. The authorized story is thus a fusion of individual versions. To illustrate this further I shall now blend my own narrative into the fusion.

I was on a second visit to Bubión. This was at the time of the annual fiesta and my friend Francisco had invited me to join him and the brothers Juan and Manuel at the church tower. They had taken on the task of ringing the bells during the procession of San Sebastian, which takes place on the last Sunday night in August. I thought this was great. I had asked Francisco if I would be able to see the procession from the church tower and he had said I could do so, although once in the tower I realized that I would not get a clear view. The village is situated on a steep mountain slope and the church is located at the square at the bottom of the village. I could see the roofs of the houses in the village rising above the square but not the streets themselves along which the procession would be passing. But even though on this occasion I did not see much, the view from the tower helped me to locate myself within the procession itself. I had walked with the procession many times before and being in the tower allowed me to reflect on my previous experience of doing so.

I was sitting by one of the windows of the tower that faces the square, watching the people who had started to gather. By eight o'clock in the evening, preparations for the procession were already underway and half an hour later it was ready to set off. The statue of San Sebastian was still in the church where a group of women had been spending the early evening decorating it. The people already gathered included the members of the annually elected committee which organizes the festivities, together with a few of their relatives, but more people were slowly drifting into the square. My observation was disturbed when Juan came and sat beside me. We had not seen each other for some time and he asked me how I was doing. I responded and turned the question back to him.

'I am in jail, you know', he said.

'Yes, I know', I said.

'How do you know?' His sensitivity towards his situation made him appear defensive.

'Carmen told me.'

'Carmen who, my mother?'

'No Carmen, Demetrio's wife. Don't worry', I added, 'she also said that you are a nice person and she told me that you get a release from jail every weekend to come home. You know, she wasn't just talking about you, I had asked her about you and she was answering my questions.' I felt as if I had to reassure Juan; he was very aware that some people detested him and he often felt marginalized.

'It's the incident your sentence is for, isn't it?' I asked.

'Yeah, it is the incident, it is the only time I have ever done anything criminal, and I know it was stupid, you know I'm not a bad person.'

We had discussed this many times before. The incident had taken place when I was doing my first fieldwork four years previously.

'It's tough being in jail', Juan said, 'but I know I deserve it.'

'But they allow you to go home for weekends', I said. 'Is that for good behaviour?'

'Yeah', he said, 'but I can't wait to get out, I want to be able to be at home. This is my place, here. I know I have done many stupid things, it is not just the incident, you know, I left my girlfriend, I abandoned my child, and then it was the car accident. I regret all this and there is no way back, but my future is still here with my mother.'

At the same time that Juan was certain about his place in the world and where he belonged, he also felt out of place. He was reflecting on his past, his journey through life and also negotiating his place in the present. Moreover, that Juan had offered to be at the tower to ring the bells during the procession reflects on this negotiation of his location in the village. This job is allocated by the Mayor of Bubión to different men every year. Although Juan's reflections indicated his marginality, he had managed to find a place at the centre of Bubión, in the midst of the fusion that would speak the synchronized version of the narrative during the procession. His role in the church tower made him indispensable to how the authorized story of belonging would be told.

The procession was starting. About two hundred rockets were set off from the roof of the Town Hall, leaving the square in a cloud of smoke, and Juan, Manuel and Francisco began to swing the bells and set the rhythm for the moving procession. People had lined up. At the front were two children from the village carrying lanterns. Following them, as every year, were some of the older inhabitants of Bubión in two rows behind. Then the statue of San Sebastian arrived, the central figure of the procession. In his life as a Roman soldier under Diocletian around 300 AD, he had lived on the margins and converted people to Christianity, for which he suffered death by arrows. He is identified as a young man, with cloth around his waist, his legs and his bare chest wounded by the arrows of Diocletian. He is carried by eight men, along with a few others who take over the statue as the procession proceeds. A brass band playing grave tunes follows the men, after which walk the Priest and the Mayor of Bubión, accompanied by the members of the organizing committee. As the procession moves up the street away from the church square, more people join in – people from the village, visiting relatives, some people that have moved in from outside of the village, as well as some from neighbouring villages.

The start of the procession establishes a partial framework for the story to be performed, and lends it a sense of authority. By ringing the bells, Juan played a direct part in setting up this framework. I continued to watch the procession as it moved ahead outside of the window. The atmosphere was grave, people bowed their heads, and the pace of walking was slow. These were people who would be following the procession, the plot of the story, from beginning to end, just as Juan would be doing, although his participation was from the church tower.

Gradually the procession left the square and began to take a circular route around the main streets of Bubión. I lost sight of it. The procession's route plays a vital role in framing the story as it creates the plot, linking the beginning to the end. It goes from the church square, following the winding streets eastwards up towards the main road which connects Bubión to the neighbouring villages and to the outside world. It then follows the main road before it takes a turn back down towards the church square, following the streets through the western part of the village. The streets that the procession follows form the central route through the village, which connects all its major neighbourhoods. Every time the procession enters a junction into a different neighbourhood it pauses, allowing people from different parts of the village to join in. Thus the synchronized walking connects neighbourhoods as it progresses, and at the same time incorporates the multiplicity of individual narratives as it spins together the tale of belonging.

Having lost sight of the procession I became immersed in the overwhelming, rhythmic sound of the ringing bells. Whilst wrapped up in it I tried to imagine the pace of the procession in order to get a sense of where it was passing. Suddenly, Juan lifted his arm and Manuel and Francisco stopped the swinging bells. There was a momentary silence. The procession had stopped where the main route passes the *Barrio de los Gitanos*, the neighbourhood of the Gypsies. In my imagination I could see how some of the people from this neighbourhood were standing on the corner or outside their houses. I could see elderly women, weeping in veneration, supported by members of their families, sons, daughters and husbands. Rosario and Amalia had once explained to me that in most cases these women are remembering deceased or lost members of the family. Amalia told me that her mother cries because of her brother who had migrated to Germany in the 1960s and had since lost contact with the family.

In the distance I could hear rockets being sent up in front of the procession. Juan gave another hand signal and the bells started swinging again. I knew that some of the people from the neighbourhood of the Gypsies would now have joined the procession, while others would continue to stand with heads bowed as it passed.

After a little while Juan gave me a sign that his arms were tired. The bell he was ringing was broken so instead of swinging it, the clapper inside needed to be swung back and forth. He asked me to take over. He steered my arms to begin with so that I would continue with the same rhythm. Before long he had to come back and put his hands on my arms to redirect me to the rhythm that, unlike him, I had little sense for. I carried on ringing the bell until the procession stopped again, this time on the main road. This is where the inhabitants from Capileira carried the statue of San Sebastian down to Bubión, and it is the road that connects Bubión to its neighbouring villages and, from there, the whole of the Alpujarra to the outside world. The largest number of people joins the procession at this point: expatriates, other local people and their visiting relatives, even tourists. They all stream out of the houses, the bars and the restaurants to witness the procession as it passes by and becomes a part of the atmosphere.

From the main road the procession takes a turn down into the village again and continues at the same rhythm with the same regular pauses. It has grown during its course. When it enters the church square it heads towards the church entrance and is brought to an end when San Sebastian is honoured there. The bells stop ringing and there is total silence as the men carrying San Sebastian lift his statue up off their shoulders. They then call loudly: 'Viva San Sebastian!' This is repeated, and then the statue is carried back into the church to its location by the altar. People gather together in the church whilst the priest gives a short sermon, followed by one final call of 'San Sebastian'.

In the meantime the square has been filling up with more people for the finale of the story that everybody is waiting for: the firework display. In the square, in front of the church, big decorative fireworks are set up on stands. The last is the biggest and circles around a picture of San Sebastian. Again, people call out 'Viva San Sebastian!' After this firework, hundreds of smaller fireworks rain over the people standing in the square, who try to protect their heads and faces with their hands, under the eaves of the houses, or in doorways. There are not many places to escape to and when the rain of fireworks is over, people press their hands on their ears, as they know the final and loudest firework, *la gorda* ('the big one'), is about to explode. *La gorda* marks the end of the firework display, the end of the procession and the end of the story. Nevertheless, although the plot may have been brought to a finale it does not end the narrative, for inhabitants continue to plot their own personal biographies as the ongoing dialogue of belonging continues.

Conclusion

Walking can be said to be a form of storytelling. My discussion has focused on the productivity of walking during the course of the procession of San Sebastian in Bubión. The structure of the procession, with its synchronized rhythm and directionality, plots a tale of belonging and weaves together the sound of time. My argument is that this way of telling is a particular form of authorizing the way in which people share their sense of belonging to a place. As Bruner, however, writes: 'the full power of a story is never felt unless it is realized in an experience' (1984, 73), and thus to get a sense of this power one needs to walk with the procession as it moves along. Whilst walking the story, the dynamic of the plot appears in the ways participants bring forward their own biographies and fuse them together to assist in telling the authorized story. People choose to participate differently in the procession. Some walk at the front, some in the middle and others at the back. Some choose to take a stand along the route where the procession passes and watch in silence or, indeed, in tears. Some join in as the procession passes while others choose not to do so. There are also those who choose to leave the village during the fiesta and not take part in the procession at all. These are often expatriates who claim that the festivity has lost its authenticity as more people seem to gather for it every year. This diversity in participation and commitment nevertheless contributes to a sense of place as it is lived and experienced and, most importantly, shared.

'What people make of their places', Keith Basso writes, 'is closely connected to what they make of themselves as members of society and inhabitants of the earth, and while the two activities may be separable in principle, they are joined in practice' (1996, 7). In this chapter I have shown that this joining can happen as walking narrates the place of belonging. The narrative creates what Jackson (2005, 356) calls a 'potential space' between the individual and the environment. It is a space in which 'every individual negotiates, albeit unwittingly, his or her own particular compromise between what is given and what he or she effectively brings into being' (ibid.). Consequently, although the narratives may express displacement they also, as de Certeau states, 'organize places through the displacement they describe' (1984, 116). Thus, taking part in the procession in all the different ways described here brings together personal narratives and experiences, binding every particular life to the lives of others, and yielding a sense of connection and continuity in a place to which one belongs.

References

Basso, K. (1996), *Wisdom Sits in Places: Landscape and Language Among the Western Apache* (Albuquerque: University of New Mexico Press).

Bender, B. (2001), 'Landscapes On-The-Move', *Journal of Social Archaeology* 1:1, 75-89.

Benjamin, W. (1970), 'The Storyteller', in Arendt, H. (ed.) (1970), *Illuminations*, trans. H. Zohn (London: Jonathan Cape).

Boissevain, J. (1992), 'Introduction', in Boissevain, J. (ed.) (1992), *Revitalising European Rituals* (London: Routledge).

Bruner, E. (1984), 'Dialogic Narration and the Paradoxes of Masada', in Bruner, E. (ed.) (1984), *Text, Play, and Story: The Construction and Reconstruction of Self and Society* (Illinois: Waveland Press).

Certeau, M. de (1984), *The Practice of Everyday Life*, trans. S. Rendall (Berkeley: University of California Press).

Christian, W. (1972), *Person and God in a Spanish Valley* (New York, London: Seminar Press).

Coleman, S. and Eade, J. (2004), 'Introduction: Reframing Pilgrimage' in Coleman, S. and Eade, J. (eds) (2004), *Reframing Pilgrimage: Cultures in Motion* (London: Routledge).

Connerton, P. (1989), *How Societies Remember* (Cambridge: Cambridge University Press).

Crain, M. (1992), 'Pilgrims, "Yuppies", and Media Men', in Boissevain, J. (ed.) (1992), *Revitalising European Rituals* (London: Routledge).

Dirks, N. (1994), 'Ritual and Resistance: Subversion as a Social Fact', in Dirks, N., Elay, G. and Ortner, S. (eds) (1994), *Culture, Power, History: A Reader in Contemporary Social Theory* (Princeton: Princeton University Press).

Green, S. (2005), *Notes from the Balkans: Locating Marginality and Ambiguity on the Greek-Albanian Border* (Princeton: Princeton University Press).

Ingold, T. (2000), *The Perception of the Environment: Essays on Livelihood, Dwelling and Skill* (London: Routledge).

—— (2004), 'Culture on the Ground: The World Perceived Through the Feet', *Journal of Material Culture* 9:3, 315-40.

—— (2007), *Lines: A Brief History* (London: Routledge).

Jackson, M. (1983), 'Thinking Through the Body: An Essay on Understanding Metaphor', *Social Analysis* 14, 127-48.

—— (1998), *Minima Ethnographica: Intersubjectivity and the Anthropological Project* (Chicago: University of Chicago Press).

——(2002), *The Politics of Storytelling: Violence, Transgression, and Intersubjectivity* (Copenhagen: Museum Tusculanum Press).

—— (2005), 'Storytelling Events, Violence, and the Appearance of the Past', *Anthropological Quarterly* 78:2, 355-75.

Lund, K. (1998), *Landscape, Memory and Tourism in Southern Spain* (Unpublished doctoral dissertation, University of Manchester).

—— (2005), 'Finding Place in Nature: "Intellectual" and Local Knowledge in a Spanish Natural Park', *Conservation and Society* (Special Section) 3:2, 371-87.

—— (2008), 'Walking and Viewing: Narratives of Belonging in Southern Spain', in Coleman, S. and Collins, P. (eds) (2008), *Dislocating Anthropology?: Bases of Longing and Belonging in the Analysis of Contemporary Societies* (Cambridge: Cambridge Scholars Press).

Myerhoff, B. (1982), 'Life History Among the Elderly: Performance, Visibility, and Remembering', in Ruby, J. (ed.) (1982), *A Crack in the Mirror: Reflexive Perspectives in Anthropology* (Pennsylvania: University of Pennsylvania Press).

Solnit, R. (2000), *Wanderlust: A History of Walking* (New York: Penguin Books).

Stewart, K. (1996), *A Space on the Side of the Road: Cultural Poetics in an 'Other' America* (Princeton: Princeton University Press).

Chapter 8

Taking a Trip and Taking Care in Everyday Life

Jo Lee Vergunst

A path is sometimes easy to walk along, and sometimes not.[1] Among hill-walkers and mountaineers, stories are often told about mishaps such as injuries, losing the way, lost or forgotten equipment, or bad weather. Here is one I heard during a walk in the hills of north-east Scotland:

> A few years ago I was out walking, and we went up Clachnaben. And on the way down, I slipped on a little bit of shale, you know, and broke my ankle. I had to hop all the way down. It actually wasn't painful, it was very very tiring. I was very lucky it was a very small fracture, it was a spiral fracture, so it kind of supported itself. But I couldn't put any weight on it.

And another, recounted whilst walking on an icy path in the same region:

> There's a Munro over in Kintail called Laith Beinn, Grey Mountain, and we went over to the Falls of Glomach and decided we'd climb it on the way back and in the guide book that's literally all it says about it. One of these mountains that you can easily climb on the way back from the Falls of Glomach. Was it heck. We hit it in blizzard conditions, which cleared, and then I led the way up the final slope, because I was the only one that day who had crampons. Some of the other lads had ice axes and I had crampons, and there I was cutting steps up it up to the top. And it got barely a paragraph, a couple of sentences in the guide book!

The success and media coverage of the book and film *Touching the Void* (Simpson 1998) taps into a certain fascination with when things go wrong, telling the story of a physically and socially catastrophic fall into a glacier. Richard Storer's popular book *The Joy of Hillwalking* similarly devotes a chapter to 'hillwalking accidents'. As he writes, 'the longer the fall, the more excruciating the pain, the greater spillage of blood, the more salivatingly relished the tale' (Storer 2004, 117). All these biographical narratives convey an intensity of experience, when something 'really happened' during the journey. In the first of the above anecdotes the walker is injured, though not as seriously as it first seems, by a tiny movement or disjuncture, a slip between the boot and the shale, and the character of the walk changes radically.

---

1   I would like to thank all those who have given their time and shared their walks with me, in particular David Coleman and friends and Cath Jackson. The research was funded by a grant from the ESRC for the project 'Culture from the Ground', award number RES-000-23-0312.

In the second, the Munro that seems insignificant in the guide book rears up in the reality of the weather to present a serious challenge to the walkers. Although such stories are often told in a humorous or entertaining style which is appropriate to the easy sociability of hill walking, they also say something about what is so often most meaningful for walkers in many different environments: the actuality of walking itself, the sheer presence of the body in the world. It is the actual underfoot and enveloping conditions that constitute the experience of the walk.

One aim of this chapter is to add these 'grounded' experiences to the guide-book-style representation of walks, and in so doing to explore ethnographically the ways that walking happens in the city and the countryside in north-east Scotland. I base the discussion in some of the mishaps that can occur in walking – in particular, tripping, slipping and losing the way. Secondly, through a focus on the textures of the environment, I aim to conceptualize the environmental relations of the walker in a way that brings out the mobile and mutually-embedding relations of walking. Finally, running through these themes is the idea of 'everydayness' as a way of sensing and knowing the environment, and I end by questioning the emotionality of the everyday.

Grounding the romanticized walk

The Romantic movement in literature and art in Europe in the early nineteenth century was also the beginning of a very particular sensibility towards the environment. It depended more than anything on the experience of being in a place, and of using that experience for reflection on the self and the environment. As described by Wallace (1993), Bate (1991) and Robinson (1989), walking was an important part of this sensibility as the means by which such experiences could occur. The poet William Wordsworth is closely associated by Anne Wallace with what she identifies as a 'peripatetic' genre of literature, based for its advocates on a sense that 'the natural, primitive quality of the physical act of walking restores the natural proportions of our perceptions, reconnecting us with both the physical world and the moral order inherent in it' (Wallace 1993, 13).

In their discussions of Wordsworth's poetry, however, literary critics have not generally been concerned with the tread of the walk itself. Things would happen to the mind or the feelings of the walker, and to the person – encounters with other people, views, and the discovery of places – but the actions of the walking body and the rhythms of walking as the source of creativity and 'eventness', the happenings *in* the walk, can easily be passed over. But Wordsworth himself had some interesting things to say about these, particularly when commenting – as did the walkers in the excerpts cited above – on the difficulty of walking. An extract from the beginning of *The Excursion* (Wordsworth 1977 [1814]) illustrates this:

> Across a bare wide Common I was toiling
> With languid steps that by the slippery turf
> Were baffled; nor could my weak arm disperse
> The host of insects gathering round my face
> And ever with me as I paced along.
>
> (I. 24-5)

This is a specific description of the narrator's steps and the immediate conditions in which they took place. There is a contrast between these passages (another example is in *The Excursion*, Book II, 323-28) and the perhaps more well known Wordsworthian mode that Wallace discusses. In the latter, the environment frequently unfolds as a series of effects of the weather in its interaction with the hills, lakes, fields, and so on, which as a totality is often personified as 'Nature', and which in turn affects the development of the mind. In the former, by contrast, the action of the body is emphasized. In Wordsworth's autobiographical *The Prelude* (Wordsworth 1964 [1805]), the actions of rowing during a childhood trip are described in a famous passage, part of which runs as follows:

> I dipp'd my oars into the silent Lake,
> And, as I rose upon the stroke, my Boat
> Went heaving through the water, like a Swan;
> When from behind that craggy Steep, till then
> The bound of the horizon, a huge Cliff,
> As if with voluntary power instinct,
> Uprear'd its head.
>
> (I. 402-8)

When the narrator is moving, all around him also moves. There are no views of peaceful Nature to be contemplated at a distance and at leisure, but rather an all-encompassing and rather frightening experience of water, mountain and cliff that almost overwhelms the rower. There is a close-up engagement with the surroundings that seems very different from Nature beheld as a view. In toiling over slippery turf, or heaving a boat over water, the Romantic ideal of the 'natural proportions' of sensations and actions (implying either a static viewing or a relatively effort-free and smooth movement) is subverted, leaving in its place a more everyday sense of doing one's best to get around in a difficult environment. This is, perhaps, part of Wordsworth's achievement: in locating his own development in specific fields of action and experience, he demonstrates the very physical qualities of walking and their contribution to his own biography.

Bate (1991) describes Wordsworth's walking as radical partly because of the search for encounters with other people that often form the basis to the poetry, and partly in locating significance in particular environments and places rather than the more commonly-cited social structures (such as of class or gender). Henry David Thoreau, by contrast, found most meaning by walking alone, in seeking wilderness, and by forcing a separation between engagements he described as 'worldly', such as politics, and those of his immediate environment (Thoreau 1862). His was not quite a walk of escape, however, because he argued that whilst walking one's attention should be completely within one's surroundings, and that by this means one could attain a state of mind that was most real and vital. If anything, the life outside of nature, in the world of work, was the more intangible part, though it might linger annoyingly in the walk.

By now, we have the common use of the word 'walk' reified as a noun in English, which is rare in Wordsworth, although the *Oxford English Dictionary* records the earliest example of this sense of the word from Chaucer in 1386. 'The walk' as an event is constituted by the person walking along a particular route at a particular time, and the description serves to mark it off from the practical aspects of life. The implication is that 'a walk' is carried out for the purposes of leisure or exercise, and that a person going for a walk has accorded it a special non-work status. Writers such as Wordsworth and Thoreau took the notion of non-work walking and through it they explored various kinds of personhood: a self connected to physical and moral orders, particularly by way of the identification of Nature.

Yet Wordsworth's passages on his own physical exploits, along with the tales of walking mishaps told at the beginning of this chapter, suggest an alternative rendering. The suggestion is that the way the actual steps are made (or not made) is integral to how the walk takes place. This is very different from the experiences drawn from the visions of walking in the Romantic mode, which is also the standard mode of writing in guide books. In these there is a gap or distance between the walker and the surrounding environment, to be spanned by the walker's appreciation of that environment. Can we reconcile walking as an action of stepping and as a source of emotional impact? One way of beginning to do this is to look in more detail at how everyday walking actually takes place, paying particular attention to some of the slips, trips and mistakes that can happen. They involve a rather different kind of knowledge, a 'becoming-aware', which I argue is characteristic of everyday walking.

Walking mishaps in an everyday environment

'Everyday' walking through an 'everyday' environment needs some explanation. Sociological discussions of the everyday have centred on the ways of life of non-elite parts of society, particularly in the industrial West, and on the extent to which there are hidden influences on what is immediately apparent. Highmore (2002) distinguishes between Freudian analyses, suggesting that our covert desires and fears need constantly to be kept in check for the everyday to function properly (and where failures result in Freudian 'slips'), and Marxist analyses, in which the forces of production structure our everyday modes of living, unbeknownst to us. The everyday, Highmore writes, is positioned between the general and the particular, and between power and resistance. Taussig (1992, 141) is more specific in outlining a sense of the everyday: 'Surely this sense includes much that is not sense so much as sensuousness, an embodied and somewhat automatic "knowledge" that functions like peripheral vision, not studied contemplation, a knowledge that is imageric and sensate rather than ideational.' Sensuousness rather than study thus pervades the everyday. We move away from the special or distinguished 'studied' walk of the Romantic writers in order to explore the underlying ways of dealing with the environments being traversed. Following Walter Benjamin, Taussig distinguishes the everyday from generalized notions of 'the public' and 'the masses', suggesting that while there are likely to be many varieties and versions of everydayness, it may still be possible to find some kinds of solidarities upon which common understandings may be based. It is worth considering the extent to which ways of moving through environments might furnish such common ground. The focus here is not on what is hidden, as in the Freudian or Marxist concepts of the everyday, but on what is *explored* by way of movement. While environments produce surprises and mishaps, I argue that these can be at the very heart of walking in a way that actually constitutes 'the everyday'.

Mishaps occur in all walking environments. I am interested in those that tell us something about the relationship between the walker and his or her immediate surroundings, because paradoxically they involve kinds of knowledge that are very close to Taussig's sense of everydayness. Of these I would like to discuss trips and slips, and then losing the way. I approach them abstractly in the first instance to get an idea of the general processes involved. At the heart of *tripping* is an intrusion from the environment into the movement of the person. Contact between an object, which thus becomes an obstacle, and one of the feet happens during the lifted phase of the foot's movement, when it should be travelling unhindered above the ground. The rhythm of the foot is brought to a shuddering halt, and the leg lifts and tries to hurdle the obstacle. The other foot, meanwhile, is normally planted on the ground but may jump forward in reaction and compensation, if the obstructed foot is unable to move. The momentum of the upper body may carry the walker so far forward as to prevent the regaining of balance by either foot, and the stumble becomes a fall forwards.

Observing tripping is not a simple exercise because of the speed of these movements, which take a mere moment to occur. The person tripping is unaware of the technicalities and is more or less surrendered to the interaction of forces and impacts. But adjustments can be made. I have seen tripping take place on uneven pavement slabs in the streets of Aberdeen, where the walker moves the arms forward to help regain balance, sometimes may trot for a pace or two to come out of the stumble, and sometimes looks down or behind at the pavement. Walking through heather on hillsides is likely to result in a trip sooner or later, as the clumps are of uneven height and it is hard to judge how high the foot needs to be lifted for each step. On hillsides, trips often occur when the foot moving above the ground hits against something – a rock, perhaps – and knocks into the back of the standing leg. In one sense the walking rhythm is disrupted by the invasion of the obstacle into the foot's movement, but what is interesting is the readjustment of the body that allows the movement to continue. The walker skilfully rebalances: quickly lifting a foot, planting the other down in a different spot, shifting weight with the arms and the back. The trip becomes just one set of adjustments amongst others. It forms an episode of the journey rather than something outside it.

The *slip* contrasts with the trip in some interesting ways. Whereas the trip is an interruption of the moving foot, the slip forces movement of the foot which is usually still. Walking generally relies on a firm grip on the ground by the standing foot, above which the body pivots and the free foot steps ahead. If there is insufficient grip, the standing foot moves forward with the momentum of the body through the heel, at the same time as the free foot is moving in front of the trunk. The first reaction is, like the trip, an attempt to correct the situation with the free foot, which immediately slaps onto the ground with the impact on the ball of the foot. If the free foot is not fast enough in restoring steadiness, or cannot gain purchase and slips itself, the standing foot continues sliding forward. It either halts when it is able to grip again, or moves above the ground and causes the walker to fall backwards. Here there is an excess of movement: in the part of the step where we rely on the ground to stop the foot moving, the foot instead slips onwards, and the rhythmical rolling motion of the foot is changed to fast-forward acceleration. In the slip, the environment does not intrude enough into the movements of walking, an inversion of the over-intrusive environment of the trip.

**Figure 8.1 A walker slipping on a hillside. His right leg moves out of line,
but balance is regained with the help of a stick**

Another contrast between the slip and the trip lies in the extent to which people are aware of and can prepare for slipperiness. Trips and slips are both fairly common walking events, but, among people in and around Aberdeen, slips are much more reflected upon and held in the mind during walking. It may be that tripping is such an unexpected event that there is no real avoidance procedure apart from the standard manner of lifting one's feet during the walk. Most trips are also very minor inconveniences, as the tripped foot is usually able simply to lift itself above the obstacle. The slip, on the other hand, can more easily cause a complete loss of balance and a fall. The fall backwards is also more likely to damage the body trunk, by contrast to the leg and arm injuries expected in the forward fall of a trip.

Awareness of slipperiness among walkers is apparent from conversations and sharing walks with people. In the city the topic may come up in talking about the physical make-up and condition of the pavements and streets, often in relation to footwear. Many of the pavements in the centre of Aberdeen in particular are made of granite, a hard but smooth stone that can become slippery in wet weather. Walkers sometimes change their footwear according to the likelihood of slipperiness, preferring flatter moulded rubber and plastic soles to higher-heeled shoes or leather 'smart' shoes, for example. One said to me as we walked towards her workplace: 'I have these shoes on today [leather shoes with a small high-heel], but when it rains, the pavement there is getting quite slippery.' During periods of snow and ice in the city it is common to see hiking boots being worn as protection against both slipperiness and wetness. Such boots allow a fairly 'normal' stride to be maintained: a straight back, extension of the legs, and feet lifting from the ground during the step. Others sometimes use quite different styles of walking, such as shuffling through the snow with very little foot-lift, spreading the feet quite widely apart and walking with something approaching bow legs, or taking very small steps. The variation apparent in walking through snow in the city shows how changed environmental conditions do not produce uniform responses. Rather, each person finds his or her own way of moving through the difficult environment. The differences are apparent in the contact that the feet have with the ground: brief or lingering, frequent or spaced out, narrow or spread. The variety of footwear is another dimension of the relationship between the walker and the environment, as is the weather. A slip will involve all of these aspects – even more so, perhaps, than the trip.

Slipperiness is also associated with particular places, as one of the walkers introduced above explained in relation to pavements. Approaching a wet wooden bridge in Aberdeen, another walker described her fear of slipping on it: 'I hate walking across this bridge. I'm so scared I'll fall.' She walked with small steps, watching where she was putting her feet, and holding on to the side rail at the edge of the bridge. Some walkers face cobbled or causewayed streets with similar trepidation, where the uneven but very smooth stones can cause difficulty in terms both of balance and of the extra physical effort needed to walk over them. In the countryside and in the hills paths often become iced over where otherwise they would have been merely wet, and again there are skills involved in negotiating them safely. Sometimes walkers intentionally skid along such tracts of ice, preventing a slip by keeping their centre of gravity over their feet, or use other techniques – shuffling, testing, balancing with arms – that are also used in the city during snow. But this is not to say that slips cannot be as unexpected as trips are. I witnessed a man slip and fall backwards while starting to cross a road. There was a smooth and sloping kerbstone (designed to allow wheelchair or pram access between the pavement and road) on which his smooth-soled brogues found no purchase. The haste with which he got up and left the scene (and my impromptu attempt to conduct some fieldwork, or at least to see if he was all right) revealed an embarrassment that testified to the control that individuals are expected to exercise over their walking, particularly in the city. The precautions we take and adjustments we make to avoid mishaps are, of course, never infallible.

Figure 8.2 A granite pavement in Aberdeen

Perhaps counter-intuitively, these actions fit into Taussig's conceptualization of everyday sensuousness, an embodied 'knowledge' involving particular ways of perceiving and acting. Again in his reading of Benjamin, he summarizes this as the everyday tactility of knowing (Taussig 1992, 143), constituted by coming into contact with things rather than contemplating them from a distance. The manner in

Figure 8.3 A walker on Arthur's Seat in Edinburgh

which the free foot attempts to hurdle the obstacle in a trip, or plants itself on the ground in a slip, demonstrates the small skills involved in walking, relying on a direct feel for the environment rather than a more distanced and ideational study of it. There are also associated skills of judging the conditions of walking both before the walk and as it continues, and of adjusting one's walking technique to suit them. Many people who walk the same or similar routes very regularly, whether for 'work' or 'leisure' purposes, have commented on the seemingly endless variability that their journeys present to them in practice. There are different sights, different weather conditions and different things going on around them, not to mention the varying mood and physical condition of the walker from day to day (Lee and Ingold 2006). Environments are re-explored and re-learned every day, as routes as well as in each footstep along them. Mishaps are particularly pointed examples of becoming aware of what an environment is *really* like.

At this stage we can think again about what the walker's surroundings actually consist of. The qualities I have emphasized so far are those of protrusion or flatness, stickiness, roughness or smoothness, felt according to the conditions of the feet and the judgement of the eyes. They are textures. Unlike surfaces, textures do not clearly separate what is above from what is below as the person moves along. They are rather experienced relationally, through the degree and kind of friction caused by contact in movement between two substances. A wet pavement is slippery for a smooth-soled shoe, and a dry sandy beach allows a bare foot to sink in and slip through it. A tired walker during a long hike is more likely to trip over loose rocks or tree roots. The intrinsic properties of the environment or the person are therefore only important in so far as they become part of a textural interaction, which then affords or hinders various kinds of movement. As Ingold has shown (2000, 241), the ever-variegated, textured ground of this movement is a far cry from the isotropic, planar surface that, in the traditions of Western navigation and cartography, has been projected by way of an imaginary 'bird's eye view' – or rather, an impossible everywhere-at-once view. Moreover, texture implies a tactility that, as Taussig suggests, can engender specifically everyday or non-contemplative forms of environmental knowledge.

Walked ground itself takes on a different character according to the patterns of use and social networks that encompass it. It can be pitted or smoothed by regular use, or become indistinct through lack of use. Harrison (2004) describes how overgrown paths in the Middle Sepik in Papua New Guinea are a sign of deteriorated relations between villages that were once socially close. Allowing a path to fall out of use is, he writes, an active forgetting of social relations in a changing riverine landscape geared to forgetfulness rather than remembrance. In pre-colonial times, new cut paths would be intentionally left to become overgrown in order to disguise their use and prevent enemy ambushes. Paths also index social relations in north-east Scotland, albeit in rather different ways. For example, many villages and small towns are developing new footpaths for leisure and access, to conform to recent Scottish Outdoor Access legislation.[2] Work usually involves partnerships of active residents, landowners, local government and a variety of nature conversation, access, and development organizations. The paths embody the social networks of their production, including the entrepreneurial forms of local development where

---

2   As part of the Land Reform Act (2003), all local authorities in Scotland are obliged to establish 'Core Path Networks', which will be managed routes intended to increase access to the outdoors.

partnership working and funding bureaucracies have to be dealt with. In one village, Tarland in Aberdeenshire, new paths became overgrown in the spring and summer months when the surrounding vegetation grew too strongly for the normal pattern of use to keep them open. The local Development Group then found new funding from the local council for cutting equipment, financially and mechanically overcoming the lack of use that would have closed the paths. Moreover the paths are meant to be a stimulus to 'development', encouraging visitors to the area and setting the village itself on a new course. They are thus a testament to the total field of relations in which they stand, from the footsteps of their walkers and the whirring of the strimmer to the efforts of local development organizations and national politicians. The particular textures that emerge are consequent upon the literal embedding of paths in the world.

Taking care

The way to walk through a textural environment is *carefully*: one must take care. In the ethnographic terms of my fieldwork, 'take care' is most obviously a spoken phrase used either as a parting at the end of a conversation or as a specific warning in a dangerous or difficult situation. In English-speaking countries, we spend a fair amount of time imploring each other to take care. However, part of what we mean is surely to encourage attentiveness towards the environment in Taussig's sense of the tactility of knowing, or as in Wordsworth's descriptions of his physical exploits (as opposed to his Romantic visions). It is the kind of attention that may not be always at the forefront of our thoughts but nonetheless should protect us from mishaps, or at least help us to recover when a mishap occurs, in contrast to the distant contemplative mode of seeing the environment.

Footsteps are the primary means by which walkers take care. As described above, each footstep produces a distinctive relationship through which the walker comes to know something of his or her textural environment. In the reactions of the feet and the body to what is found, we see how taking care happens physically: the adjustments and readjustments of balance, of walking technique and of apparel such as clothing. There is, however, something more to taking care than the individual footstep, and this is reflected in a more generalized attentiveness that relates to the rhythm of walking. One episode of walking in particular led me to consider this idea. I joined an informal club of around fifteen friends for a day's hike in the hills of Deeside close to Aberdeen. Near the start we climbed the side of a valley up a steep narrow path in single file, and I found myself watching the footsteps of the person in front as we ascended. The path had many uneven bumps and ridges, as well as being steep. It was peaty, mostly wet and soft enough to leave footprints but occasionally frozen and icy, and sometimes with stones embedded in it. Shin-high heather sometimes brushed onto the path, and patches of snow lay around it. I saw how the feet turned at the ankle and the legs shifted weight in different directions up the path. Sometimes there was a pause between footfalls as a decision was made on where to step, and short steps were interspersed with longer reaches up the path. The arms swung, kept balance, and occasionally gripped a stone or the heather, or leant on the path itself.

Amongst these irregular movements, what kind of rhythm can be said to be present in the walking? It certainly did not seem to fit with the common notion of rhythm as an evenly-timed recurrence. Many walkers identified 'rhythm' as one of the most attractive and enjoyable features of walking, and yet the actions I observed were anything but regular. It seemed rather that the rhythm of walking took its lead and its tempo from the environment of which it was part. In a path of contrasts and unevenness, the rhythm of the body in its movement was precisely attuned to the continuation of movement up the path. In a paper on the phenomenology of human movement, Van den Berg identified a way of moving in which 'the body itself is forgotten, eliminated, passed over in silence for the occupation or for the landscape for whose sake the passing is necessary'. The body, he wrote, 'is realised as *landscape*' (Van den Berg 1952, 170, original emphasis; Lorimer and Lund 2003, 138). Climbing the path, according to my observations, entailed a movement of precisely this kind. It involved concentration, of course, but this concentration was focused on the maintenance of a rhythm of movement that complemented the path itself. The body alone was passed over in favour of an awareness of the textures produced by the feet and hands in their surroundings.

The second aspect of rhythm I would like to discuss relates to Lefebvre's contention that it is difference that distinguishes rhythm from mere repetition (Lefebvre 2004, 78). If an event takes place in exactly the same way as its predecessor and successor, the sequence is repeated rather than rhythmic because there is no possibility for variety. A defining characteristic of rhythm is that it is not fixed but continually answerable to perturbations in the conditions of the task as it unfolds. It is this responsiveness that allows practitioners to 'carry on', in Ingold's (2006) terms. Thus, in walking through a variegated and textured environment (rather than on a solid, isotropic and planar surface), no two steps are precisely the same. A walk along a steep and uneven path requires a rhythm that is full of variety – even more so than in the task of sawing a plank that Ingold uses to illustrate his argument – and yet it is this variation that makes it possible for the walk as a whole to be carried on. However walkers would rarely speak of this sense of rhythm except when it is felt to be absent: as one hill walker said, 'there are some days when you just can't get in a rhythm'. The very 'carrying on' of walking can sometimes prove difficult.

Distinctive social relations are also apparent during this kind of walking. While hiking in a group is generally a very sociable experience, walking up a steep hill is usually undertaken without talking. The personal effort and concentration of climbing take precedence – one walker commented to me after an ascent: 'you've just got to take it at your own pace, haven't you'. Groups often break up at the bottom of the hill and reconvene at the top (or at a staging post), where the celebration of reaching the summit serves to bring everyone together again as they collectively gather their breath (Lorimer and Lund, this volume). On the way down a group can become similarly strung out as the techniques of walking downhill are practised: keeping low to the ground and testing the path before putting weight on it, for example. In the same way that paths reflect the social relations in which they are produced, so the rhythms of walking along them have distinctively social aspects.

Taking care happens through these various rhythms of walking. It is by maintaining a rhythm that the walker is able to be careful, to be attentive to the body-and-environment in Van den Berg's sense. Although careful walking, as I have described it here, is often undertaken in what seems like a more solitary manner, walkers follow each other very closely, sometimes to the extent of walking in each others' footsteps. In the city, coming across environmental hazards such as slippery ice, broken glass, or traffic when crossing a road, will often elicit a simple spoken 'take care', a call to attentiveness. Picking a route through a crowd of people involves a similar kind of care: a tactility not so much of the feet but of the whole body, and an awareness of the routes of others (Lee and Ingold 2006). Although taking care does not remove the possibility of slips or trips, it does serve as a particular orientation to the environment, and is essential to the flexible performance of everyday skills. And if we do take care, then the mishaps that inevitably befall us may have less serious consequences.

Finding and losing the way

Other senses of taking care are less amenable to the adjustments of the body discussed so far. Among these are the care needed to find a route to walk along, and then not to lose it. Here the walker is not so concerned with the immediate tactility of the footstep and the path, more with their overall sense of self and personhood. How, then, do these rather different concepts of taking care relate to the everydayness described earlier? How are episodes of finding and losing the way sensuous activities, and what do they tell of the small or un-thought-of skills of moving around?

Losing the way and getting lost are not quite the same thing. Losing the way requires the existence of its converse, namely having or following a route in the first place. There are degrees to which this is the case in any particular walk. In my fieldwork it was occasionally pointed out to me (perhaps to bring me down to earth, as it were) that walking is for the most part simply a way of getting somewhere, and a definite route is often a part of this kind of walking. There is a difference, however, between the route as a pre-planned line between places, which is in effect acted out by the walker in the manner of an actor following a script, and the route which is improvised in the course of the walk itself. The latter comes from always knowing where one is and where one wants to go, but enjoying the freedom to choose and explore alternative routes as the walk proceeds. Many walkers in the city engage in this kind of improvisational route finding in their walks to and from work and in other regular trips.

I joined a Community Warden, a neighbourhood patroller employed by the local council to be the 'eyes and ears' of the police and to maintain good community relations. Though planned to cover the general area of the neighbourhood, our walks actually answered to much more immediate choices. These included timing, such as the need to be at a local school when the children were leaving; a sense of covering the ground, where certain streets were chosen on that day and others not; and personal opportunities for the Warden to rest on a wall, buy a drink from a shop, or, sometimes, walk along a pleasant grove of trees near a river. Walks of this kind are not confined to a single 'way', which is either kept to or lost, but unfold episodically. Walkers can feel confident that they will not become lost, so long as they keep to areas of the city they know (whether or not the specific streets are familiar) and maintain an overall sense of direction – such as heading towards or away from the town centre.

There are hints here of the tradition of aestheticized urban wandering identified in European cities from the nineteenth century onwards by Benjamin (1999), and also described by Careri (2002) and Lucas (this volume). From the *flâneurs*, self-consciously flaunting the capitalist organization of urban time and space, to the Dadaists in their excursive resistance to it, the streets and locations of the city have been deliberately appropriated for the purposes of wandering (Careri 2002). The tradition entails an active rejection of the pre-planned itinerary in favour of the more organic constitution of the route during the walk. One can only lose the way if one was sticking to a particular route in the first place – and this is the very type of walking many walkers try to avoid. The example of the Community Warden, however, shows how such wandering can also be part of a strategy not just of integrating the walker into the surroundings, but also of enabling the city authorities to exercise some control over them.

Walkers making their way through farmed or low-level countryside in north-east Scotland often have much more limited possibilities for taking alternative routes than do either urban or hill walkers. Farm tracks and estate roads may be available, but people are often reluctant to walk around farm buildings. Walkers are not usually keen to walk along roads without pavements, although minor roads are sometimes incorporated into walking routes. In these cases the problem lies more in finding a way in the first place than in choosing between options or taking care not to get lost. Residents of a particular village often know routes in their immediate area, for strolling or walking their dogs, but rarely venture on foot beyond this area. The network of footpaths actually taken is usually modest but, as described earlier, it is growing in the vicinity of many small towns and villages. The number and extent of long-distance waymarked countryside routes in Britain is low compared to European countries such as France, The Netherlands and Austria. Most walking guidebooks rely on readers having access to a car to transport them to the beginning of the prescribed route. A major difference in the current situation in Britain, compared to earlier eras, is that rural roads are now surfaced with asphalt, allowing cars to pass so quickly as virtually to preclude the use of these roads by walkers. This has certainly been the fate of many of the old cattle and pony drove roads running through the valleys of Scotland (Haldane 1997 [1952]).

Hill walkers face few of these problems. The possibilities for routes are partly shaped by the physical terrain – the valleys, hillsides, ridges and so on – and partly by the paths that already exist in the hills, themselves produced through the activities of previous walkers. Lorimer and Lund (this volume) note how a desire to reach the tops is an important influence on how walkers find their ways around the hills. Given the ability to walk off-path, however, the variety of ways that can be made is virtually without limit. But alongside the freedom to choose and create routes is the much greater potential for getting lost than is usual in urban or low-level countryside settings. In the hills particularly, the skills of walking include not only those of way-finding that come from familiarity with the landscape, but also those that come through the use of documents and tools such as maps, compasses, Global Positioning Systems, and guide books. Lorimer and Lund (2003, 140) describe some of these processes in detail, concluding that 'the complexly layered and continuous dialogue of modifications between hill-walker, compass, map, the ground passed over and prevailing weather conditions ... dictate situated practice'. They emphasize the prior selection of the route by hill walkers and the efforts made during the walk to keep to it.

Inevitably, walkers sometimes lose the way and get lost. Walks with people in the city and low-level countryside areas have not, for me, led to many identifiable occasions of being lost, for the reasons discussed above. I have however been present in episodes of losing the way in the hills. During one hill walk, cloud descended around the hill tops as we proceeded and eventually hid the shapes of the hills and valleys that had been guiding us along with our maps. But the nominal leader of the walk was confident that if we continued in the same direction we would soon hit a larger path. After some time we had not found the path, and he stopped and formed a small coterie to look at the map. We decided that heading across and down the hill should bring us out into the valley we were aiming for in our circular walk. But now the dynamics of the group became rather different. The easy sociability of the group disintegrated into a quiet and more purposeful walking, the pace increased and individuals would peer into the cloud to try and make out the surrounding hills. The halting of normal conversation was part of our being lost, or at least of our having lost the way, a predicament that now took over and occupied our thoughts. A quiet seriousness is always apparent on these occasions. Being lost emphasizes in its absence the comfortable groundedness that is normally felt during a walk when one has found or is on the way. When lost, the ground feels less firm; the route is less confidently 'made' by each footstep for fear that it is leading one astray.

To lose the way is to experience a disconnection or a disjunction from one's surroundings that is perhaps not so different from that of the slip or trip. Where the slip or trip interrupts the rhythm of the footsteps, losing the way interrupts what Lorimer and Lund, in the passage cited above, call the 'continuous dialogue' between walker, tools and environment intrinsic to routemaking. In both cases the walker tries to re-establish proper contact with the ground – contact that is stable and allows for the walk to carry on. Similarly, it is when we trip or slip, or when we are injured as a result, that the skill and the groundedness of ordinary walking are brought home to us.

Two further points about losing the way deserve emphasis. The first concerns the formation of the 'coterie' in the walk: this is a distinctive gathering in many hill walks where a larger number of people are present. Often, three or four people huddle over a map slightly apart from the main group and discuss the progress of the hike. It is another social dimension to taking care, where the responsibility is spread beyond the one or two more or less formal 'leaders' that groups usually have. But social relationships are strained by getting lost. 'Whose fault was this?' 'She shouldn't have walked off so fast.' 'Why should we listen to him?'

Secondly, the extent to which one has actually lost the way is not always or immediately apparent. To return to our example, we descended from the hill and came to a small wood, which we finally recognized as one we had passed earlier on the way up the hill. Having intended to walk down a different way, we were quite far off our route. It was only now that we realized how far we had gone astray, yet simultaneously the stability and groundedness of knowing where we were was then restored. There is not necessarily any easily definable moment of losing the way, unlike the moment of the slip or trip. The state of being lost can start with a mere thought, or may only become apparent in retrospect.

Conclusion: towards an emotionality of the everyday

Wordsworth's poetry is not just about growing into a love of nature. Some of it, at least, explores how moving through an environment is a very physical process that can be difficult, mistake-ridden and troubling. Walkers in Aberdeen and north-east Scotland demonstrate these aspects of walking in manifold contexts: in the city, in the countryside and in the hills; alone or in groups; in different weather and with variable conditions underfoot. To understand walking as an everyday activity is not, then, to attribute mundanity or repetitiveness to the sphere of the everyday. Rather, I have followed Taussig in arguing that a particular sensuousness and a tactile way of knowing are central to everydayness. In walking this sensuousness allows the environment to be known through a textural relationship between the walker and the ground. The small skills of walking, of balancing and recovering balance, of taking care and making routes, do as much to constitute the experience and meaning of the walk as do the grand vistas along the main street of the city or from the top of the mountain. They are also perhaps closer to the heart of the everyday.

Ultimately the mishaps of walking become part of the rhythm of walking itself. At an immediate level a slip, trip, or loss of the way seems to interrupt the walk in a manner that is different from pauses to rest, to talk or to admire a view. The mishap is unplanned and unwanted, sometimes painful and potentially catastrophic. Yet mishaps are incorporated within the overall tale of the journey, much as other events are. They serve to emphasize the actuality of the walk, the fact of its taking place in the real world with its protrusions and intrusions and textures of slipperiness or stickiness. The rhythm of walking encompasses all that happens to the body that allows it to carry on, somehow, in environments that are as often difficult as easy to move through.

One question that emerges is how mishaps are linked to the emotions of a walk, and thus how emotions become part of our environment. The ever-present possibility of mishaps can engender fear in walkers. They may be afraid of slipping over, and some may be so fearful of getting lost that they are unable to walk in the hills. Many city walkers fear being attacked, in certain places or times of day, and here the mishap takes on an even more sinister guise. For Wordsworth and the storytellers quoted at the beginning of the chapter, however, mishaps seem also – if only in retrospect – to form part of the joy of walking, in the pleasure of an experience of hardship overcome or learnt from. To inquire into the emotionality of the everyday is to ask how these forms of sensuousness engender feeling. If walking is understood to be a relational and textural activity, then *where*, in experiential terms, is the emotion? To confine it to the body is, after all, to fall back on the very distancing of body from environment that is antithetical to everyday living.

References

Bate, J. (1991), *Romantic Ecology: Wordsworth and the Romantic Tradition* (London: Routledge).

Benjamin, W. (1999), *The Arcades Project*, trans. H. Eiland and K. McLaughlin (Cambridge, Mass. and London: Harvard University Press).

Careri, F. (2002), *Walkscapes: Walking as an Aesthetic Practice* (Barcelona: Gustavo).

Haldane, A. (1997 [1952]), *The Drove Roads of Scotland* (Edinburgh: Birlinn Press).

Harrison, S. (2004), 'Forgetful and Memorious Landscapes', *Social Anthropology* 12, 135-51.

Highmore, B. (2002), 'Introduction: Questioning Everyday Life', in Highmore, B. (ed.) (2002), *The Everyday Life Reader* (London: Routledge).

Ingold, T. (2000), *The Perception of the Environment: Essays on Livelihood, Dwelling and Skill* (London: Routledge).

—— (2006), 'Walking the Plank: A Meditation on the Process of Skill', in Dakers, J. (ed.) (2006), *Defining Technological Literacy: Towards an Epistemological Framework* (New York: Palgrave Macmillan).

Lee, J. and Ingold, T. (2006), 'Fieldwork on Foot: Perceiving, Routing, Socializing', in Coleman, S. and Collins, P. (eds) (2006), *Locating the Field: Space, Place and Context in Anthropology* (Oxford: Berg).

Lefebvre, H. (2004), *Rhythmanalysis: Space, Time and Everyday Life* (London: Continuum).

Lorimer, H. and Lund K. (2003), 'Performing Facts: Finding a Way Over Scotland's Mountains', in Szerszynski, B., Heim, W. and Waterton, C. (eds) (2003), 'Nature Performed: Environment, Culture and Performance', *Sociological Review Monographs* (Oxford: Blackwell).

Robinson, J. (1989), *The Walk: Notes on a Romantic Image* (Norman and London: University of Oklahoma Press).

Simpson, J. (1998), *Touching the Void* (London: Vintage).

Storer, R. (2004), *The Joy of Hillwalking* (Edinburgh: Luath Press).

Taussig, M. (1992), *The Nervous System* (London: Routledge).

Thoreau, H. (1862), 'Walking', *Atlantic Monthly* 10 (June 1862).

Van den Berg, J. (1952), 'The Human Body and the Significance of Human Movement: A Phenomenological Study', *Philosophy and Phenomenological Research* 13:2, 159-83.

Wallace, A. (1993), *Walking, Literature and English Culture: The Origins and Uses of Peripatetic in the Nineteenth Century* (Oxford: Clarendon Press).

Wordsworth, W. (1977), *The Poems (Volume One)* (London: Penguin).

—— (1964 [1805]), *The Prelude, or Growth of a Poet's Mind* (Oxford: Oxford University Press).

Chapter 9

Walking Through Ruins

Tim Edensor

In this chapter, I consider the effects of walking through industrial ruins. Having undertaken many journeys on foot throughout the United Kingdom over the past three years, I have walked through structures of varying age and states of decay, buildings and sites ranging from old mills to warehouses and foundries to vehicle workshops, and a host of derelict sites whose prior use could not be determined. While in Britain the de-industrializing Thatcher years were the era most productive of landscapes of ruination, there remain many urban areas that are littered with industrial ruins, typically in cities which have failed to prosper in the intense competition for new investment. Along railways and canals, in old industrial estates and interstitial, neglected urban areas, ruins continue to crumble and decay. While such sites are frequently vilified as despondent realms, spaces of waste and blights on the landscape, they support a range of human activities and a plethora of non-human life forms, as well as offering aesthetic, somatic and historical experiences at variance to the often over-coded, themed spaces of urban renewal. They are thus able to talk back to these apparently seamless processes of regeneration and provide spaces within which counter-aesthetics and alternative memories might emerge. Different encounters with objects and materiality, peculiar sensations and ineffable impressions may be experienced. Accordingly, I will highlight how travelling by foot through an industrial ruin or derelict site opens up walking to critical speculation and offers a diversity of distinct experiences which defamiliarize the encounter between feet and world.

Firstly, I focus on the possibilities for improvisational walking offered by the industrial ruin, and the ways in which impediments to linear passage and the presence of danger simultaneously defamiliarize space and enervate the walking body. Secondly, I consider the sensual characteristics engendered by strolling through ruins, drawing attention to the encounter with the ruin's peculiar affordances and unusual materialities, productive of a range of sensory experiences that coerce the walking body into unfamiliar states. Thirdly, I discuss how walking through the ruin involves a particular way of looking at the environment passed through and how this invites speculation about the characteristics of walking and vision. Finally, I critically interrogate the much-mooted metaphorical relationship between walking and narration, suggesting that such parallels are overdrawn. The illegible, fragmented experience of passage through a ruin suggests that walking is not usually amenable to authoritative representation.

Walking in the regulated city

All forms of walking – and indeed other ways of moving – are invariably constrained
and enabled by a range of factors, including the material characteristics of the terrain
moved across, and the particular regulatory regimes that overtly or more subtly
coerce normative modes of movement. Against the various schemes for ordering
urban space I will counterpose the disorderly space of the ruin, but first I want
to consider the ways in which walking is constrained – though never totally – by
particular regulatory procedures. Most obviously, the activities, routes and numbers
of city pedestrians are increasingly subject to surveillance by CCTV cameras,
which extend across ever-larger areas of urban space (Fyfe 2004). While those
monitoring the screens are unable continually to observe everything that is going on,
all pedestrians under surveillance are potentially subject to scrutiny. The dawning
awareness among pedestrians that they may be under observation is apt to affect
movement and constrain practices, especially if they congregate in crowds, engage
in 'unsociable' activity ('creating a disturbance' or 'loitering'), or practise begging,
busking or street-trading, and they may then be subject to intervention from police
and security guards. The denial of dwelling space or passage to homeless bodies
generates a condition of 'perpetual movement' borne of placenessness; movement
undertaken by the homeless not 'because they are going somewhere, but because
they have nowhere to go' (Kawash 1998, 322-9). These modes of control 'purify'

space (Sibley 1988) and identify the things, people and practices that are held to be 'out of place' in such spaces (Cresswell 1996).

These ordering regimes are accompanied by an internalization of performative conventions among pedestrians themselves. These conventions govern how and where one may walk, including preferred techniques, styles of comportment and bearing, and disposition to the surroundings. People wandering through cities are expected to walk at moderate pace and to progress in a linear fashion. They should not express themselves in ways that are too unexpected or overly expansive, nor should they dance, run, or display a jouissance of movement – 'never a clenched fist, a passionate kiss, a giddy wink, a fixed-shoulder stride' (Boddy 1992, 123-4).[1] Not only is deviation from normative modes of walking met with disapproving glares and comments; these modes are also cultivated by self-monitoring, through an embodied self-awareness which delimits the range of potential manoeuvres, gestures and styles. This self-reflexive disposition might particularly apply to the 'postmodern' city where, according to Csordas, the body has become 'primarily a performing self of appearance, display and impression management' (1994, 2). Here, walking figures as a choreographed performance in which bodies communicate meaning through stylized movements and stances and are cloaked in self-consciousness

In the Western city, tourists, workers and shoppers follow preferred, signposted routes along bounded walkways and conveyors which form part of larger systems of circulation. This conveying of bodies is part of a process through which the range of activities, styles, forms of comportment and mobilities is restricted. Such restriction stands in marked contrast to the exuberance of differently regulated cities outside of the West. I have referred elsewhere to the characteristics of the Indian bazaar (Edensor 2000b), where a much wider range of social activities is permitted, including those that would be considered private in a Western context, along with diverse domestic, commercial, convivial, political, consumption-oriented and playful activities which may coincide and are subject neither to soft control nor to more stringent regulation. Similarly, the range of people, vehicles and animals travelling across space in a complex matrix of multi-directional movements of varied pace is part of he normative mix whose vigour makes Western cities appear sterile by comparison.

Of course, the Western, 'postmodern' city might also be conceived as 'labyrinthine, free-flowing and uncontrollable' as well as 'containing and trapping' (Briginshaw 1997, 35): a space not only of fear and alienation, but also of sensual, fantastic and erotic possibility. But these opportunities are restricted by powerful conventions that limit expressive physical performance and more unhindered engagement with the material world, and by received assumptions that situated objects and orderly space are inviolable. In accordance with such assumptions and conventions, outsiders are identified, barriers maintained, notions of property upheld and single-purpose spaces produced. However, irrespective of the prevalence of walking norms, certain

---

1   I have written elsewhere (Edensor 2000a) about the ways in which recreational walking is performed in the countryside, arguing that certain discourses, preferred equipment, values and aesthetics follow distinct modes, often in contest with each other.

alternative realms emerge 'in the interstitial spaces between dominant orderings' (Stanley 1996, 37) to constitute the *terrain vague*, described by Levesque (2002) as

> an indeterminate space without precise boundaries ... a place ... outside the circuit of the productive structures of the city, an internal, uninhabited, unproductive and often dangerous island, simultaneously on the margins of the urban system and a fundamental part of the system ... the counter image of the city, both in the sense of a critique and a clue for a possible way to go beyond.

Industrial ruins belong to this *terrain vague*.

The possibilities for walking in ruins

In contrast to the deliberate channelling of movement in the regulated city, the physical structure of ruins invites and constrains walking in a distinctive fashion. Under conditions of continuous decay, material structures and routeways are not distributed according to an ordering scheme but emerge according to happenstance. This means that instead of moving towards objects and objectives, those present in ruins tend to walk contingently and improvisationally, their multiple manoeuvres, moods, gestures and rhythms belying any sense of walking as a singular practice. This contingent improvisation is particularly evident because the historical organization of any industrial site required the very opposite, namely the hierarchical, sequential arrangement of space in accordance with the demands of production lines – an intense regulation that scrutinized the movement of bodies, subjecting them to strict regulation and confining their movements across space and time.

With the erasure or blockage of once carefully maintained sequential routes, along with the collapse of walls and doors, large ruins often resemble labyrinths in which path-making is arbitrary and open to multiple options. Decisions about which directions to follow are taken according to chance, intuition and whim rather than governed by the coercion of material structuring, surveillance and internalized walking conventions. Unforeseen openings may emerge – sometimes into previously inaccessible spaces – and conversely, apparently self-evident paths are blocked by a pile of insurmountable rubble or terminate in a vertical descent. Accordingly, we might wander according to numerous geometries. Rather than following a signposted route, a map or the guidance offered by linear arrangements of space, we might repeatedly cover the same circuit, go up and down stairs, walk on the roof or in a cellar, chart an enjoyable obstacle course between fallen fixtures, successively explore the rooms adjacent to a large shop floor area, walk in criss-cross fashion inside and outside the remaining standing walls, or according to all sorts of other ad hoc procedures. A path evolves as the walker is called forth by curiosities, potential channels of movement, tempting surfaces and gradients, and peculiar impulses.

Stopping where we like, diverted by peculiar sights or fixtures, or drawn to micro-spaces that pull us in with inexplicable promises, the passage of walking in ruins is likely to take on a stop-go character, a staccato rhythm rather than a repetitive pulse. Likewise, the notion that a journey is composed of segments is confounded by the lack of any evident sequence in a path to nowhere, for the temporal structure of a walk through a ruin is not ruled by conventions about how long the trip should take (such as that a mile is covered in 20 minutes of above average walking speed). Rather than limiting the range of movements available, the disarrayed affordances of the ruin prompt the body to stoop, crouch, climb, slither, leap, swerve and pick its way to avoid lurking hazards. Walking cannot follow a regular rhythmic gait because of the variability of the surface underfoot and the uneven textures that force high and either small or extended steps. It is often impossible to progress in an uninterrupted, purposive fashion towards a predetermined destination. The continual bodily improvisation in interaction with ruined space usually begins at an entry point where access requires the physical effort to climb over an unstable wall, hack a path through tangled vegetation or squeeze through a small window or the crack of a partially opened door. Once inside, numerous obstacles from fallen masonry and old machinery to debris of all descriptions must be manoeuvred around, jumped over, avoided or balanced upon.

The constantly evolving anti-structure of the ruin contrasts with the supervised linearity which determines much movement through the city, and opens up a host of spaces that may never normally be traversed and occupied. Despite the signs which warn of penalties for trespass, there is little surveillance of those walking through ruins. At most, a security guard might be glad of some brief company or a temporarily housed homeless resident might guard their space, but otherwise there are no rules or personnel to prevent the walker from venturing anywhere. Moreover, the proprietary codes of walking performance that constrain expression and dramatic improvisation are irrelevant in a space largely devoid of human presence. There are no social impediments to movement, no temporal limits on the appropriate time to be spent there, and no need to adhere to the self-conscious monitoring of one's own body in a city of surveillant onlookers. All these elements allow visitors to ruins to walk without being regulated by others. We can stop for long periods, dawdle or run, with no objective at all.

Walkers in ruins may wander along dormant production lines and on top of obsolete machines, spin round in office chairs, slide down chutes, climb up ladders and fire escapes, climb into attics or descend into murky cellars. Other spaces that once embraced order may now be violated. We may skate across the boardroom table or lounge in the foreman's chair. Walking is thus apt to be augmented by several other physical endeavours. There are empty corridors to dash along, stairs to run up, windows and other spaces through which to scramble. There are trap doors to be avoided or through which to drop down or hurl objects. Crawling through dense undergrowth, scrambling over walls and under fences, leaping over hurdles and across gaps, kicking debris of various qualities along the floor, throwing rubble at chosen targets and dancing and sprinting across stretches of flooring generate a rekindled awareness of the gymnastic, expressive movement of childhood. Flights of fancy inspired by popular cultural imagery can be enacted by clattering along rooftops or careering down decrepit fire escapes. Because of these incentives to expressive and ludic movement, signs of playful exercise abound in ruins. Rope swings hang over wooden beams, burst footballs and improvised goalposts litter floors, bottles are lined up in shooting galleries, wheeled vessels are utilized as impromptu forms of transport and football pitches are extemporized. Ruins are alternative playgrounds for children and adults outside the 'over-determined, narrow, striated orders of adult being, adult spaces and adult assemblages' (Cloke and Jones 2005, 330). Interstitial spaces such as ruins serve as venues for adventures, den-making and imaginative play, not only those which chime with romantic and bucolic versions of childhood.

Extensive, abandoned and cleared shop floors make possible the performance of spectacular and dangerous adventures. Cupboards, store-rooms, cellars, lofts and offices provide snug, felicitous spaces which can serve as dens and hidey holes. Feats of balance, agility and bravery may be accomplished in these unsupervised playgrounds which, full of risk, clash with the regulated, recreational spaces of the more ordered world outside – that is, with officially designated 'playgrounds' – which limit the range of permissible practices to 'appropriate' and largely risk-free activities. Ruins allow a return to a less self-conscious engagement with space and materials without purposive planning or a view to utility.

Besides liberating bodily movement, ruins can offer strange and disruptive spaces in which to walk. Moving into dark interiors confounds senses that have been attuned to an ever-illuminated world in which all is open to scrutiny and the eyes are able to chart a path through space. In the gloom, tentative progress is facilitated by sudden awareness of a delicate, improvisational balancing of the body, movement that needs to feel its way across unpredictable space, keeping in touch with surroundings. A further uncanny sense of bodily presence is engendered by walking across a huge expanse of empty space, perhaps across the concrete flooring of a chamber which was formerly a shop floor, where the footsteps echo and one's body is the only moving, living thing in an uncluttered realm. This can induce a sudden sense of isolation. Other peculiar experiences emerge through confronting the textures of decay. I have for instance walked across a vast sea of wooden flooring which, penetrated with damp, has buckled to form waves, creating a visual surprise and a challenge to walking. These material contingencies demand unfamiliar movements in unfamiliar spaces, provoking an awareness of the effects of the body's movements – the sounds produced by walking on peculiar surfaces, the displacement of matter and the footprints left in the dirt of decay – and a sense of its unpractised capabilities.

The walking body, habituated to safe and seamless movement, must also tackle the unusual risks of slippery timber, loose floorboards, protruding nails, trap doors, rickety stairs, swinging light fixtures and electrical wiring. Walkers in ruins thus need to take account of the unstable or slippery floors they encounter, and must distinguish stable surfaces from those too dangerous to walk upon. Improvising in accordance with the encumbrances that confront it, the body after a while develops a feel for ruined space, a sense of where and where not to tread.

Walking through ruins also violates the usual, common-sense boundaries that inform us about the nature of a place – between inside and outside, past and present, rural and urban, natural and cultural. The widespread apprehension and acceptance of such boundaries is, of course, inherent in the ways pedestrians reproduce space and perform within it. Yet in ruins the compartments once constructed to shore up these boundaries and to reduce to a minimum the scope for their transgression, are broken apart and merge. Roofs, walls and windows lie open to the elements, belying a distinction between interior and exterior. Plants grow in profusion and animals move into spaces that were formerly delineated as interior. We cross the tracks of assorted non-humans, the flight paths of pigeons, rabbit and fox trails and the traces of smaller creatures such as woodworm. The ruined world is alive with moving non-human life forms that are usually consigned to marginal spaces. Moreover, walking through ruins produces a complex sense of time, as I discuss in more detail below, and this acts to decentre easy divisions between past and present. For instance, derelict spaces are often replete with obscure signs of the past, a past that is rarely comprehensible, but they are also full of new forms of life.

The industrial ruin, then, presents us with a defamiliarized space in which modes of passage are improvisatory, uninformed by conventions, continually disrupted and expressive. Instead of a self-contained bodily comportment, with fixed stride, steady gait and minimal gestures which limit interaction with the environment, objects and other people, the body is inadvertently coaxed into a more flamboyant and expressive style, awakening performative possibilities beyond those to which it has become habituated. Both the material characteristics of the ruin and the absence of forms of surveillance and social pressures permit ways of walking that foster an extension of bodily experience and expression by contrast to the largely constrained disposition of the urban pedestrian. This defamiliarization is further brought out by the strange sensualities of the ruin.

The sensual affordances of industrial ruins

To develop some of the ideas discussed above, I now turn to a more detailed account of the material affordances and sensual properties of industrial ruins. I do so partly in order to counterbalance an emphasis in the literature on the narration of walking as an experience through which the world is looked at and represented. These accounts present a curiously disembodied view of what is an intensely somatic experience. Downplaying the relationship between the feet and the rest of the body, as well as the space that is walked through, they tend to neglect the fuller sensual experience that walking affords.

I have already alluded to the ways in which the experience of walking through Western cities has been increasingly desensualised. Richard Sennett (1994, 15) goes so far as to argue that urban space has largely become 'a mere function of motion', engendering a 'tactile sterility' which in turn leads to a pacifying of the body. Sennett contends that the imperative to minimize disruption and distraction for pedestrians and drivers – to keep them focused on shopping, working and playing in preferred ways – means that movement is typified by rapid transit without arousal. He concentrates on the minimal interaction with space typified by the 'micro-movements' of car-drivers, which desensitize travellers to their environment, prioritizing the 'desire to move freely ... over the sensory claims of the space through which the body moves' (ibid.). This desensualised environment impacts, in turn, upon the ways in which the world is sensed through the feet. The sterile, flattened surfaces – the smooth tactilities of urban paving – ensure that the feet and legs are not enlivened by contact with the ground, and need not operate contingently in apprehending irregularity. In these material circumstances, it may only be when feet become tired that experiential awareness of ground contact really makes itself felt.[2]

My concern with the impact of materiality upon the sensory experience of walking is fuelled by an insistence that walking can never be conceived purely as shaped (or constrained and enabled) by performative conventions, ideological and romantic presuppositions or other social and cultural understandings, for this is to abstract walking from the material world. As Feld notes, 'as place is sensed, senses are placed; as places make sense, senses make place' (1996, 91). Here it is useful to draw on the concept of affect to denote 'the shifting mood, tenor, colour or intensity of places and situation' (Wylie 2005, 236), in so far as they are embedded and embodied in (temporary) configurations of matter and object-hood. Place thus impresses itself upon the pedestrian body, for its affordances are inevitably created out of the relationship between its physical and material qualities on the one hand and the social and subjective experience of walking on the other, along with the cultural precepts through which the practice is interpreted. The sensory, according to Seremetakis, 'is not only encapsulated within the body as an internal capacity or power but is also dispersed out there on the surface of things as the latter's autonomous characteristics, which can then invade the body as perceptual experience' (1994, 6).

The highly regulated, familiar space of the city is organized to allow for continuity and stability, so that its materialities and sensualities minimize disruption of normative performances, cajoling the body into enacting regular, normative modes of walking which mesh with dispositions consolidated through repetitive routines. The regulation of urban space is often concerned with managing the sensual world, keeping strong smells, loud noises and rough textures at bay. While commodified scents of incense, coffee and bread pervade shopping areas, smells of sewage, food and industry are reduced to a mimimum, creating what Drobnick calls 'blandscapes', those 'aseptic places, created by the modernist drive towards deodorization, that

---

2 Once again, the contrast with the Indian city deserves to be noted. Not only do parts of the Indian city foreground disruption and non-linear movement; they also offer an array of tactilities – including varied gradients, unevenness, fragment-strewn paths, soft and hard surfaces, organic and constructed planes – that contrast with the reduced textures underfoot typical of cities in the West (Edensor 2000b).

are so empty that they lead to an alienating sense of placelessness' (2002, 34). Similarly, sound is carefully controlled, abatement procedures limit loud noises and muzak-filled soundscapes are engineered by laying smooth textures underfoot which silence the body's movement. Crucially, this manufactured smoothness ensures that the body is undisturbed in its progress and is able to move unhindered towards its destinations.

In encountering ruined space, by contrast, the body is enlivened and challenged by a wealth of multi-sensual effects – including smells, sounds and tactilities – which thwart any distancing manoeuvres that prioritize the visual. I suggest that the affective experiences and expressive activities that centre upon ruins are made possible and pleasurable because they take place in a space replete with rich and unfamiliar affordances. Here I am referring to characteristics such as the textures, form, weight, consistency and state of decay of the objects in ruins, along with other redistributed matter and materials around and across which walking takes place. Walkers experience the unfamiliar textures of decaying materials, the stark, hard, cold feel of a piece of industrial metal machinery, the splintery and pulpy texture of a damp wooden work bench, the delicious sheen of a wooden hand rail worn to smoothness over decades, the mouldering dampness of wallpaper and plaster, the weight of oil drums and steel boxes, the profusion of peculiarly shaped off-cuts and fragments of manufactures that were never assembled, the thick greasiness of chains and cogs, the encrusted exteriors of foundry fittings, the pliability of wires and thin metal strips, the cushioned consistency of moss and the sliminess of wet, rotting wood.

Walking on surfaces of varying tactility and texture – splintering floorboards, hard concrete, rubble strewn flooring, shards of glass, mixed surfaces of foliage and crumbling masonry – conjures up an awareness of what Deleuze and Guattari (1987) call 'becoming animal'. For me, familiarity with ruins fosters a heightened sensitivity towards matter and space comparable to sensations apprehended during a long distance walk through Scotland. After a few days, a deeper, non-cognitive, sensual form of appreciation developed for the terrain traversed, experienced through the feet and legs, promoting an adaptation to the environment through a heightened sense of corporeal balance. Similarly in the ruin, an awareness of physical dangers develops a more sensually attuned body which takes account of, and learns how to negotiate, risky space.

The improvisational performances of the walking body in response to the ad hoc structure of the ruin can trigger unfamiliar or half remembered manoeuvres that jolt the body out of the complacent, fixed composure and habitually inexpressive and self-conscious performances played out on the city's streets. The adult body can thus engage in a more expansive physical engagement with its surroundings, a somatic disposition redolent of sensual childhood play. Initially disruptive, the materiality of the ruin can cause the body to open up to sensation and interact with space in a playful, unselfconscious fashion, allowing us to engage both corporeally and sensually in a context in which our actions are likely to have little impact on propriety and property.

Though the experiential modalities of walking through a ruin are peculiarly varied and contingent, they also mirror the broader experience of walking. They are however compressed in the ruin, where we can walk from one micro-space to another, sensing different atmospheres, becoming aware of different soundscapes and smells, along with other, more indescribable intimations. The act of walking can attune us to the (ever-changing) sensualities of place if socialized dimensions are consigned to the background. Movement through space produces unfolding moments of varying intensity, which bring into relation walkers, objects and non-human life forms. The experience is distributed in its intensity and richness between these relational elements, and shaped by their qualities (Amin and Thrift 2002). Walking is intertwined with the ruin and its numerous, unpredictable constituents, and experience and interaction with these derelict environments, like others, is deepened by experience over time so that the body becomes skilfully habituated to sensations, dangers and attractions, and develops alternative ways of thinking, sensing and moving. As Wylie puts it, through walking 'self and world overlap in a ductile and incessant enfolding and unfolding' (2005, 240), in the encounter with the distinct affordances of places and spaces.

Seeing while walking: vision and the ruin

One aspect of walking through purified, highly regulated urban space is the dominance of vision and the marginalization of other kinds of sensory experience. In his discussion of tourist space, Rojek argues that it is typically designed to shut out 'extraneous, chaotic elements' and reduce 'visual and functional forms to a few key images' (1995, 62). Tourists, as Urry claims, can 'take possession of objects and environments, often at a distance' (2002, 147). By framing views, drawing attention to privileged sights and highlighting particular cultural themes, tourist managers and designers foreground the visual consumption of place. Similarly, spectacular urban space is subject to intensive aesthetic control which in archetypal theme parks, heritage attractions, festival marketplaces, residential districts and shopping areas, mobilizes a coding that 'brands' space and reduces it to a few key themes or designs.[3]

Ruins violate disciplinary aesthetic schemes in which objects are carefully situated, difference is domesticated and contained, 'clutter' which might complicate sight-lines and passage is continuously removed, and the bright and the smooth are maintained. For in ruins, there has been no assiduous attempt to keep up appearances. The scene is one of disorder, disarray and the mingling of usually unlike categories of things. This material excess, in which things and matter have moved away from their assigned locations, is initially disturbing to habituated aesthetic sensibilities. In the ruin we confront an alternative aesthetics, one which rebukes the seamlessness of much urban design and opens out heterodox possibilities for appreciating beauty and form. Unusual or anomalous sights can jolt the body out of any quiescent immersion in the process of walking. Strange or accidental sculptures, things located in odd situations, juxtapositions of things and eccentric compounds of matter disorder a gaze attuned to visual orderliness. Moreover, distanced visual apprehension is impracticable when attention must focus upon obstacles in the way and when material contingencies must be dealt with. A mindful, preoccupied mode of movement is engendered by the need to manoeuvre, but we may also suddenly become aware of bodily strain, the texture of the immediate surroundings and the eruptions of memory.

In aesthetically regulated urban space, the gaze of pedestrians is organized so as to repress the kinaesthetic qualities of vision, which becomes desensualised through the distancing of the tactile, auditory and aromatic qualities of what is beheld. The aesthetic thematization and regulation of urban space obscures how (ever-changing) space is visually apprehended as landscape, which is itself constituted out of distinct materialities and effects that impact upon – indeed are enmeshed with – our sense-making capacities. The qualities of light, for instance, continually facilitate and restrict vision, from which we may infer that we see not just in, but

---

3   By contrast, a walk through an Indian bazaar thwarts the predominance of the visual as experiences are confounded: as people, animals and vehicles move in many directions, as varied smells, sounds and tactilities overwhelm sensory apprehension, and in the absence of any stringent attempts to maintain aesthetic order or of rigid understandings about how space should be designed and used (Edensor 2000b).

with, the space that surrounds us. Walking always raises the possibility that as our attention is intermittently drawn from the immediacy of the feet to sights nearby or further afield, we may sense these sights in ways other than the visual, for sights may conjure up an apprehension, for instance, of texture, weight and smell. This is primarily because whatever we gaze upon now can evoke apprehensions from the past. Accordingly, while we walk we always travel elsewhere, not just along the immediate path but outwards to distant sights and scenes, back to the past and to places in the imagination, and to remembered smells, noises, and non-visual sensations, often those which are stimulated by the sights of the journey.

This blending of the visual with other senses – coupled with the recognition that there is nothing inevitable about the dominance of vision – is especially apparent when walking in the ruin. It is an environment, as Latham puts it, that fosters 'a way of looking and experiencing the world in which the eye does not act to hold external objects in a firm contemplative gaze ... it is a way of looking that feels its way round that place it finds rather than fixing that place with a distancing look ... [it is] intensely tied up with the other sensations of the body ... ' (1999, 463). Looking, in such an environment, is particularly multi-sensual, inextricably embedded in the work of all the other senses in the body's interaction with its surroundings.

Temporality, narrative and walking: the incoherent stories of ruins

In discussing the potential for expressive and sensual performance that might be realized by walking through the unregulated space of the ruin, I have foregrounded the effects of the material characteristics of space. I have done so deliberately, in order to counteract the tendency, in much scholarly writing on the subject, for the materiality of walking to be sidelined by a focus on narrative, both as a means to render accounts of walking and as a metaphor for walking itself. Walking is often assumed to be like a narrative, in the sense that walkers in the city are held heroically to inscribe their presence and meanings on space. Most famously, de Certeau (1984) maintains that they produce 'turns of phrase' which act against the meta-language laid down by the powerful. But by foregrounding the metaphor of walking as narrative inscription, the affective, sensual dimensions of walking are apt to disappear.

When considering the politics of walking as narration, it is important to acknowledge that walking narratives have been highly complicit in entrenching representations of otherness. Like travel narratives that attempt to capture in sequence the 'essential' elements of a journey, accounts by Westerners of walking in 'exotic' spaces are colonizing manoeuvres that assert an authoritative understanding of the land. Through walking, the expert confidently discerns cultural traces in the landscape, and charts its 'natural history' along with other 'key features' which mark the space traversed, so that otherness – whether natural, cultural or historical – may be 'known'. These walking narratives not only identify preferred ways of understanding space in the realm of the other; they also map numerous routes through which walkers may orient themselves to their surroundings – for instance, by following annotated guides to long-distance footpaths.

Attempts to employ walking as a narrative technique to defamiliarize the spectacular, regulated, commodified space of the city, so as to yield alternative readings that multiply its meanings (Lefebvre 1995), are undoubtedly useful. Yet like surrealist modes of walking, and the psychogeographic accounts of Sinclair (2003) which particularly privilege the occult, the criminal, the literary and the political, they curiously decentre corporeal, sensual interaction with the material world. Narratives of walking typically create the illusion of linear progress through sequential time: this or that feature is passed, discussed, and then the next, and so on until the end of the walk (Kearney 2002, 129-31). Yet while there may be a clear beginning and end, the temporal experience of walking is usually far from a flow of successive, episodic events. This is particularly evident while walking through ruins, which highlights complex temporalities and thus draws attention to the limits of narrative both as a technical means to represent walking and as a metaphor for walking. Walking through ruins characteristically involves circularity and a choreographic repetition through which the same ground is approached and traversed from different perspectives.

Walking is suffused with a kaleidoscope of intermingling thoughts, experiences and sensations, so that the character of a walk is continually shifting. This applies to the numerous non-linear temporalities which, as elsewhere, are 'multiple, composite, simultaneous, open-ended and changing' (Adam 1995, 5). Here I draw upon Adam's convincing depiction of the overlapping temporal experiences of aeroplane travel (ibid., 12-13), in which numerous temporalities overlap: the suspension of ordinary temporal routines and their transgression by eating and drinking alcohol and viewing films at unorthodox times, the rhythms of the aircraft, sudden memories of other travels, the peculiar effects of jet-lag and temporal disorientation, the awareness of the effects of the body clock with regard to hunger and thirst, a sense of anticipation and a longing to arrive.

In its quest for an orderly account, narrative cannot effectively capture the momentary impressions confronted, the peculiar evanescent atmospheres, the rhythms, immanent sensations and physical effects of walking. While walking through a ruin might be particularly disruptive of temporal and physical linearity, it encapsulates the broader inadequacy of narrative for describing both walking and the city's fluidity (Reid 2005). In ruins, there are moments of reverie and recollection, an awareness of the cyclical characteristics of capitalist production, innumerable and obscure traces of the past, shocking reminders of long-forgotten phrases and popular cultural icons, abrupt alarms or surprises, a sudden grasp of the demise of a particular industrial future, pangs of hunger, temporal rates of decay and natural growth which continually alter the characteristics of the site, the different routines of animal inhabitants, and the fragmented rhythms of corporeal experience. Ironically, this sense of temporal disorder contrasts strongly with the necessarily rigid scheduling and time-management that facilitated industrial production, and signs of these defunct temporalities persist in clocking-on devices and schedules on notice boards.

I particularly want to draw attention to the ways in which walking conjures up other times and places that disrupt any linear flow. For instance, as my body was forced to confront the aforementioned buckled, wooden flooring, I was hurtled back to a childhood visit to the Funhouse at Blackpool Pleasure Beach, in which an array of devious contraptions – moving stairs, whirling discs, wobbly stepping stones, huge revolving tunnels – challenged my ability to walk upright. At other times, I have become acutely aware of long-dead working class relatives whose lives were shaped by the harsh routines of industrial labour, and also of memories of my own labour in factories. More obscurely, we are haunted in industrial ruins by the signs of the past that project us back to things we half know or have heard about, recollections of a past we can hardly recognize, and carry us outwards to other places, in the memory or imagination. With our steps we trace out the everyday routines of the previous habitués of the ruin, and are in this sense possessed by them. This spectral aspect extends to walking along all well-marked paths, where we follow in the footsteps of numerous others.

These effects, along with others that remain only as traces that are barely recognizable, hardly understood or partially apprehended, tell us that stories about walking through ruins can only be speculative, cannot rely on hard knowledge or understanding, and cannot readily be composed into coherent temporal sequences. Stories that are fragmented, non-linear, impressionistic and contingent are better suited than traditional linear narratives to the experience of walking in ruins. Alongside de Certeau's (1984) acknowledgement of the multiple enunciations of walking, Solnit has argued not only that walking generates particular 'rhythms of thinking' (2000, 5) but also that 'the recounted walk encourages digression and association, in contrast to the stricter form of a discourse or the chronological progression of a biographical or historical narrative' (ibid., 21). Improvisational rather than analytical or pre-ordained like the guided tour, most walking narratives are fluid and irregular. But in any case, to privilege the narration of walking is to consign its immanent, embodied, sensual characteristics to secondary importance, for the story effaces the physical interaction with space and its sense-making techniques are usually mobilized only in a post-hoc, reflexive conceptualization. Words can but feebly allude to sensations and the selective content of an account can refer to no more than a tiny proportion of what is experienced. Tell stories we may do – although their impact typically depends upon the skill of the teller – but we should be aware of their partiality and their peculiar tendency to underestimate temporal, spatial and somatic experience.

Conclusion

> Walking is one way of maintaining a bulwark against (the) erosion of the mind, the body, the landscape and the city, and every walker is on guard to protect the ineffable (Solnit 2000, 11).

I have suggested that walking through a ruin, although possessing its own peculiar characteristics, leads us to question broader conceptions and depictions of walking. It can, for instance, provide us with a critical awareness with which to interrogate the over-smooth, regulated fabric of much urban and suburban space – and perhaps manicured forms of nature as well. I also propose that the richly embodied, sensual experience of walking through ruins can suggest ways in which we might enrich urban pedestrian environments and experiences in Western cities. As Thrift (2004) points out, apart from the careful manufacture of a 'buzz' which makes a city attractive to residents, investors and visitors, accounts of affect are neglected in discussions about urban culture, or drowned out amidst the torrent of debate about urban representations and practices. Walking through industrial ruins highlights the progressive benefits of affect, for it 'allows us to be open in receiving new affectively charged disclosive spaces' (ibid., 70) – the unrepresentable spaces that feature the 'little, the messy and the jerry-rigged' (ibid., 75). Despite the seemingly rigid organization and orderly appearances of the city, there always co-exist interstitial spaces that are amenable to different approaches to walking which cut across the orderly and the disorderly, and constitute a 'series of interruptions and reprises, fragments of constructed city and unbuilt zones that alternate in a continuous passage from full to empty and back' (Careri 2002, 186). Such fragmentary spaces highlight the mutability of the city that enables the walker to 'intervene in their continuous becoming by acting in the field of the *here and now* of their transformations' (ibid. 26). Intermittently then, urban walkers enter the *terrain vague*, a realm which 'offers a counterpoint to the way order and consumption hold sway over the city [and] ... room for spontaneous, creative appropriation and informal uses' (Levesque 2002).

My discussion of walking through ruins conjures up the *deambulations* through which Dadaists attempted to disorientate the walker from bourgeois norms of apprehending the city, liberating their affective responses to the unexpected, unclassified and unfathomable in banal urban spaces. It also reminds us of Surrealist attempts to use walking to call forth the 'unconscious' realms of the city which 'elude planned control and constitute the unexpressed, untranslatable component in traditional representation' (Careri 2002, 88). Perhaps most obviously, my account chimes with the Situationist *dérive*, through which key islands of affect were identified by breaking established urban rules and inventing playful others in their stead. Similarly, Robert Smithson searches for a 'territory free from representation', space in 'continuous transformation' and the 'rejects of thought and culture' (Careri 2002, 166). He finds such elements in abandoned suburban sites of industry, in 'entropic territories' 'made of refuse and disruption' (ibid., 168). In a different vein, the walking art of Richard Long combines the material, faunal and floral, sensual, action-oriented and embodied dimensions of walking without privileging any one of them (see Edensor 2000a). However, apart from Long's works, these attempts to defamiliarize walking downplay the sensual, affective, material and spatial specificity of the terrain, as if the human subject were free to interpret and experience at will, irrespective of the qualities walked upon and through. In this chapter I have attempted to put the materiality of space and its effects on the body back into the relationship between the walker and the world.

References

Adam, B. (1995), *Timewatch: The Social Analysis of Time* (Cambridge: Polity).

Amin, A. and Thrift, N. (2002), *Cities: Re-imagining the Urban* (Cambridge: Polity).

Boddy, T. (1992), 'Underground and Overhead: Building the Analogous City', in Sorkin, M. (ed.) (1992), *Variations on a Theme Park* (New York: Hill and Wang).

Briginshaw, V. (1997), '"Keep Your Great City Paris!" – The Lament of the Empress and Other Women', in Thomas, H. (ed.) (1997), *Dance in the City* (London: Routledge).

Careri, F. (2002), *Walkscapes: Walking as an Aesthetic Practice* (Barcelona: Gustavo Gili).

Certeau, M. de (1984), *The Practice of Everyday Life* (Berkeley: University of California Press).

Cloke, P. and Jones, O. (2005), '"Unclaimed Territory": Childhood and Disordered Space(s)', *Social and Cultural Geography* 6:3, 311-33.

Cresswell, T. (1996), *In Place/Out of Place: Geography, Ideology and Transgression* (London: University of Minnesota Press).

Csordas, T. (1994), 'Introduction: The Body as Representation and Being-in-the-World', in Csordas, T. (ed.) (1994), *Embodiment and Experience* (Cambridge: Cambridge University Press).

Deleuze, G. and Guattari, F. (1987), *A Thousand Plateaus: Capitalism and Schizophrenia* (Minneapolis: University of Minnesota Press).

Drobnick, J. (2002), 'Toposmia: Art, Scent and Interrogations of Spatiality', *Angelaki* 7:1, 31-46.

Edensor, T. (2000a), 'Walking in the British Countryside', *Body and Society* 6:3/4, 81-106.

—— (2000b), 'Moving Through the City', in Bell, D. and Haddour, A. (eds) (2000), *City Visions* (London: Prentice Hall).

Feld, S. (1996), 'Waterfalls of Song: An Acoustemology of Place Resounding in Bosavi, Papua New Guinea', in Feld, S. and Basso, K. (eds) (1996), *Senses of Place* (Santa Fe: School of American Research Press).

Fyfe, N. (2004), 'Zero Tolerance, Maximum Surveillance? Deviance, Difference and Crime Control in the Late Modern City', in Lees, L. (ed.) (2004), *The Emancipatory City?* (London: Sage).

Kawash, S. (1998), 'The Homeless Body', *Public Culture* 10:2, 319-39.

Kearney, R. (2002), *On Stories* (London: Routledge).

Latham, A. (1999), 'The Power of Distraction: Distraction, Tactility and Habit in the Work of Walter Benjamin', *Environment and Planning D: Society and Space* 17, 451-73.

Lefebvre, H. (1995), *Writings on Cities* (Oxford: Blackwell).

Levesque, L. (2002), 'The "Terrain Vague" as Material – Some Observations', <http://www.amarrages.com/textes_terrain.html> (accessed December 2005).

Reid, B. (2005), 'A Profound Edge: Performative Negotiations of Belfast', *Cultural Geographies* 12, 485-506.

Rojek, C. (1995), *Decentring Leisure: Rethinking Leisure Theory* (London: Sage).

Sennett, R. (1994), *Flesh and Stone* (London: Faber).

Seremetakis, C. (1994), 'The Memory of the Senses, Part One: Marks of the Transitory', in Seremetakis, C. (ed.) (1994), *The Senses Still: Perception and Memory as Material Culture in Modernity* (Chicago: University of Chicago Press).

Sibley, D. (1988), 'Survey 13: Purification of Space', *Environment and Planning D: Society and Space* 6, 409-21.

Sinclair, I. (2003), *Lights Out for the Territory* (London: Penguin).

Solnit, R. (2000), *Wanderlust: A History of Walking* (London: Penguin).

Stanley, C. (1996), 'Spaces and Places of the Limit: Four Strategies in the Relationship Between Law and Desire', *Economy and Society* 25, 36-63.

Thrift, N. (2004), 'Intensities of Feeling: Towards a Spatial Politics of Affect', *Geografiska Annaler B* 86:1, 57-78.

Urry, J. (2002), *The Tourist Gaze* (2nd edition) (London: Sage).

Wylie, J. (2005), 'A Single Day's Walking: Narrating Self and Landscape on the South West Coast Path', *Transactions of the Institute of British Geographers* 30, 234-47.

Chapter 10

Walking Out of the Classroom: Learning on the Streets of Aberdeen

Elizabeth Curtis

Introduction

The sight of children walking the streets armed with clipboards is a common one in Aberdeen (Figure 10.1). About two thousand children between the ages of 5 and 12 set out on walks led by one of the staff from Aberdeen Environmental Education Centre (AEEC) as part of their school year. I have had a connection with AEEC for over ten years; as a student teacher, class teacher, volunteer trail writer and as one of the development officers who create materials for teaching and lead guided walks. Currently as a lecturer in Primary Education, I am interested in the ways in which learning occurs and knowledge is created during guided walks offered by AEEC. For the purposes of this chapter I have drawn from my own practices and experiences of both using and providing the service which AEEC offers to explore the relationship between walking and learning during structured trail activities.

My title, 'walking out of the classroom', suggests that children are out and free for the day, and in the minds of many parents and children the trip to AEEC is indeed a day away from work. I will argue, however, that the learning which occurs during these walks is nevertheless shaped by and valued in terms of national educational priorities that underpin the school curriculum, and that are designed to foster positive attitudes and dispositions in children towards the environment as a whole. By becoming the spaces in which children explore and learn through structured activities, the streets themselves are transformed into a classroom. Embedded within the children's walking, as I shall show, are rules of pupil-teacher interaction, codes of behaviour and principles of learning that are no different from those that apply within the school.

My account of walking and learning in AEEC activities alludes to a number of trails that focus on the built environment, including the *World War II Experience*, the *Victorian Trail* and *Exploring Buildings*. I have also drawn on evidence from AEEC trail booklets, teacher evaluation forms and pupils' letters to staff, as well as from Scottish Executive documents that direct and support environmental education in schools in Scotland.

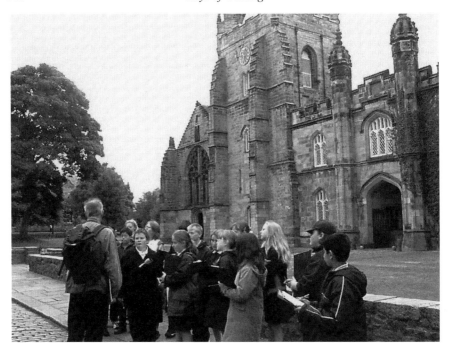

Figure 10.1 Primary 7 pupils and AEEC leader outside Kings College, Aberdeen

Walking with the Aberdeen Environmental Education Centre

The approach to walking and learning taken by AEEC is underpinned by the belief that by learning through 'direct experiences in the environment individuals are able to make informed decisions about issues affecting the environment from a position of knowledge' (Paterson and Stewart 1998, 1). The Centre was originally established in 1978 by Grampian Regional Council as the Aberdeen Urban Studies Centre, one a number of similar centres established in the UK during the 1970s and 1980s. The core staff originally included a director, a development officer and an IT support officer, all of whom were experienced teachers with an active interest in environmental education. Their role was to develop and to lead environmental trails through the urban environment, with a view to extending the scope of environmental studies beyond rural field centres and outdoor education. The Director of AEEC, Allan Paterson, has commented that 'first hand experiences in the environment heighten pupils' awareness and provide strong and meaningful links with the real world' (Paterson 2004). This view is also shared with class teachers who use AEEC. One teacher from an Aberdeen primary school commented on her evaluation form that she had chosen to take her class to the Centre 'because it offers pupils direct experience of how Aberdeen was affected by WWII'. Another noted that for her class of ten-year-olds the visit had 'opened their eyes to Victorian evidence in Aberdeen'.

Notes

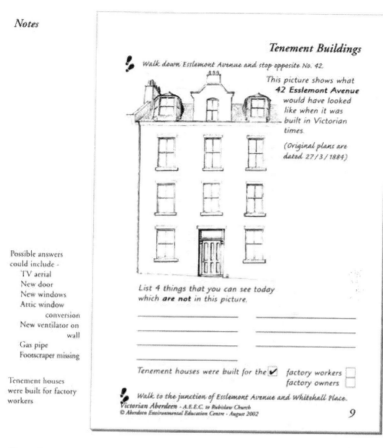

Possible answers
could include -
   TV aerial
   New door
   New windows
   Attic window
            conversion
   New ventilator on
            wall
   Gas pipe
   Footscraper missing

Tenement houses
were built for factory
workers

Extension

* Should we change old buildings?

Investigate planning regulations affecting buildings.

Look for an old building in your area which has been changed in some way. Discuss the changes.

Find out what a listed building is. Do you have any near your school?

How is permission obtained to change a listed building?

   p.16 & 22 No.42 Esslemont Avenue

**Figure 10.2 Tenement buildings at 42 Esslemont Avenue, home of the
            fictional Jamie Craig and evidence for working class Victorians
            in Aberdeen**

As well as having strong links with the urban studies movement, the founding Director of AEEC was influenced by the work of Parks Canada, which has emphasized the importance of learning through direct experience (Elizabeth Hay, pers. comm.). Their creation of annotated trails through national parks was particularly influential, and led AEEC to develop a series of urban trails which drew attention to historical, social and aesthetic aspects of the urban environment. The trails create a known place out of which it is hoped that children will also develop positive values and dispositions towards the environment. Anna, a nine-year-old pupil who had taken part in the *Victorian Trail*, commented in her thank-you letter to staff that 'I was really surprised by how much evidence the Victorians left to prove they lived there. I had no idea how much things there were around Aberdeen'. No longer did the streets merely comprise rows of grey buildings: for Anna, her experience on the trail had helped her to understand that the streets she had walked along and the houses which she has seen in the present had been there for over a century. Bound up in Anna's remark is her understanding of the relationship between time passing, the formation and detection of evidence and concern for posterity, along with an acknowledgement of her part in the future care of Victorian Aberdeen. The extract from the *Victorian Trail* leader's booklet reproduced in Figure 10.2 gives an example of the kinds of evidence that Anna had collected and thought about whilst on the trail. Through the identification of twenty-first century features of the tenement at 42 Esslemont Avenue, Anna could also work out how much of the original building had survived. The 'extension' question at the foot of the page encourages the group leader to challenge children to consider the value of building conservation, asking 'should we change old buildings?' (Stewart 2002, 9).

It is significant that AEEC chose the idea of the trail as the focus for children's learning. The idea is suggestive of being guided through new territory. Rather than exploring the completely unknown, following a trail involves being led along a route that has been carefully created to allow opportunities for discovery in a safe environment. In the trails developed by AEEC children work together in adult-led groups to discuss ideas and to identify and record evidence on their walks. The extract from my own copy of the children's booklet for the *World War II Experience* (Figure 10.3) shows my annotations regarding the most effective places to begin each of the questions, which reflected my own and other guides' experience of leading children on this particular trail. My note at '3', 'holes in the wall' served not as the answer to the question ('Where did the metal come from?'), but as a reminder to ask the children why they thought there were holes in the wall before they read the answer to the question in their booklet.[1]

---

1   The wall in question separates the pavement from the front yards of adjoining houses, and had once supported iron railings. As these were removed to provide metal for wartime munitions, only the holes remain.

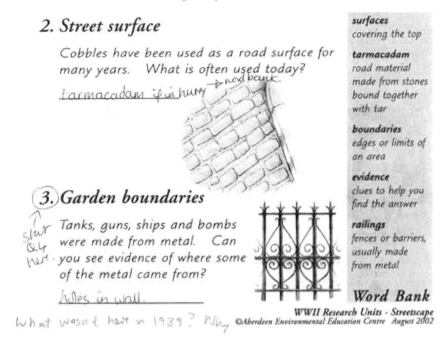

2. Street surface

Cobbles have been used as a road surface for many years. What is often used today?

tarmacadam if in huny ~~pnod bank.~~

surfaces
covering the top

tarmacadam
road material
made from stones
bound together
with tar

boundaries
edges or limits of
an area

evidence
clues to help you
find the answer

(3.) Garden boundaries

slur *Q4* *hver* Tanks, guns, ships and bombs were made from metal. Can you see evidence of where some of the metal came from?

holes in wall.

railings
fences or barriers,
usually made
from metal

Word Bank

WWII Research Units - Streetscape
©Aberdeen Environmental Education Centre August 2002

What wasn't here in 1939? Why

Figure 10.3 Annotated booklet used by the author when working as an AEEC Guide

Transforming the street into the classroom

Emphasizing the integrated nature of environmental education, AEEC highlights various aspects of the learning that takes place while walking. For example, in the introduction to the teachers' notes for the *Victorian Trail* the links between participation in a trail and specified areas of the curriculum are emphasized. These include a wide range of subjects from the *5-14 National Guidelines* published by Learning and Teaching Scotland (LTS 2000), such as Social Subjects, Technology, Mathematics, Language and Expressive Arts. The importance of the Centre's explicit linkage of the potential learning from each of their trails with specific elements of the *National Guidelines* is verified by teachers who have chosen to use the service it offers. One teacher from a small rural school in Aberdeenshire justified her choice of the Centre for the study of Victorians on the grounds that the *Victorian Trail and Classroom* 'matched the 5-14 criteria perfectly'. The key skill of 'developing informed attitudes' is shown to be supported by discussions arising out of walking through conservation areas which enable children to question why buildings from the past are looked after and to consider some of the practical implications of local planning legislation in conservation (Stewart 2002, iii-iv). The leader's introduction to the *World War II Experience* (Bennett et al. 2003, iii) also highlights links to 'Education for Citizenship' which recommends that 'the citizenship that formal education should seek to promote and foster needs to be thoughtful and responsible' (LTS 2000, 10).

The relationship between positive behaviour and effective learning is an important part of current practice in classroom organization and management and this is another reason why teachers like to include the guided walks in their plans for the delivery of environmental studies. As well as curriculum-focused learning intentions, leader's notes also discuss the learning of social conventions that takes place during trail-based activities, such as acceptable modes of behaviour in walking. In the introduction of the leader's notes to the *Exploring Buildings* booklet, there is an explicit set of 'Rules for Working Outside'. These include reminders that pupils should: 'Walk well back from the kerb and road, Look and listen for traffic at all times, When crossing any roads, cross with your teacher or group leader and be aware of other pedestrians' (Atherton et al. 2003, iv). These rules are not reproduced in the pupils' books as it is expected that group leaders will share them with children at the beginning of the trail and remind them of particular points at appropriate intervals during their walk. For teachers, it is important that the rules echo those of the classroom.

Exploration and learning through walking along the streets of Aberdeen affords a rich opportunity for kinaesthetic learning. In the trails related to the built environment, children are invited at some point to feel with their hands the different textures of building materials like granite, concrete or sandstone. Stones can feel hot, cold or damp and these physical experiences help children to shape their understanding of the different properties of particular building stones and their knowledge about why architects, builders and consumers choose the materials they do. On the *Victorian Trail*, children are asked to 'stop opposite No. 180 Skene Street and listen. Can you hear the sound of running water?' (Stewart 2002, 12). At this point in the street there is no sign of the tiny Denburn which flows in a culvert beneath the street. It is often very difficult to hear the sound of the water as it is drowned out by that of the traffic on the main road.

While exploration is encouraged and fostered, play is not part of the explicit agenda on the historic trails. Part of the reason for this lies in attitudes to play in primary school. It is considered axiomatic that pre-school children and those in the early years of primary school cannot learn without doing. It is expected that a class of five- to six-year-olds studying street furniture around their school will want to play, and taking account of their safety, children are allowed to run, skip, shout, point, hop and shuffle by their leaders. The trails designed for younger children allow leaders to help children learn through a structured but playfully oriented walk. A teacher whose class of Primary 1 children had taken part in a *Scottish Homes* trail around their school commented on his evaluation form that the 'class really enjoyed the house/homes walk and hunt, seeing the environment with different eyes'.

But by the time children are over the age of around eight and in the middle stages of their primary school education the expectation is that they will be able to learn by observation and discussion rather than through explicit forms of play. Walking as an older child is a much more orderly business. For example a comment on the leader's notes of the *Victorian Trail* booklet urges teachers to ensure that 'pupils should not be allowed to roam all over the church' (Stewart 2002, 16). Variant forms of walking are considered to be distractions. Leaders prefer children to concentrate on the task of learning about the historic environment through which they are walking.

However, comments from children in their thank-you letters to staff show that older children do engage in games developed out of more formal parts of the trail. Jenny, a ten-year-old who had been learning about Aberdeen during the Second World War, wrote that 'I liked spotting the hooks on tops of houses which used to be for trams'. This game had started off as a result of the children's attention having been drawn to the remains of one of the iron roses that supported the tram wires between houses on the city's Rosemount Place.

Creating the trail

The Centre currently offers a range of 12 trails which relate to different aspects of learning in, about and through the environment. Among the choices offered are the *Victorian Trail*, the *World War II Experience*, *Scottish Homes*, *Traffic First*, *Exploring Buildings* and *Living with Trees*. Some are historical in nature and focus on evidence for particular periods in the city's past, some are focused on the theme of biodiversity and others relate to urban design including the management of traffic. The trails also differ in the way the routes are determined. All of the historical trails follow predetermined routes through particular places in Aberdeen, such as the Rosemount area for the *Victorian Trail*. Other trails, particularly those focused on the exploration of urban design, have routes which are negotiated with the class teacher and within walking distance of pupils' schools. The degree of structure within the trails is also variable. As the historical trails follow a set route, the children create their own narrative account of the trail. They thus develop a key historical skill: building narrative from historical evidence. The trails which focus on biodiversity and urban design have a more open structure with less emphasis on creating a narrative so that children can choose where they stop and which features they will explore in detail.

One of the most regularly walked historical trails is the *Victorian Trail* (Stewart 2002). Following a route through part of Aberdeen with buildings largely dating from the nineteenth century, this trail takes children from a city centre area of three- to four- storey tenement flats surrounding a cotton mill to an area of large granite houses in the wealthier Victorian city suburbs. Many shops are situated on the ground floor level of the tenements on the main street and there are several nineteenth century churches. Over the last 15 years the *Victorian Trail* has been developed in terms of both the distances children walk and the scope and direction of enquiry. When it was first designed, the trail was laid out in the area immediately surrounding the Centre and children walked for about an hour. It now takes about two hours and follows the grocery run of a fictional character, Jamie Craig, in the novel *Danger by Gaslight* (Ramsay 1998), which was commissioned by AEEC to support the trail. After a visit to the Centre with a class of 10- and 11-year-old children studying the Victorians, one teacher commented that 'the children learned a great deal about the subject and it brought to life "Danger by Gaslight"'. This was particularly important as the class had travelled from a country school about forty miles south of Aberdeen. School classes participating in this trail often take part in another activity to create a whole-day excursion, typically a role-play activity in a reconstructed Victorian classroom in the building adjacent to the main part of the Centre.

Unlike the *Victorian Trail, Exploring Buildings* was designed to be used in any urban environment. Its purpose is to 'raise awareness of building design *through direct experience* in the environment', and to extend pupils' experience 'of buildings of particular significance in the local area' (Atherton et al. 2003). *Exploring Buildings* focuses on the exploration of building design and construction, and the ways in which evidence is collected and recorded are significantly different from the conventions used in the *Victorian Trail*. Adopting an explicitly child-centred approach, *Exploring Buildings* was designed to give children more freedom to choose what to record from their observations, including selecting which building to record and putting more emphasis on children's own drawings. Rather than creating narratives on their trail, children taking part in *Exploring Buildings* are introduced to a range of sketching techniques before they embark on their walk. AEEC's director believes that after completing these exercises, children are ready to be 'taken out into the environment to record shape, texture and architectural features' (ibid., 4).

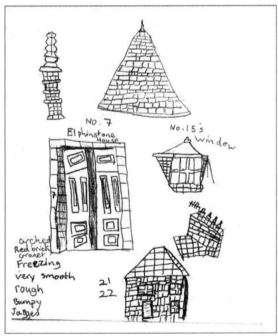

12.

Dream Box

Record any ideas that you have during your
walk in the box below.
You can use your ideas to help you
with follow up work back in class.

Figure 10.4 and Figure 10.5 AEEC 'dream box' in which to record thoughts and feelings as well as drawings of places experienced on the walk, as the basis for imaginative building back in the classroom

Whereas the *Victorian Trail* emphasizes the recording of selected features by writing and annotating illustrations, children taking part in the *Exploring Buildings* programme are encouraged to consider other ways of gathering evidence, including touching buildings and listening to sounds around them, and then to incorporate their feelings into their own field sketches rather than responding to a series of predetermined questions. The language of *Exploring Buildings* is less prescriptive than that of the *Victorian Trail*. It encourages children to record their thoughts, feelings and responses to particular buildings and places on their walk. This is done through the creation of so-called 'dream boxes'. Figure 10.4 shows a 'dream box' completed by a Primary 7 pupil who explored Old Aberdeen with his class. The annotated drawings reveal aspects of his journey along the High Street, walking and stopping to look carefully at houses and making a detailed record of numbers 7, 15, 21 and 22. His additional notes demonstrate his experience of the different textures of building materials which he felt on his walk: the smoothness of some, roughness and jaggedness of others, all contributing to a very rich record of this child's embodied experience of walking. Back in the classroom this deep knowledge then became the basis on which he created his own imaginary buildings.

Children participating in this kind of exploratory activity have the opportunity to take the lead in their learning, and their success is conditional on their existing knowledge and understanding of how to carry out an urban investigation. It is also governed by their predisposition to self-motivated learning. A teacher commenting on a class from a school where a number of the children had educationally challenging backgrounds noted that although the *Exploring Buildings* programme had a great deal of potential, and while some of the members of the class were very interested in what they were doing, for others 'it was too much. [It was] difficult keeping those of low concentration on task.'

Walking from point to point

Both the *Victorian Trail* and *Exploring Buildings* involve children in walking and observing the architectural features of buildings, and then in making inferences based on these observations to explain the reasons why the buildings were designed in particular ways and how the architecture reflects the lives of the people who lived or worked in them. Children do not however walk continuously; they follow a trail punctuated by planned stops. These stops are designed to enable them to observe and explore in safety, away from traffic, though occasionally they are asked to look for street names or to look out for particular buildings as they walk. Explicit instruction in environmental studies – for example, learning the vocabulary associated with architectural features – thus happens in the pauses when children stop and are asked to observe and to think.

Figure 10.6 Children pausing to think at Footdee

Before setting out on the *Victorian Trail*, children are expected to familiarize themselves with the route they will follow by studying a map in their trail booklet. It shows the route of the walk and the points at which they will pause to address particular questions and to observe particular features in the streetscape. The first task is therefore for children to 'find where you are on the map and put an "x"' (Stewart 2002, 6). They are then expected to follow the footprints on the map, which mark where they will be walking. At various intervals children are told to locate their place on the map and so identify where they are on the ground, such as: 'Continue walking and stop just past St Mary's Church. Look along Albert Terrace to help you answer the following questions' (Stewart 2002, 12, 13). Interestingly, the map extract in the trail booklet is not recent, but taken from the 1899 revised edition of the Ordnance Survey, so the comparison between map and ground is historical as well as geographic. Other AEEC trails take the same approach, with a walk around the streets of early modern Old Aberdeen using an extract from a 1661 map. The way in which children are encouraged to carry out their investigations reveals a strong visual emphasis. Instructions such as 'look for', 'look up', 'look across', and 'find three things which you can see today' form the basis of the structured enquiry which children carry out on the *Victorian Trail*. By comparing the buildings they see with drawings and photographs of the buildings a century ago, children are encouraged to make inferences relating to changes that have taken place and the reasons for them, as well as to consider why some parts of town are now accorded 'conservation status' while others are not.

A striking feature of the trail booklets is that apart from instructions and directions about where to go, there are few references to the practice of walking itself. Thus, despite walking along the route taken by the fictional Jamie Craig on his grocery round, the emphasis on exploring architectural features in the *Victorian Trail* does not encourage children to empathize with how it might have felt for Jamie walking the same route a century earlier, with or without shoes, on cobbles or dirt roads. Nor does the *World War II Experience* ask what it might have been like to go about on foot for the children's grandparents, when they were youngsters, during wartime blackouts. Only once is the experience of walking explicitly suggested as offering an empathetic link with the past. When children walk from AEEC to the building which contains the Victorian Schoolroom they dress in Victorian clothes and are made to walk silently in twos with straight backs and hands by their sides. As a leader of this activity you can visibly see the children change shape and attitude as they become images of Victorian children.

Although it is normally expected that children taking part in the *Victorian Trail* will have learnt how to behave appropriately in public and will walk accordingly, in my experience as a trail guide classes are still praised for their ability to line up neatly and walk in a straight line in twos. Most comments about walking therefore focus on the practice as one that brings potential dangers that have to be prevented through taking proper precautions. For example, the leader's notes for the *World War II Experience* highlight the importance of pupils coming appropriately dressed with 'warm, waterproof clothing and sensible footwear for walking' (Bennett et al. 2003, v). Similarly, advice to leaders at the beginning of the *Victorian Trail* reminds them of the need to observe road safety rules at all times. Teachers are asked to ensure that children walk in pairs away from the edge of the pavement (Stewart 2002, ii). Although not an explicit learning outcome of participation in an AEEC trail, it is clear that certain skills of walking are considered to be very important.

Conclusion

The language of the *5-14 National Guidelines* for Environmental Studies and that of AEEC suggests that the environment is external to children: it is *out there* to be encountered and ultimately mapped and recorded. Consequently, for most of the time children are walking, their learning is clearly focused on the rules of road safety and sensible behaviour. Walking itself is not generally regarded as a vehicle for sensory understanding. Children record their experiences when stationary, and yet whilst they are walking they are fully aware of, for example, the length of their walk, the weather (I have walked these trails several times in the pouring rain, snow and also in warm sunshine), the width of the streets, the sounds of traffic and the height and density of housing. There is no doubt that walking profoundly affects the experience of the children taking part in trails, and that it contributes through this experience to their learning. This contribution, however, is scarcely acknowledged. In the *Victorian Trail*, the value of walking receives no mention at all. In the case of the *Exploring Buildings* programme, while it does not follow a predetermined trail, the physical experience of walking is incorporated more fully. By moving away from a knowledge-centred approach to one with a greater emphasis on the individual child's experiences, it marks a first step from traditional models of classroom learning towards something more in keeping with how children themselves go about learning what they do.

References

Atherton, D., Baxter, L., Paterson, A. and Pirie, N. (2003), *Exploring Buildings* (Aberdeen: Aberdeen Environmental Education Centre).

Bennett, A., Pirie, N. and Stewart, S. (2003), *World War II Aberdeen's Experience* (Aberdeen: Aberdeen Environmental Education Centre).

Learning and Teaching Scotland (LTS) (2000), *National Guidelines: Environmental Studies, Society, Science and Technology 5-14* (Edinburgh: Queen's Printer for Scotland).

Ramsay, E. (1998), *Danger By Gaslight* (Edinburgh: Scottish Children's Press).

Paterson, A. (2004), *Space and Place*, CD-ROM (Aberdeen: Aberdeen City Council).

Paterson, A. and Stewart, S. (1998), *Scottish Homes Programme Overview* (Aberdeen: Aberdeen Environmental Education Centre).

Stewart, S. (2002), *AEEC to Rubislaw Victorian Trail Leader's Notes* (Aberdeen: Aberdeen Environmental Education Centre).

Chapter 11

Enchantment Engineering and Pedestrian Empowerment: The Geneva Case

Sonia Lavadinho and Yves Winkin

Urban walking: a research agenda

The material presented in this chapter is drawn from a series of teaching and research collaborations between the authors that encompass ethnography and urban planning. These developed through jointly conducting the Anthropology of Communication course at the University of Geneva on the theme of walking in an urban context. At the time Lavadinho had begun an evaluation of urban walks developed within the framework of the Pedestrian Masterplan launched by the City of Geneva. Winkin, meanwhile, had been encouraging students to observe people interacting in public. We started to work with students on the premise of a simple question: 'what is it to walk, to wait and to observe in the city?' Every one of us, when acting as a pedestrian – walking around, or standing in wait for a friend, a bus or a green light – observes other people as they come and go, and draws from these observations, and the impressions they make, certain social inferences (Goffman 1971).

Relying on maps, notes and readings,[1] Winkin encouraged students to write papers on these ordinary aspects of ordinary social life – so ordinary, indeed, that they become almost invisible, even though they constitute the very ground upon which contemporary urbanity grows. The course was lively, alternating between theory and field practice. A number of articles on urban walking, written in the wake of this work, helped us to define a common research agenda on urban walking (Lavadinho and Abram 2005; Lavadinho and Winkin 2005a; Lavadinho and Winkin 2005b; Lavadinho 2005; Lavadinho 2006; Lavadinho and Pini 2005). Here we can present no more than a summary.

Firstly, we want to take walking seriously, and to find ways to valorize walking behaviour and initiatives that are conducive to pedestrian empowerment. Secondly, we consider walking to be neither merely a leisure activity nor simply an alternative means of transportation, but rather an enlightened everyday practice, useful for going to work, going shopping, and so on. Ideally a successful walking route should respond to multilayered users' representations. Furthermore, we propose to deal with pedestrian circulations as complex communicative interactions rather than simply as functional displacements. We also want to probe the ways in which pedestrians

---

1   For a comprehensive review of methods of research on urban life, we used Grosjean and Thibaud (2001). Thibaud (2002) turned out to be very useful for theoretical grounding.

appropriate public space and invest in it through their daily movements. Thirdly, while we ground our work in fieldwork-based urban anthropology and sociology, we are pragmatic enough to hope that our arguments will be of interest to decision makers and urban planners alike.

Enchantment engineering

Over the past few years Winkin has been dealing with the notion of enchantment understood as 'willing suspension of disbelief' (Coleridge 1817). In his perspective, such suspension is produced in specific places through collusion between 'enchantment engineers' and visitors. Though the latter may be well aware of how phoney a place may be, they nevertheless want to sustain the illusion for as long as possible. Enchantment, then, is to be understood as the product of crafted engineering and sustained denial (Winkin 2001).

According to an initial typology developed by Winkin, the places in which enchantment is produced are of three kinds. The first comprises settings purposely built for illusion, such as Disneyland resorts, Las Vegas casinos and cruise ships. The second includes settings permanently reframed for the purpose of reviving the past, such as touristic sites, or for reviving utopic ideals, such as Club Méd villages and academic conference centres (Winkin 2005a). The third consists of settings defined temporarily as 'off zones' in which relations are 'reversible' (that is, inconsequential), such as carnivals, public relations events or group dynamics seminars. Commercial centres based on the marketing notion of 'fun shopping' also aspire to this latter category.

Winkin was not entirely happy, however, with the idea that enchantment is contained in close-bound places, which seems to imply a causal relationship between physical structures and specific conduits. He was also curious to find out how enchantment may be produced with no engineers around, and how it may be sustained in porous places such as historical walking trails. As he walked along the trail toward St Jacques de Compostelle, he examined how the fragile enchantment frame is maintained or ruptured and how the Catholic Church still acts as a powerful engineering institution (Winkin 2005b). Urban walking thus became the logical next step in his explorations of the realms of enchantment.

Years ago, Winkin conducted an observational study of the outdoor cafés of his native city of Liège. Drawing on Goffman (1953; 1961), he defined them as euphoric as opposed to dysphoric places. The idea that certain places may be conducive to interactional euphoria was not far from that of urban pedestrian enchantment. In extending the idea to walking in the city, however, we faced a double challenge. Firstly, the traditional equation between euphoria and leisure had to be suppressed. Urban euphoric places had been cast as locations for slow, almost languid sitting or walking, inviting idle talk and *flânerie*. When we embarked upon the study of urban walking, we opted for a more functional vision of pedestrian movement: feet get you to places and back. How could we build a bridge between active, goal-oriented pedestrian itineraries and enchantment? Secondly, while enchantment engineers can clearly be seen at work in places such as tourist resorts or group dynamics seminars, it is harder to make out their presence in ordinary urban settings. In spectacular urban renovations, well-known architects, urbanists and artists clearly play the role of enchantment engineers. But to extend the role to administrators in urban planning or parks and gardens departments may be stretching things a bit far.

Another humble actor, however, may well help us explain how enchantment comes about in urban walking scenes: the pedestrians. Thus the answer we found to both questions lies in the notion of empowerment, to which we now turn.

Pedestrian empowerment

As we all know, the notion of empowerment is very difficult to define (and impossible to translate into French). Empowerment may be personal, as the result of one's own 'work' or 'development' (to borrow two favourite terms from the self-help literature). It has to do with an increasing capacity to make one's own decisions, to consider a territory as one's own, to move through life with autonomy and determination. Empowerment can also be collective, leading to group formation, if not to claims to recognition as a new social category (Anderson 1983). In the latter case, the process of awakening may be triggered by special events out of which leaders may emerge, and group consolidation may be guided by these leaders, accompanied by the media and reinforced by the construction of specific buildings and amenities.

Once we had come up with the idea of pedestrian empowerment, we were struck by its capacity to capture how urban walkers are nowadays aware of the growing role they play in the city – to the point that they sometimes consider themselves to be an emergent group with precise needs and claims. We also realized that more and more cities are listening to, responding to, and even anticipating their demands. Let us consider these issues more closely.

Personal empowerment

The notion of personal pedestrian empowerment refers to the way walkers actively engage both in the act of walking and in the construction of their own identity as walkers. We began by collecting data on the use of a range of walking accessories. Some accessories facilitate walking, such as shoes and other equipment borrowed from the sporting world. Then there are devices that accelerate the pace of walking, aptly named NFM for 'New Forms of Mobility' (rollers, skates, segways and similar devices). A third category comprises body-accessories (multi-functional watches, mobile phones, walkmans, ipods and other music players) along with the equipment designed to carry other accessories (backpacks, caddies, rolling suitcases, banana-belts, if not glasses with miniature speakers). Finally, we identified a mixed category of wearables, including accessories so small or so minutely crafted that they are carried on the body itself, such as Swatch watches of the 'Skin' series, micro earphones, cameras or USB keys. For several years now, 'intelligent clothes' which integrate phones, heat captors and other functions have also been in the making.

All these accessories are far from being mere gadgets, or age or status symbols. They carry an important symbolic load precisely because they reinforce the functional autonomy of their wearers. They are signs of the new freedom and self-reliance claimed by walkers, whose 'territories of the self' (Goffman 1971) have expanded, both in surface area and legitimacy. Walkers may thus consider themselves, to an ever greater extent, to be fully-fledged urban actors rather than the weakest victims of the urban jungle, to be protected and parked in specially designated zones.

Personal pedestrian empowerment also derives from the personal appropriation of various spots and sites of the city. Many writers have described how they felt enthralled, for example, by the discovery of a particular point of view over the city or by the recurrent beauty of the flowing water under a particular bridge. Ordinary walkers may also be possessed by such scenes, and may possess them in turn; each scene is their own little movie, and they may make a detour en route to their work in order to run it one more time. Nowadays most cities build amenities for their many pedestrian users, from pavements to parks. Some amenities are strictly functional, such as zebra crossings. But many amenities can be both functional and aesthetically sound. We will speak of symbolic amenities[2] when they are conducive to appropriation by their users, who will make a personal effort to go through them because some form of satisfaction is at hand. Here is enchantment at work again.

Collective empowerment

Personal pedestrian empowerment leads to collective pedestrian empowerment. This occurs firstly because urban walkers realize how many of them there are on the road every day. They may even use the strategy of 'togethering' (Ryave and Schenkein 1974) to cross a street while the red signal is still on. But this is still informal collective empowerment. Formal collective empowerment goes a step further. When associations of urban walkers, vocal leaders, and written supports of expression coalesce, we witness the emergence of a self-designated, specific group calling for specific measures. Most of the proposed measures still tend to focus mostly on pedestrian safety in regard to car traffic, and continue to frame pedestrians as dominated and victimized. In recent years, however, the focus has slowly but surely been sliding towards a new trend more along the lines of enhancing pedestrians' quality of life. This is apparent from the evolution of the designs awarded with the annual Swiss 'Prize for innovation in pedestrian mobility'. One further step in this process of collective empowerment has to do with the re-establishment of an equal footing, so to speak, of pedestrians with car users and other city dwellers. Ultimately, collective empowerment will reach a stage of personal embodiment when walkers, even alone, will produce 'symbolic togetherings', and the awareness of their power

---

2   The symbolic dimension of these amenities, on either a personal or a collective level, is constitutive of pedestrian empowerment. We use the word symbolic here to stress the performative dimension of infrastructures and accessories alike: beyond their materiality, their effectiveness arises from their being appropriated by the walkers themselves.

will thus be intimately incorporated. By then walking will have recovered its forgotten status as the pacing rhythm of the city.

Let us now move to our urban field, the city of Geneva.

The Geneva case

Geneva benefits from a strong manifesto for walking: the Pedestrian Masterplan. Adopted by the City Council in 2001 and approved by the Geneva State Authorities in 2004, the Pedestrian Masterplan is the result of a longer process that started out in 1995 following the early signature of the Aalborg Charter that had just been launched by a number of European cities in the wake of the 1992 Rio conference. The first of the five main axes developed within the scope of the Masterplan is specifically devoted to the promotion of walking for both leisure and daily activities: it aims to encourage walking by developing and promoting walking routes within and between districts. In addition, the City of Geneva chose to reinforce the visibility of the Masterplan by editing a series of maps retracing developed walking routes. The City has conceived two lines of action: to create walking routes and to promote a coherent network that connects the city with its suburbs and adjacent municipalities, bypassing administrative borders to focus on real walking practices.

From pedestrian areas to encounter areas: policies of shared space

Public amenities aimed at putting the different users of public space on an equal footing may considerably reinforce both personal and collective pedestrian empowerment. We now see emerging throughout Europe boldly reorganized urban zones in which speed is limited to 20km per hour. Pavements and zebra crossings are eliminated, and walkers go as they please while cars have systematically to give them the right of way. Significantly enough, these reframed public spaces are called 'encounter zones in Switzerland.

Geneva, like many other Swiss and European cities, has lately tried to implement a sustainable transport policy based, among other measures, on the promotion of human-powered mobility through the multiplication of traffic-calming schemes and the implementation of encounter areas. To that end, the emergent logic of mixed fluxes was opposed to the once prevalent logic of separated fluxes in (re)designing public spaces. Within this new logic, human-powered mobility may thrive only so far as traffic speed is moderated and pedestrians gain priority over other transport modes. Mutual respect and personal responsibility are the new rules by which all users are to abide. Perpetual negotiation thus becomes a sign of urbanity. These new urban designs are not so much infrastructure-oriented as behaviour-oriented. If sharing is the key word, so is belonging: pedestrians rely solely on themselves to appropriate as much space as has been provided for their use. New frames of perception and action are required to deal with these new trends in urban design.

Figure 11.1 Encounter areas in Switzerland, a rising trend

While the radical pedestrianization of commercial streets that took place in the 1970s and 1980s remains necessarily bound to tiny islets within the inner cores of cities and is relentlessly criticized for suffocating business, a different approach has been taken of late regarding the expansion of pedestrian-friendly zones to residential neighbourhoods and areas of mixed land-use throughout the whole city. These new urban policies admit that different mobility needs have to be addressed in different ways, but that no particular set of needs (and thus no mode of transportation) is superior to another. It is a first step towards full public recognition of urban walkers as members of a new social category.

Personal enchantment engineering

On their way to work, shopping or other daily activities, pedestrians may decide to use an oblique itinerary, slightly costlier time-wise, simply because they will cross a particular park, bridge, or side alley which will produce a tiny enchantment. Suddenly and for a short while, they are away – as if on vacation – on a delicious memory trip. All the ingredients of enchantment are present. On the one hand, there are the enchantment engineers who designed the amenity; on the other, there are willing visitors, ready to surrender to a brief denial of reality. Engineers alone cannot produce the temporary illusion. Only passers-by may hold the magic wand. We may even add that the more open and the more available to personal investment are the amenities offered, the more ready are the conditions for enchantment. This is another way of saying that personal empowerment – that is, personal appropriation through enchantment – does not necessarily depend on spectacular amenities designed by major enchantment professionals. When their work is too tight, they offer no screen for personal imagination and history, and they might as well return to their material basis – flat surfaces of concrete inviting graffiti.

We will look at four strategies of enchantment engineering in Geneva. The first two are very humble; they entail planting tiny gardens throughout the city and making simple pathways along the lake. These clearly have to do with personal enchantment and empowerment. The third is a much more ambitious operation of urban cosmetics, which can be seen as explicit enchantment engineering; it has however sometimes provoked negative reactions from the public, which can be heard as: 'leave us to do the job; we are our own enchanters'. It suggests that collective enchantment and empowerment cannot be decided by the authorities but can only come about through the active collaboration of the local population. The fourth example is of a successful strategy of collective enchantment and empowerment that has been going on for decades now, fascinating generation upon generation of 'promeneurs'.

Les jardins de poche

Small-scale, hardly noticed amenities such as the 'Jardins de Poche' (pocket gardens) currently being planned throughout Geneva (Barbisch 2005) may create an enchanted thread that momentarily suspends disbelief for speedy walkers on their way to work or other daily activities. Their modest greenery and their almost hidden benches may even slow the walkers' pace for a few minutes, since walking in a place of enchantment is usually slow and smooth. Though these proximity amenities are by no means spectacular, their regular appearance throughout the urban tissue strengthens the continuity of the walking network. A person may relate to each of these gardens as his or her own personal space, nearby the home or office, but the similarities in design and purpose allow people to link these particular spaces with others located elsewhere in the city. Green walls and benches dot every itinerary at regular intervals and contribute to the reading of the itinerary as a continuous thread – one of many making up the urban fabric – rather than as an assemblage of disconnected segments dotted erratically around the city.

The Jardins de Poche thus furnish a simple yet coherent key to ordinary urbanscapes. We know how ordinary walking is made up of the most insignificant of events, of short glimpses of bliss as much as repetitions and banalities. Walking across the city thus means both being reassured, through indices of predictability, rites and rhythms, that one is following a given itinerary, and simultaneously experiencing the surprise and pleasure of small, unexpected discoveries. Though potentially at the disposal of all city dwellers, the Jardins de Poche may, precisely because of the modesty of their dimensions and the simplicity of their amenities, become vectors of personal appropriation which can be felt as one's own, a feeling roughly translated as 'my own little garden'. They constitute themselves as 'ambiences', conducive to the (re)discovery of a feeling of pleasure in being in town (Amphoux et al. 2004).

**Figure 11.2 Jardins de Poche: The bench acts as a framing device
for enchantment**

Au fil du Rhône

Other amenities, such as the ones developed within the framework of a waterfront
revitalization project called 'Au fil du Rhône', aim to give coherence and strength
to the walking routes along the river, using the flow of water as their uniting thread.
These amenities function both as connectors and as symbolic landmarks. They frame
urbanscapes in unique ways for those who move through the walking grounds, and
attract people precisely because of their landmarking and landscaping properties.
The framing power of such an installation is immediately perceptible. While below
ground its real uses remain a mystery, people feel free to interpret the urbanscape it
creates above ground. It has become a favourite place to watch the fading light over
the river and let life flow slowly by.

Both the Jardins de Poche and Au fil du Rhône initiatives privilege the redesign
of proximity amenities as a way to enhance ordinary public spaces and punctuate
itineraries throughout residential neighbourhoods otherwise rendered illegible by a
lack of recognizable landmarks.

**Figure 11.3 The Passerelle du Seujet, where the passing waters and
the passing people mingle together as one**

Les Yeux de la Ville

Another initiative that privileges proximity amenities is an ephemeral annual event,
launched in 2002, 'Les Yeux de la Ville' (The Eyes of the City). The staging of this
event is a complex process bringing together several actors. Firstly, City officials
identify some particular streets and places where there is a desire to experiment with
new mobility solutions, solve traffic nuisances, tackle long-existing problems or
plan new uses of public space for the future. Most of these demands emerge from the
population itself, either directly through petitions or letters from inhabitants or relayed
by local associations. After discussing the pros and cons with the local population
and other stakeholders through consensus conferences and similar participatory
methods, the City officials then decide if they are to close the streets to traffic for
three consecutive months. When such a decision is made, fine-grained interventions
take hold of the perimeter, through artistic, cultural and social animations. Many
people take part into these interventions: artists, architects, schools of landscape and
urban design, local associations and, last but not least, the inhabitants themselves.
Terraces are installed in the middle of the streets, allowing people to walk and gather
in places to which they could not previously gain access (Trayser 2005).

At the end of the summer, a balance sheet is drawn up for the whole of the
season. If the ephemeral installations are proved to have been successful, the City
may consider the possibility of settling them on a permanent basis, and will then
revert to a more classical *modus operandi* in urban planning, with the advantage of
having recruited the public to its cause beforehand.

Figure 11.4 Walking art

This is not always the case, however. Enchantment engineering sometimes backfires. Some interventions remain obscure and incomprehensible to the population, who cannot relate to the ways their familiar space has been rewritten – to the point that installations may be removed early in the face of overwhelming resistance. This happened recently among the inhabitants of Eaux-Vives neighbourhood, and was relayed by the media in such a virulent manner that the City quickly renounced the intervention altogether. It is generally the case that numerous critiques, both positive and negative, surface in the media throughout the summer period and controversies sometimes arise, leading to the mobilization of different actors for or against particular interventions. This is what empowerment is all about: the freedom to choose whether or not to adhere to a certain vision of public space that is being constructed through explicitly professional enchantment engineering.

The main interest of such an operation remains that it provides a way of 'concerting through acting out'. Every urban actor may thus see with his or her own eyes – the eyes of the city – what would happen if a different scene was played out on the streets. This 'what if … ' intervention is not far from our notion of enchantment, in that it literally gives room to people to imagine what their street could become if it did transform into a pedestrian's kingdom. It remains to be seen, however, whether local people and passers-by are willing to proceed to a collective 'suspension' of the kind: 'Sure, I know it is still my good old dreary street, but I will act as if it had dramatically changed for the better.' When the order comes from above, it is not always certain that inhabitants will want to cooperate; if the artistic intervention in the perimeter is not understood or appreciated, they may suspend their suspension instead. Or they might just play the game from time to time, knowing that it may be over by the end of the summer. *Permanent* collective empowerment is something else altogether; it happens at the 'Bains des Pâquis', our fourth and last case study.

Collective enchantment through collective apropriation

Some places in Geneva have acquired a 'suspended' status long ago, and its citizens think it is a status worth fighting for – to the point that they mobilize themselves to vote against its remodelling and subsequent loss of identity. The 'Bains des Pâquis', a public bathing area built around Lake Geneva, is just one of those places.

This immensely pleasurable leisure area – founded more than a hundred years ago and remaining pretty much the same since the 1930s – illustrates the notion of a 'place of enchantment' as we have defined it above, not least because its historicity allows people to inscribe themselves within a continuous line of affiliation that stems from the past. 'Restoration of behavior' (Schechner 1985) thus takes place, in which past and future mingle within this single moment of eternal present, where the Bains remain once and for ever 'the same'. Every season people stroll around its ancient trees and the lighthouse at the end of the promenade, only to find out that it is still there. Then they rest (re)assured that everything is as it should be – each place, as it were, is indeed in its place.

During fieldwork devoted to the Bains, as Genevans familiarly call them, Lavadinho developed the notion of 'life hub' to describe this impressively multifaceted area – comprising multiple spaces that allow for diverse activities and complex agendas and timeframes – that acts as a main attraction not only for leisure but on the way to and from work and other daily activities for many city dwellers (Lavadinho 2002).

From enchantment engineering to pedestrian empowerment

From these case studies we may infer that there is more to enchantment engineering than meets the eye. Inevitably, no walking promotion policy can reach its goal unless walking is adopted by the population itself. Thus it is not enough to plan walking routes, draw maps on paper and stack them at the nearest tourist office, nor is it enough to design amenities in certain well-defined areas of the city, specifically for leisure purposes. Indigenous walkers expect a whole range of public places, much broader in scope and much nearer to their daily activities, since they usually anchor these walking routes to their daily agendas.

Although walking for walking's sake is quite possible, more often than not people are motivated to walk in their pursuit of a combination of several activities besides the leisurely stroll itself. The more that walking routes adapt to these other reasons for people being where they are, or going where they will, the greater the investment in them. A successful walking route tends to dissolve against a wider background of high-quality urban fabric that can accommodate the multifunctionality called forth by users' daily practices and that responds to their equally multilayered representations. Ideally, public places along this route evolve into hybrid places capable of fulfilling leisure expectations as well as more utilitarian needs, while the former and the latter tend to reinforce each other as they revolve around interlocking circadian and hebdomadal rhythms. Walking settings, as we hope to have demonstrated, are more than functional, they are emotional: they provide us with places to grow and to remember, places to sit back and relax and enjoy life, places to meet people that we care about, places to fall in love with. The practice of walking can only be fostered by taking into account the values attached to it, as people consider walking as either rewarding or stigmatizing. We thus need to address, as a priority, the issue of how to reinforce the positive dimensions of walking as a mode of self-presentation and representation. For the best urban improvements in terms of walkability may turn into fiascos if they are not embedded in the ways people 'walk in their minds'.

References

Amphoux P., Thibaud, J.-P. and Chelkoff, G. (eds) (2004), *Ambiances en Débats* (Grenoble: A la Croisée).

Anderson, B. (1983), *Imagined Communities: Reflections on the Origin and Spread of Nationalism* (London: Verso).

Barbisch, C. (2005), *Les Jardins de Poche* (Geneva: Service d'Urbanisme de la Ville de Genève).

Coleridge, S. (1817), *Biographia Literaria; or Biographical Sketches of my Literary Life and Opinions* (London: Rest Fenner).

Goffman, E. (1953), *Communication Conduct in an Island Community* (Unpublished doctoral dissertation, University of Chicago, Department of Sociology).

—— (1961), *Encounters: Two Studies in the Sociology of Interaction* (Indianapolis: Bobbs-Merrill).

—— (1971), *Relations in Public: Micro-studies of the Public Order* (New York: Basic Books).

Grosjean, M. and Thibaud, J.-P. (eds) (2001), *L'Espace Urbain en Méthodes* (Marseille: Parenthèses).

Lavadinho, S. (2002), *Promenades sur la Rade: L'Imaginaire de l'Eau aux Bains des Pâquis: Flux Proxémiques, Rituels d'Interaction et Mythologies de Communication Urbaine* (MA thesis, UNIGE, Geneva).

—— (2006), 'Evaluating Walking Promotion Policies With Regard to Mobility Representations, Appropriations and Practices in Public Space', in Mander, U., Brebbia, C. and Tiezzi, E. (eds) (2006), *The Sustainable City IV: Urban Regeneration and Sustainability* (London: WIT Press).

—— (2005), 'Walking, From Policy to Practice: The Geneva Case', in *Walk 21*, Conference Proceedings, Zurich.

Lavadinho, S. and Abram, L. (2005), 'Webwalk: Using GIS Mapping to Compute Door-to-door Routes on a Web Platform', in *Walk 21*, Conference Proceedings, Zurich.

Lavadinho, S. and Pini, G. (2005), 'Développement Durable, Mobilité Douce et Santé en Milieu Urbain', in *Développement Urbain Durable*, Symposium Proceedings, Lausanne.

Lavadinho, S. and Winkin, Y. (2005a), 'Quand les Piétons Saisissent la Ville. Éléments pour une Anthropologie de la Marche Appliquée à l'Aménagement Urbain', *MEI* 22.

—— (2005b), 'Les Territoires du Moi: Aménagements Matériels et Symboliques de la Marche Urbaine', in *Développement Urbain Durable*, Symposium Proceedings, Lausanne.

Ryave, L. and Schenkein, N. (1974), 'Notes on the Art of Walking', in Turner, R. (ed.) (1974), *Ethnomethodology* (Harmondsworth: Penguin).

Schechner, R. (1985), 'Restoration of Behaviour', in Schechner, R. (ed.) (1985), *Between Theater and Anthropology* (Philadelphia: University of Pennsylvania Press).

Thibaud, J.-P. (ed.) (2002), *Regards en Action: Ethnométhodologie des Espaces Publics* (Grenoble: A la Croisée).

Trayser, M. (2005), *De l'Éphémère au Durable, ou les Aménagements Éphémères Étudiés Sous l'Angle de la Durabilité: Le Cas de l'Opération les 'Yeux de la Ville' à Genève* (MA thesis, UNIL, Lausanne).

Winkin, Y. (2001), 'Propositions pour une Anthropologie de l'Enchantement', in Rasse, P. et al. (eds) (2001), *Unité-diversité: Les Identités Culturelles dans le Jeu de la Mondialisation* (Paris: L'Harmattan).

—— (2005a), 'Communiquer à Cerisy', in Heurgon, E. et al. (eds) (2005), *Cent Ans de Rencontres Intellectuelles de Pontigny à Cerisy* (Paris: Editions de l'IMEC).

—— (2005b), 'Le Chemin de St Jacques', in Alizer, M. and Kihm, C. (eds) (2005), *Fresh Theory* (Paris: Léo Scheer).

Chapter 12

'Taking a Line for a Walk': Walking as an Aesthetic Practice

Raymond Lucas

> It is not given to every man to take a bath of multitude; enjoying a crowd is an art; and only he can relish a debauch of vitality at the expense of the human species, on whom, in his cradle, a fairy has bestowed the love of masks and masquerading, the hate of home, and the passion for roaming (Baudelaire 1970, 20).

Walking has long been regarded as offering the potential for aesthetic practice. In this chapter I seek to understand the uses made of walking by twentieth century artists and art movements, with particular reference to the city. Siting the investigation in the city reflects my own interests which are rooted in my architectural training. It also serves as the context for my own creative practice, particularly a project entitled *Getting Lost in Tokyo*, the subject of a solo exhibition in 2005 and at the core of my research on inscriptive practices. My inquiry begins, however, with the engagement of theorist Walter Benjamin with the nineteenth century Parisian poet, Charles Baudelaire. Around the figure of the *flâneur*, which has become familiar from their writings, there has grown a vast secondary literature, exploring various aspects of our interaction with the urban environment (Tester 1994). Benjamin's work is reflected in the interests of art and self-professed anti-art groups such as Dada, Surrealism, and the Situationist International. For these visual artists, poets and performers, the city provided a site for investigation both relevant to their condition and breaking with earlier forms of patronage. Besides considering their work, I explore some of the ways in which walking has furnished a metaphor for creative practice itself. In the aphorism that gives this chapter its title, Paul Klee conceptualized the line as a trace resulting from a continuous gesture (Klee 1961, 105). The 'walk' of the brush or pen over a surface generates the line. The action of inscribing a line has the potential to be so deeply ingrained that it can inform our thinking across many disciplines and practices.

Following a discussion of urban aesthetic walking, in particular *flânerie*, I present an example from my own work. *Getting Lost in Tokyo* is a project based on my observations of Shinjuku subway station in Tokyo. It engages with walking explicitly, and seeks to generate new architectural spaces out of my experiences of a specific place and time. The work involves a series of transformations and translations from one inscriptive practice to another.

On the fascination of the *flâneur*

Architectural and urban theory, especially at the height of modernism and the International Style, has often been criticized for considering the city in isolation from those who inhabit its territories. This problem does, indeed, run through modernism's dealings with urban space, to the extent that its *tabula rasa* approach and strict single-use zoning denied much of the historic place-making that originally created the city. The early roots of what we now know as modernism, however, had a strong humanist element. Charles Baudelaire, writing at the cusp of the movement's beginnings, and later Walter Benjamin, writing in its early phase, both identified with the urban character known as the *flâneur*. Baudelaire spoke movingly of how this character, who would go 'botanizing on the asphalt', was vanishing in his time as a result of Baron Haussmann's boulevards, in opposition to and competition with the arcades, which were the native haunts or hunting grounds of the *flâneur*.

> [In] those days it was not possible to stroll about everywhere in the city. Before Haussmann wide pavements were rare, and the narrow ones afforded little protection from vehicles. Strolling could hardly have assumed the importance it did without the arcades (Benjamin 1997: 36).

By the time Benjamin wrote about the *flâneur*, however, Paris had just been transformed into a city of boulevards, with the arcades only surviving as a partly hidden route running north to south of the right bank.

A parallel can be drawn here between walking in the city and practices of reading. As Tim Ingold (2007) has shown, medieval and modern readers would approach a text in very different ways. The medieval reader would stalk its pages like a hunter-gatherer on the trail, seeking out meaning in its smallest signs (Ingold 2007, 15). While this way of reading still persists, most modern texts are aimed at readers who expect information to be presented in an orderly, chronological sequence, in the manner of reportage. In the mode of reading that emerged with modernity, meaning is imparted rather than sought and found. The differences between these modes are reflected in many other disciplines. The theory of cinema, for example is split between the ideas that spectators actively discover meaning for themselves and that they are passive recipients sutured into their entertainment. In a nutshell, this is the difference between so-called art-cinema and movies. This dichotomy is present in other art forms as well: the fine arts, architecture, music. Likewise, in modelling the city, the *flâneur* and his ilk may be opposed to the shopper, tourist and commuter.

> Basic to flânerie, among other things, is the idea that the fruits of idleness are more precious than the fruits of labour. The flâneur, as is well known, makes "studies". On this subject, the nineteenth-century Larousse has the following to say: "His eyes open, his ear ready, searching for something entirely different from what the crowd gathers to see. A word dropped by chance will reveal to him one of those character traits that cannot be invented and that must be drawn directly from life; ... most men of genius were great flâneurs – but industrious, productive flâneurs ..." (Benjamin 1999, [M20a,1] 454).

How, then, does the *flâneur* see the city? Here we can turn to Benjamin in his extended studies of the character, related to his reading of Charles Baudelaire. Benjamin's major unfinished work, *The Arcades Project*, devotes an entire section to the *flâneur* (Convolute M: The Flâneur; Benjamin 1999, 417-55), placing him alongside such phenomena as fashion (Convolute B); iron construction (Convolute F); prostitution, gambling (Convolute O); and photography (Convolute Y). Indeed, the *flâneur* is understood as a phenomenon.

> Preformed in the figure of the flâneur is that of the detective. The flâneur required a social legitimation of his habitus. It suited him very well to see his indolence presented as a plausible front, behind which, in reality, hides the riveted attention of an observer who will not let the unsuspecting malefactor out of his sight (Benjamin 1999 [M13a,2] 442).

The dilettante wanderer is an unlikely hero for a writer associated so strongly with the left, Adorno and the Frankfurt school. His concern, however, is to show that there is joy and comfort to be found of the urban environment. Far from decrying the modern city as inhuman, Benjamin celebrates its anonymity, the way in which one can be lost and at home in a crowded street or on public transport. The *flâneur* is a figure who understands this sheer enjoyability of the modern city – the exhilaration, and display, of promenading to see and be seen. It is all part of the urban character. The *flâneur* inscribes upon the city, writing rather than reading it. This is an important distinction: his spectatorship is an active one, which imposes his will upon the city streets, creating a narrative as he goes along. In what follows we shall see that different modalities of being in the environment contribute to different understandings of inscribing and of spectatorship. It is important to understand that practices of reception can be as creative as those that inscribe in the first place.

Flânerie as a thinking tool

> "Sous les pavés, la plage."
> [Beneath the paving stones, the beach.]
> Situationist slogan, Anonymous, c. 1968.

Flânerie has long been regarded as a creative tool. Francesco Careri of Stalker, a contemporary Italian interdisciplinary urban workshop group, establishes a trajectory for the use of this tool from the Dada anti-art movement, through Surrealism, the Situationist and Fluxus movements to the work of Robert Smithson and Richard Long (Careri 2002). Some of the best documented examples are found in the works of the Situationist International with the notion of *dérive* or drift.

As one among various Situationist methods, *dérive* is a technique of transient passage through varied ambiences. The *dérive* entails playful-constructive behaviour and an awareness of psychogeographical effects, which distinguishes it from classical notions of the journey and the stroll.

> In a *dérive* one or more persons during a certain period drop their usual motives for movement and action, their relations, their work and leisure activities, and let themselves be drawn by the attractions of the terrain and the encounters they find there. The element of chance is less determinant than one might think: from a *dérive* point of view cities have a psychogeographical relief, with constant currents, fixed points and vortexes which

strongly discourage entry into or exit from certain zones (Guy Debord, *Theory of the Dérive*, in Andreotti and Costa 1996, 22).

The Situationist drifting strategy is closely tied to their notion of psychogeography (Sadler 1998). This refers to an exploration of the hidden, non-physical connections between spaces, and of the patterns of desire within a space. The group produced a number of psychogeographic maps, most notably *The Naked City* (1957) by Guy Debord and Asger Jorn, in which patches of a map of Paris were collaged with variously sized arrows including images of war and colonialism, postage stamps and a text which read 'Life continues to be free and easy'. Each map represents a drift taken by Debord and his colleagues through Paris – a series of connections that cannot be adequately represented on a standard plan of the city (Debord 1994; McDonough 2002). This drifting strategy is clearly related to *flânerie* as defined by Benjamin. It is important to stress that the movement involved is far from random. It is rather guided by various attractions and spectacles and how these act upon the drifter. I undertook a similar traversal of urban space in Tokyo, and the accompanying notations and drawings are largely the result of the various attractions and repulsions as I made my way through Shinjuku station.

The theory of the *dérive* informed much of the work of the Situationist International and beyond. An example is the work of the artist-architect Constant. Constant took the central theme of the drift and incorporated it into his attempts to create a 'unitary urbanism' based upon a view of the future in which humanity would be released from the burdens of work and accordingly free to play and occupy space however and whenever desired. This rather naïve notion gave dwelling the same weight as running and skipping, and represents a fundamental if impracticable challenge to traditional notions of architecture. It lay behind his plans and models for New Babylon – a proposition for a Situationist city, whose entire structure could be reconfigured according to the whims of its inhabitants.[1] From an architectonic perspective, indeed, the intent behind the project is of greater interest than the megalithic structures of his imaginary city, which hearken to the greatest excesses of modernism rather than, as Constant intended, railing against them.

The Situationist *dérive* may be contrasted with the Dadaist excursions to banal places, the Surrealist reconfiguration of the city through games, and Fluxus street-theatre and happenings. The aesthetic and creative implications of *flânerie* and similar wayfaring in urban situations are quite different from those encountered in what Careri (2002) calls 'wilderness', as it figures for example in the work of Richard Long. The sense of isolation in the city is of an entirely different quality from that found in the wilderness. Careri holds that the wilderness walk degrades and fades with the passing of time, whereas the urban walk perpetuates its memory in the walkers and the traces they leave behind, be they representations, reconfigured maps, or the memories of participants who may or may not have been passers-by.[2] The defining

---

1   De Zegher and Wigley (2001) and Wigley (1998) present this project, and its aims and implications, in great detail.

2   In fact by 'wilderness', Careri is referring more often than not to 'rural' and hence managed landscapes.

features of the urban walk lie in the apparatus of memory and in interaction with others who may be neither aware of nor implicated in one's actions. The *flâneur*, after all, walks to be observed, as well as to observe others. The key difference is in duration: engagement with others in the city is immediate and primarily with human observers (wildlife in the city, though present, is rarely acknowledged). Outside the urban environment, by contrast, engagements with other walkers can carry on over seasons or even years.

Engagements with the city

The leading Surrealist writer and poet Louis Aragon has given one of that movement's most coherent expositions of Paris, the focus of so much of their attention. *Paris Peasant* is a novel, but seeks to be neither a coherent narrative nor a character study. Aragon chooses to examine a small part of the city with which he is well acquainted and particularly interested: this is an arcade, the Passage de l'Opera, which was under threat at the time of Aragon's writing in 1926.

> How oddly this light suffuses the covered arcades which abound in Paris in the vicinity of the main boulevards and which are rather disturbingly named *passages*, as though no one had the right to linger for more than an instant in those sunless corridors (Aragon 1994, 13-14).

The novel combines observations of this place with excerpts from advertising or price-lists from restaurants and bars (ibid., 78-9), street signs (165) and newspaper clippings (32); all of which conform to the model of the *flâneur* and wanderer who allows the mundane and banal to grab his attention with the same fascination and ferocity as the unusual and the freakish. The gaze that Aragon turns on the Passage de l'Opera is at times disinterested or directed towards a spectacle, and at other times fully engaged towards others: indeed, while Aragon ostensibly crafts a portrait of the city of Paris, the ultimate effect of his writing is to compose a self-portrait, to give an account of himself and how it is that he, by turns, engages and disengages, physically and socially, with his chosen environment. As an actor in this place – that is to say, as an individual *with agency* – he understands the 'original' environment with a degree of neutrality:

> There is nothing more mysterious than these curious slatted shutters, set into the walls above the baths, which allow communication between the adjoining cabins in many of the Parisian establishments (those of the Rue Fontaine, the Rue Cardinet, the Rue Cambracéres, for example). No one is suggesting that the architect foresaw the use that would be made of these fittings: could the engineer who drew up the plans for the Pont de Solférino have had an inkling of the debaucheries that his arches would one day shelter? The simple hearts of architects are free of all perversity (Aragon 1994, 57).

Figure 12.1 Parisian passage

One anthropologist who has sought to understand contemporary space as radically opposed to the environment of the *flâneur* is Marc Augé. Augé's analysis rests on two complementary concepts – non-place and supermodernity. Conceptualized differently from the pre- and early-modernism of Baudelaire and Benjamin, the supermodern is a spatial phenomenon with temporal implications. Supermodernity relies upon ubiquity and evenness of space where events cannot take place and where social activity is confined to narrow channels and stripped of most of its engagement and interaction. This supermodern is exemplified in the contemporary international airport, especially when it is contrasted with the hustle and bustle of its predecessor, the sea-port. Airports present a smooth, secure and undifferentiated space in which little can happen outside of that narrow channel of permissible social activity. As a result we barely interact with such spaces, being held in a disinterested state for the duration of our stay there. While such spaces might be personalized by regular users or workers, the traveller will often identify the chains of coffee shops and other amenities as ubiquitous manifestations that conform to standard expectations. Where airports such as Amsterdam's Schiphol add art galleries and casinos, these can be read as part of the same system, conforming to the non-place rather than reacting against it.

Augé's work draws explicitly on Michel de Certeau's notions of space and place (Augé 1997, 79-95, see Certeau 1984, 117-18). But whereas de Certeau does not set space and place in explicit opposition – seeking merely to differentiate between them – Augé's notions of place and non-place are strongly opposed. This can be seen again in terms of narrowing options and the way in which travel by air or on a motorway strips any quality of place from a locality. Where nods are made in this direction (such as towards boards depicting local wildlife and nearby landmarks used as logos) they reduce locality to pure spectacle. Spectacle was, of course, one of the key concerns of the Situationist International and Guy Debord – and it forms part of a process of urbanization that has its roots in the Parisian arcades and Grands Magasins.

Of particular relevance here is Augé's work on the Paris Metro (Augé 2002). While it might seem at first that these subterranean transportation networks are examples of non-places, Augé argues that the Paris Metro is part of the genuine experience of a city which tourist activities have reduced to a theme-park itinerary of the Eiffel Tower, Arc d'Triomphe, the Louvre, and a number of other clichéd destinations. The mode of transport is, however, more important to Paris as a living, working social space. The Metro shows us the diversity of the city's occupants, and also reveals its differences from other cities such as London, New York, Moscow and Tokyo – all famous for their subways and each with a unique character of their own.

> If we look more closely, we cannot fail to notice that the activities of the subway traveller are numerous and valid. Reading is still prominent among them, mostly (although some lines are more intellectual than others) in the form of comic strips or sentimental novels of the Harlequin genre. Thus adventure, eroticism, or rose water is poured into the solitary hearts of individuals who apply themselves with a pathetic constancy, to sealing themselves off from those around them without missing their stop (Augé 2002, 34).

Before considering other activities that commuters engage in, such as using a walkman or maintaining a stony and stoic silence, Augé cites Georges Perec, who ponders what effect the enforced temporality of subway stops might have upon the reading of the text – how might this fracture control or limit a narrative?

Despite appearing to be a similarly controlled space to the airport non-place, with its atemporality[3] and immunity to the time of day, week, month or season, the subway is in reality a distinctly 'anthropological place' (Augé 1997, 42) varying in character from the first train in the morning (Augé 2002, 31) to the rush-hours, to the daytime and then evening trains. Thus the place varies over time, bringing different travellers to their destinations as diverse social groups and individuals go about their daily routines. This resembles Augé's exemplar for anthropological space, the marketplace, which is only identified as such when it is actually happening; at other times it might not be a marketplace but a city square, car-park or some other windswept expanse.

Getting lost in Tokyo

The metro is but one example, of course – and it leads me to consider its relation to my own project in the Tokyo subway. The terms of my exploration were similarly poetic and personal in their intention, even if my purpose and experience there differed greatly (after all, Augé's portrait of the Metro is drawn from a lifetime's travelling on it, whereas I was a novice visitor – an outsider in terms of both nationality and purpose). It was an experience of running counter to the system, being out of place, but this also gave the project something rather tangible to hold on to.

The city of Tokyo is organized on principles founded in the unique co-operative competition of Japanese corporations which combine their economic might with a social role, often providing financial services, childcare and even local government and broadcasting within private megastructures. It is this mix of activities in the city and, as I discovered, in the subway stations themselves that makes *flânerie* possible. The connection between modes of urban wandering and the urban environment in Tokyo is illustrated by the arrangement of subway stops, which are often conjoined with department stores. The city is structured as a number of smaller cities, each with its own centre based around a transportation, economic and social hub. Standing in for town-halls, these hubs have their left-over spaces, which substitute for town squares. The space around Shibuya station is one example. Hachiko[4] square serves as the meeting point for nights out in the ward as well as attracting hopeful rock bands that come to busk or simply to play for the joy of it. Other sides of the station attract street vendors, break-dancers and motorcycle gangs in what would fail any

---

3   This is again with reference to the commuter and irregular traveller. Given that place is a category defined by the action of people on a locality, the quality of placelessness is variable.

4   Hachiko was a professor's dog who waited on his master at the station every day. After his owner's death, Hachiko continued to return, waiting there every day. Commuters fed Hachiko with rice cakes and sushi until he eventually died. A statue was erected of the loyal Akita in the square in front of Shibuya station, that now bears his name.

architectural examination for the design of an effective urban environment with a social aspect to it. Different parts of Tokyo offer even more extreme examples of what should not work, but somehow does. Ikebukuro station and its Seibu department store have a rich social life which is far less teenager-oriented than Shibuya, but which nevertheless is understood to confer a strong and worthwhile local identity on those who participate in it.

My series of drawings, *Getting Lost in Tokyo* has its origins in two trips I made to the city, in January 2003 and 2004 (Lucas 2004; 2008). These trips were ostensibly tourist journeys to a place that has long fascinated me. It was in part Chris Marker's cinematic travelogue and search for images of beauty and happiness, *Sans Soleil*, which finally persuaded me to go. I arrived as a traveller who, though moderately informed, had no contacts or real working knowledge of the language or customs of the place. My visits to Tokyo responded to my reading of theories of *flânerie*, Situationist drift and spectacle. And of the many experiences that flowed from them, one stood out as especially interesting – that of travelling the subway and, in particular, negotiating the massive interchange stations such as Shibuya or Shinjuku, the station at the heart of this project, which has some seventy exits to the surface. Navigating these stations raised numerous questions – not least of which was 'how is it even possible to negotiate this place?' What are the characteristics of the Tokyo subway as distinct from those, say, of Paris, London and New York?

A traditional map or plan of this space is of no help in understanding or finding the way; so how do the many thousands of commuters and other users actually manage it on a regular basis? How did I manage it? Given my particular circumstances as a foreigner without any real intention or purpose, I ran counter to the flow of people in the place, when sampled in and out of the legendary rush-hour crushes. Reconstructing from memory my experience of using Shinjuku station, I found it was best represented by a flowchart diagram. This allowed me to include all the journeys I made through the space, including finding my way, getting lost, exiting or just passing through to change lines. This flowchart fragmented the account into episodes – each distinct from one another, and not tied to a specified place. The episodic nature of the flowchart allowed a complex and non-fixed totality to be broken down into manageable chunks.

This theme of the manageability of the environment runs through the work as a whole. The primary purpose of the episodic division was to allow each smaller element to be presented in Laban notation. This is a system of notation most commonly used in dance choreography to trace the movements of the dancer. In it, time is read from bottom to top, and the central vertical line represents the vertical axis of the body. The shapes on either side notate the actions of particular parts of the body as (in this case) it moves through and touches the train. The diagrams show that movement is complex, iterative and variable, and we can begin to see how notation itself can be a rather radical gesture. Each notation in the series describes the way every action impacts upon the body during its passage through the subway station.

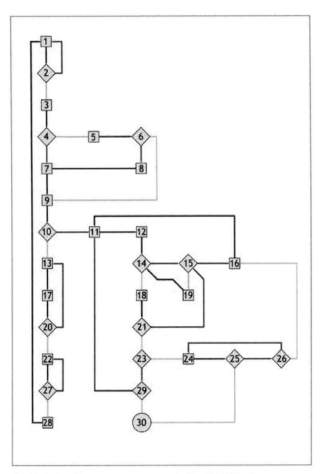

1. Stay on the train.
2. Is this your stop?
3. Stand up and wait at door.
4. Is someone else at the door?
5. Wait on them opening the door.
6. Do they open the door?
7. Press the door release.
8. Mutter, grumble and complain.
9. Exit train.
10. Are you changing lines?
11. Locate exit sign.
12. Move in the direction indicated.
13. Locate transfer sign.
14. Is there another sign?
15. Is there a transfer sign?

16. Find an open space.
17. Move in the direction indicated.
18. Move in the direction indicated.
19. Move away from that crowd.
20. Are you at the correct platform?
21. Is there another sign?
22. Wait for the train to arrive.
23. Is there more than one sign?
24. Select an exit sign.
25. Does this exit lead out?
26. Have you tried other options?
27. Has the train arrived?
28. Board the train.
29. Does this exit lead out?
30. Exit station.

Figure 12.2 Flowchart diagram from *Getting Lost in Tokyo*

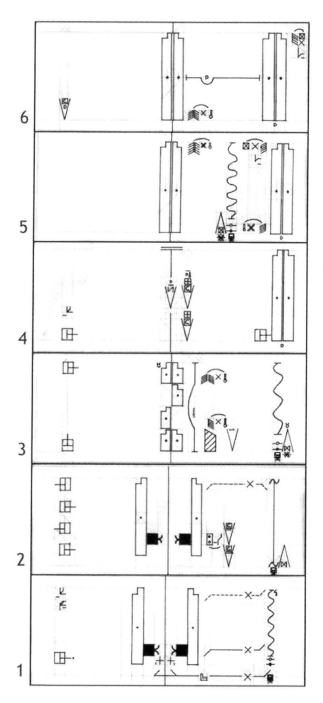

Figure 12.3 Sample of Laban notation from *Getting Lost in Tokyo*

Upon further analysis, this series of notations threw up several recurring motifs – elements from the journey that were common concerns. Out of the thirty episodes, fifteen motifs recurred in the notation, though appearing in varying degrees, positions and relationships. This repetition led me to consider the next step, the use or even *detournement* (Situationist-style misappropriation) of architectural drawing conventions. Since my aim was to reconstruct an experience within an actual architectural space, I had to avoid any attempt to reconstruct the actual plan of Shinjuku station. Adopting the projective conventions of axonometric drawing, I forced each event into a narrow corridor that represents the passage of time. I made no attempt to modulate the lighting of the space, such as placing it in north- or south-facing contexts, nor did I give any suggestion of artificial or sky-lighting. The form alone was depicted in the drawing. This enhances the feeling of non-place. Plan and section would have made it much easier to 'design in' such orientation, but I chose instead to impose a diagram – specifically a labyrinth (as opposed to a maze). The longest route within this space is taken by the labyrinth path, which spirals towards a centre. This deliberately recalls Tarkovsky's *Stalker*, where the destination is visible at most times, but only the semi-supernatural guide of the Stalker can navigate its hidden traps and pitfalls (Tarkovsky 1986).

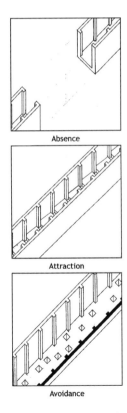

Absence

Attraction

Avoidance

Figure 12.4 Building block archetypes from *Getting Lost in Tokyo*

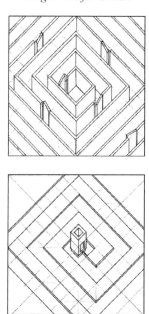

Figure 12.5 The Labyrinthine Zone arrangement derived from Tarkovsky's film *Stalker*, from *Getting Lost in Tokyo*

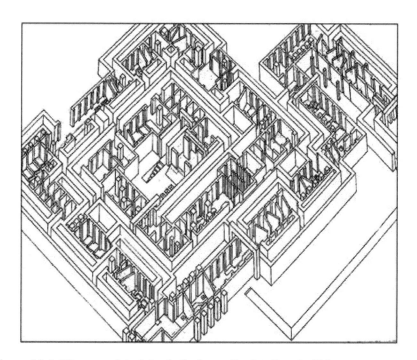

Figure 12.6 The complete labyrinth, from *Getting Lost in Tokyo*

The labyrinth

A drawing of the entire labyrinth shows us the ultimate alternative to the series. The episodic nature of the series allows us to understand one thing at a time, savouring and understanding each detail and decision, while not being overwhelmed by the totality. Indeed the drawing series could be offered as one way of answering the question 'how is it possible for a newcomer to learn how to negotiate this vast complex space, which is constantly changing with the ebb and flow of the crowds of rushing but ever polite commuters?' We can cope with one or two episodes at once, but not all thirty and not all of the possible permutations of decisions.

> The city is the realisation of that ancient dream of humanity, the labyrinth. It is this reality to which the flâneur, without knowing it, devotes himself. Without knowing it; yet nothing is more foolish than the conventional thesis which rationalises his behaviour, and which forms the uncontested basis of that voluminous literature that traces the figure and demeanour of the flâneur – the thesis, namely, that the flâneur has made a study of the physiognomic appearance of people in order to discover their nationality and social station, character and destiny, from a perusal of their gait, build and play of features. The interest in concealing the true motives of the flâneur must have been pressing indeed to have occasioned such a shabby thesis (Benjamin 1999 [M6a,4] 429).

> The masses in Baudelaire. They stretch before the flâneur as a veil: they are the newest drug for the solitary. – Second, they efface all traces of the individual: they are the newest asylum for the reprobate and the postscript. – Finally, within the labyrinth of the city, the masses are the newest and most inscrutable labyrinth. Through them, previously unknown chthonic traits are imprinted on the image of the city (Benjamin 1999 [M16,3] 447).

The horror of the totality is represented by the Tarkovskyan labyrinth, where the path to the desired centre is always clear, but can be found only by those initiated in the ways of the Zone and who can avoid its invisible dangers.

The more a source is inscribed, the more meaning accumulates. But what is the result of this accumulation? This interpretation of a distinctly urban event provided me with challenges that other exercises have not. Departing from the concentration in traditional architectural drawing upon static fixtures, I could render such things as the distraction of attention by advertising and signage, the movement of crowds against and towards your destination, and the way in which one negotiates a space. My aim was to explore the difference between this use of architectural notation and the drawing conventions traditionally used in design and construction. What is also shown, through the drawing series, is how much more there is to architectural experience than what is normally depicted in its representations – including architectural photography – which are normally devoid of any signs of occupation. By representing other concerns than the play of solid and void, we broaden the scope of what architecture and our experience of the city can be.

Figure 12.7 Examples of photographs, from *Getting Lost in Tokyo*

Inscribing the city in this way is more than a method to represent experience. There are more direct ways in which this could have been achieved, for example through prose writing or making a documentary video. The point of working in this way, through diagram, notation, drawing and photography, was to understand the experience more fully. Inscription, then, is itself a learning process.

Walking is such a fundamental human practice that it cannot fail to inform our other activities. Art, architecture and other creative practices are no different. The brief outline presented here covers only a small sample of a very large body of artistic walking. The picturesque landscape might indeed be regarded as an earlier version of the same thing, though located in the wilderness rather than the city. The particular conditions of the city require different approaches, however. As the artists reviewed above discovered, urban wandering demands different forms of representation. Taking a line for a walk, as Paul Klee described drawing, conceptualizes the surface as a territory on which one *can* walk. This is to understand artistic practice in terms of everyday common experience. What I am suggesting here is that different modes of walking involve the territory of both surfaces – of the landscape and of an artistic medium such as canvas or paper – in interesting and novel ways.

A different concept of territory is suggested by the city than by the rural or wilderness environment. It would still of course be possible to depict the contemporary city in ways ordered by Romantic landscape or Renaissance courtly painting traditions, but this would be knowingly to misappropriate forms from another context. Armed with an attitude towards such things, the artist, architect or anthropologist can make self-conscious choices regarding the representation and inhabitation of the territories of their chosen practice, be that the city itself or a sheet of paper.

References

Andreotti, L. and Costa, X. (1996), *Theory of the Dérive and Other Situationist Writings on the City* (Barcelona: Museu d'Art Contemporani).

Aragon, L. (1994), *Paris Peasant* (London: Jonathan Cape).

Augé, M. (1997), *Non-places: Introduction to an Anthropology of Supermodernity* (London: Verso).

—— (2002), *In the Metro*, trans. T. Conley (Minneapolis: University of Minnesota Press).

Baudelaire, C. (1970), *Paris Spleen*, trans. L. Varése (New York: New Directions).

Benjamin, W. (1997), *Charles Baudelaire*, trans. H. Zohn (London: Verso).

—— (1999), *The Arcades Project*, trans. H. Eiland and K. McGlaughlin (Cambridge, MA: Belknap Press of Harvard University Press).

Careri, F. (2002), *Walkscapes: Walking as an Aesthetic Practice* (Barcelona: Gustavo Gili Land and Scape Series).

Certeau, M. de (1984), *The Practice of Everyday Life* (Berkeley: University of California Press).

Debord, G. (1994), *The Society of the Spectacle*, trans. D. Nicholson Smith (New York: Zone Books).

Ingold, T. (2007), *Lines: A Brief History* (London: Routledge).

Klee, P. (1961), *Notebooks, Volume 1: The Thinking Eye*, J. Spiller (ed.), trans. R. Manheim (London: Lund Humphries).

Lucas, R. (2004), 'Inscribing the City: A Flâneur in Tokyo', *Anthropology Matters Journal* 6:1.

—— (2008), 'Getting Lost in Tokyo', *Footprint* 2.

McDonough, T. (ed.) (2002), *Guy Debord and the Situationist International: Texts and Documents* (Cambridge, MA: MIT Press, October Books).

Sadler, S. (1998), *The Situationist City* (Cambridge, MA: MIT Press).

Tarkovsky, A. (1986), *Sculpting in Time* (Austin: University of Texas Press).

Tester, K. (ed.) (1994), *The Flâneur* (London: Routledge).

Wigley, M. (1998), *Constant's New Babylon: The Hyper-Architecture of Desire* (Rotterdam: 010 Publishers).

Zegher, C. de and Wigley, M. (eds) (2001), *The Activist Drawing: Retracing Situationist Architectures from Constant's New Babylon to Beyond* (Cambridge, MA: MIT Press and New York: The Drawing Center).

Chapter 13

A Collectable Topography: Walking, Remembering and Recording Mountains

Hayden Lorimer and Katrín Lund

Introduction – the circuitry of collecting

Of collecting as a propensity peculiar to humans, the novelist John Fowles had little good to say.[1] Among collectors great and small, his most forceful rebuke was saved for those whose habit it is to acquire things from the natural world. In one sense at least, Fowles' criticism was well directed. He could write from personal experience. As a child he had been an avid butterfly collector. Thinking these boyish days long gone and enjoying the spread of middle age, the sight of a rare Monarch butterfly prompted in him an uncontrollable urge to give chase. Shocked (albeit in a most writerly manner), he found himself racing not towards the fragile quarry but instead towards a 'continent of buried memories' and the 'whole series of blind attitudes to nature' which the passion for collecting had fostered in him.

> This illustrates perfectly the deformation, the blindness, brought about by the hobby attitude to nature. It turns nature into a sort of golf-course where you go to amuse yourself at weekends; into the mirror in which you flaunt your skill at naming. It drains nature of its complexity, of its richness, of its poetries, of its symbolisms and correspondences, of its power to arouse emotion – of all its potential centrality in human existence. And far worse than the damage it does to the misguided natural historian is the damage it does to the vast majority who are neutral or indifferent towards nature. If this is the one avenue of approach, then it is no wonder they shrug and turn away (Fowles 1984, 83).

Fiercely protective of the pristine encounter, Fowles was quick to dismiss populist renderings of nature as too imposing, reductive and vulgar, 'miserably retarded' or worse still, a 'lethal perversion'. Misanthropy would, of course, secure for Fowles a certain notoriety. Aloofness and pomposity aside, what is of chief interest is his insistence that an elevated appreciation of nature is commonly subordinate to what he perceived as a much diminished, lesser form of knowing. His message was clear: for as long as the conceptual urge to classify, document, list and tick prevailed, our common response to nature would be much the poorer. 'Not so!', we would respond,

1   Thanks to the individual walkers and hill walking clubs who in their welcome and hospitality made this research possible. Thanks to Tim Ingold for advice and insight and to Felix Driver for his comments on an earlier conference version of this chapter. The research reported here is drawn from an ESRC Research Award (Ref: R000223603).

as these provocations have a direct bearing on this chapter and its consideration of
how walking and collecting correspond as forms of social encounter. In it we wish
to reveal a more complex weave where collecting happens on foot in the midst of
epistemic ambition, and emotional and embodied response.

Fowles' essay offers further critical resources to think with. The 'blinded eye',
which gave his piece its title, is a reminder of how the collector's passion for amassing
things has, at its centre, a powerful optic. A collection is, first and foremost, something
treasured by being seen. To appreciate collecting we need to learn to see things
through the eye of the beholder. Once put on display these assemblies are truly the
objects of our gaze. Visibility notwithstanding, a collection also has tactile appeal.
Securing ownership can confer exclusive rights to the sensations of touch. We might
recognize this as an acquisitive claim: '*I* have and *I* hold' (Blom 2003). Among those
who possess – and those entrusted to curate, value or admire – the possibility of
physical contact with a collection's contents is a privilege. Meanwhile, across diverse
collecting communities, tasks of judgement, organization, inspection, preservation,
re-inspection and comparison happen as a series of correspondences between nimble
hands and discriminating eyes. Our codification of each of these perceptual exercises
as visual-*manual* could easily pass without comment. In much recent academic
literature it is often assumed that haptic awareness is experienced through the work
of fingers, thumbs and palms. For commentators on collecting, likewise, the circuitry
of cognition remains resolutely heady stuff. Strains of psychoanalysis have pushed
the desire to accumulate downwards. In this presentation, we want to descend further
still, to bodily extremities. Taking up Tim Ingold's (2004) invitation to better fuse
cognition and locomotion, we want to prioritize patterns of collecting behaviour first
encountered through toes, heels and soles, and to consider what happens – and what
difference it makes – when feet make collecting possible.

Collecting as a topographical tradition

The collectibles underfoot, and under scrutiny here, are 284 mountain summits in
Scotland, each one rising to an elevation of at least 3,000 feet (914 metres) above
sea level. As physical places they differ greatly in appearance and character: ranging
from rocky peaks and rounded tops to the flattened highpoints of rolling, expansive
plateaus. As objects of interest, these mountain summits fall into an unusual category
for the collector. Thanks to laws of gravity and open public access, they cannot
be physically moved or completely withdrawn from general circulation by private
ownership. As immovable artefacts, it is fair to say that Scotland's mountains are a
democratic space for collecting.

In aggregate, the mountains are commonly known as 'The Munros', after Sir
Hugh Munro, mountaineer and landowner, who originally drew up the system of
classification based on an altitudinal mark during the 1880s. Combining labours in
footwork, mapwork and draughtsmanship he made a significant contribution to the
topographical surveying of the Scottish Highlands. Although in its execution the
project was demandingly muscular, Munro's production of a series of topographical
'Tables', standardized according to altitude and regional section, was driven in equal

measure by his ambition to advance scientific knowledge. Munro did not foresee in his classificatory system for topography any mass recreational appeal, nor did his fellow pioneers of the Scottish Mountaineering Club who underwrote the survey exercise and published its results. Today, those who collect the Munros number in the tens of thousands, and are not limited to people resident in Scotland. The Scottish Mountaineering Club has continued to administer Munro's Tables, retaining overall responsibility for various programmes of revision prompted by technological change leading to improved surveying and cartographic techniques. That topographical 'facts' are sanctioned through a continuous institutional arrangement has been important in cementing the system's historic status (Lorimer and Lund, 2003). While the Munros are a collection that cannot be housed in conventional terms, the founding systematic structure does have a recognized spiritual-institutional home. Managerially, the upkeep of the Tables is no insignificant task. Once mountains have been awarded Munro status and 'promoted' to the Tables (or have lost their status and been removed) this decision is quickly reflected in the number of walkers and climbers who choose to make an ascent. Footpaths become visible on mountainsides from afar where once any obvious route of ascent might have been difficult to discern. Erosion and water-logging occur in places where they had never before been in evidence (Access Forum 2000). Thus, categorical decisions taken in the committee room have an immediate environmental impact.

Today, as a semi-formalized and nationally arranged mechanism that enables people to organize the way they climb mountains, Munro's Tables have no obvious rival (though for comparative cultures, see Solnit 2000). As a community with a shared recreational passion, walkers-cum-collectors are richly diverse and self-differentiating. Long before academic analysis intervened, 'Munroists' had their very own politics of identity and position. To claim that you are 'doing the Munros' is considered by some to be too explicit and naked a statement of intent. It burdens walking with anxieties about failing to meet expectations, and can be unhelpfully self-regulating in decisions about *what* mountain should be climbed. For those among whom either an acquisitive impulse or a competitive streak burns most intensely, the term 'Munro-bagger' is saved. The label conjures up a character who takes a perfectly acceptable exercise and seeks 'to have it all done with' in far too much of a hurry. Not quite a slur on character, but not wholly complimentary either, the label 'bagger' is one that few walkers willingly volunteer in self-description. Given the possibility of such stigma, walkers can be guarded or veiled about their collecting in any presentation of self. What they offer are less direct explanations or motivations for spending time in the mountains. Fuller commentaries on collecting can be the stuff of the quieter confessional. In company it is commonly preferable to cultivate the status of the lapsed collector, the reluctant collector, or the self-parodying collector. Efforts to collect the Munros are often relegated to a side-project. Careful to evade their own typologies, walkers are reluctant to ascribe a single purpose or priority to walking-collecting. Many identify shifting sorts of significance across years, and decades, of walking. Commonly a narrative emerges of initial youthful urgency to build up a collection that gradually dissipates into a 'more mature' form of conduct less driven and given to suffocating regulation. Equally, it is not unknown for walkers to claim a loss of interest in the overall collecting 'game', or to have abandoned any hope of completion, while continuing secretively to accrue summits.

The Munros are *the* significant phenomenon of Scotland's mountain leisure scene: whether considered as a great secular pilgrimage, as a rising environmental issue, as something bordering on an obsessive condition, or as a commercial, marketing opportunity (Highlands and Islands Enterprise 1996; Dempster 1995). Indeed, recognition of the Munros is not restricted to practitioners and active collectors. Markers of the mountains as everyday cultural currency are diverse: posters in public buildings and workplaces encourage people to take the stairs, and so to convert accumulated floors climbed into Munros; weekend weather broadcasts provide specific information on meteorological conditions expected above the 3,000-foot mark; guidebooks and photographic celebrations are staple enough sellers that high street bookstores devote to them prominent and permanent shelf space. This flourishing popular culture of mountains and the diverse stages for its representation could be subject to more detailed review, however in this chapter the material drawn upon – documented during participatory research with hill-walking clubs and groups of 'hill-walkers' – sticks close to the action as it happens on foot. Keeping the company of walkers, and on an equal footing, we want to treat collecting as an open event and an activity in process, rather than as culturally circumscribed or already judged. To achieve this we focus on four pairings of practice which share as their setting the mountain summit: namely, orienting and identifying, accumulating and remembering, completing and fulfilling, and recording and reporting. These four pairings speak of the social worlds, and afterlives, of summits among walker-collectors. In conclusion, we draw attention to how geographies of mountain summit collecting have a different bearing on recent debate concerning the emergent and practice-based nature of seeing, collecting and thinking spatially. So, without further delay, to events on the summit…

Orienting and identifying

In the Old Testament the mountaintop – just like the desert – is a place of revelation and divine intervention. It is a place of dramatic atmospheric extremes that produce before you, perhaps within you, spiritual kinds of vision. But you can also go to summits to take different sorts of measure, and in so doing it seems that sight is the walkers' primary faculty. Seeing 'properly' usually means a halt in progress and seeing to a considerable distance. Thus, summits are the hill-walkers' favourite footrest.

Summits offer a sure and still point amid a day's movement, a place to take the measure of what surrounds, what has been accomplished, and what yet awaits. They allow for a natural hesitation in pedestrian progress, and have come to be understood – at least in British recreational culture – as the morally proper place for pause; or for idling. During precious moments on the mountain summit the character of walking slackens and drifts. No longer unilinear, no longer driven or so fixed in purpose, though no less deliberately styled, here energetic locomotion gives way to wandering. With any urgency to push on temporarily suppressed, and the expectation of still higher ground to come now gone, it is slowness that circumscribes the summit's immediate terrain and its social scene. Wind speeds and other weather conditions permitting, the purpose of the exercise is to take time. Maundering would seldom describe human activity as it happens elsewhere on the great bulk of a mountain. If rest and contemplation are understood to be 'deserved' on summits, what is uppermost in these places is a certain quality of awareness. From summits, people draw in the view through the social practice of orienting and identifying. Among good companions and complete strangers, that view – or the lack of one for that matter – is an easy and wholly acceptable source of casual conversation. While taking in a panorama, exchanges turn comfortably on the identification of ranges and peaks. Imagine, on having reached a summit, overhearing these questions (and answers) of geography:

"What's that big, bulky one way over that way? To the left."
"What one? That one?"
"No. That one. The one with the cloud just covering the top."
"Could it be Creag Meagaidh?"
"No, no, I think it's even further to the left, past the crest rising from the little notch."

There are practical explanations for such dialogue, telling enough in their mundane nature. Ordnance Survey sheet maps of the British landscape are organized into area sections, and thus can only guide the eye so far, and then not by equal distance to all points of the compass. So while orientation is a traditional requirement of safe 'hillcraft', an ability to discriminate between the jumble of shapes and lines, and the risings and fallings of relief silhouetted on the horizon, is also considered a useful social skill. Finding your feet as a hill-walker on Scotland's mountains involves subtle forms of apprenticeship in which topography surfaces as an ever-recurring, common lore. Whether competitive or congenial, the experience of keeping company renders the view from the mountain top as different: looking is produced as a social skill that extends the faculty of seeing. Rather than being an observation point secured for a version of Romantic, gentlemanly solitude, the summit cairn and white-washed concrete triangulation point are instead the setting for comparative, mutually assuring and continuous exercises in the production and performance of landscape (Wood 2001). In short, walkers enjoy sharing in-sights.

This airy social world of summiteering recalls something of the conduct and postures – hand held to shield eyes against the light; strongest eye sighting along the line of a pointing arm; index finger extended and outstretched – that David Matless (1999) uses to explain the term 'outlook geography'. Whereas Matless considers representations of this form of outdoor citizenship, here signature gestures and active responses afforded by a mountaintop setting are drawn from observations of conduct in person. Among walkers, known relief is something stitched together according to the visible landscape: comprised of differing profiles and relative positions of mountains, their clusters of peaks, and intervening stretches of water. Lofty only in terms of height, 'unremarkableness' is the most significant quality in such a performed presentation of geographical knowledge. We might consider this a small skill in the competent craft of the hobbyist (or amateur) geographer: a detailed knowledge of topographical form emerging through physical effort and encounter. In this fashion, geography becomes an exercise in gathering up the experience of having been to a place, or the ability to recognize a place's distinguishing surface features. Tellingly, visual expertise amassed during walking as collecting – *rather* than the details of a person's individual collection – most commonly surfaces in summit-based conversation. Just as it can be considered unseemly or indulgent to detail personal wealth, so collecting etiquette demands that fellow walkers are saved a serial re-count of Munros already 'ticked off'. In company, mountain-tops are enrolled into conversation rather differently. Recognized from unusual aspects, or by familiar angles of approach, or at the peripheries of vision, prominent Munros offer accurate sightlines and feature as waymarkers for pointing fingers and straining eyes. They allow walkers to keep on interrogating a visible landscape as it recedes, range on range, into the distance. Admittedly, this sort of topographical literacy can be articulated in quite peculiar fashion. The Gaelic names of Scottish mountains pose challenges for the majority of walkers who are not Gaelic speakers. Toponymy creates the social conditions for awkward consultation, tentative utterances and mangled pronunciation.

Accumulating and remembering

Evidently, it is not entirely productive to divide meaning stemming from physical presence into two discrete categories, as *either* collective or individualized. Even so, we do need to consider the ways that one person's collection niggles away as a private exercise in accumulation, and can be differently rehearsed during moments of introspection. To recognize this is to re-visit the common observation that 'when we collect, we collect ourselves' and to acknowledge the twist of perspective necessary for a narrative of collecting to be internalized. For the walker in meditative mood, or alone on a summit, the uninterrupted or unexpected view is a chance to remember their collection into being. In search of a way, memory branches out from (or flits between) the places recognized in a personal history. On such occasions, the landscape can be seen in long perspective and measured against the self. When paths previously taken and summits once stood upon are clearly visible, it can be pleasing – or possibly frustrating – to track progress made towards completion. What can be seen, and thereby recalled, are versions of walks in the past. Here, 'storying' with events can render landscape memorable:

> … you can stand on your first Glencoe summit and look around at perhaps forty or fifty peaks, all fairly anonymous. Once you've climbed them, and you revisit that first hill, you stand at the top and you name them all. You often remember the walk up those hills by some of the most trivial things – sometimes it will be the view, other times it will be "the walk where I forgot my gloves", or "where I watched the ptarmigan" or "when you stayed over at my house and we left early".

And so, working in tandem, a sense of direction and a personal collection grow with experience. After all, ascents made can have spanned several decades, will have happened in contrasting seasonal conditions, and the bagging of a 'bonus summit' can have been as much opportunistic as it was pre-planned. Consequently, each walker's collection emerges as a unique constellation of high-altitude points. Were it to be accurately mapped – and such graphic displays *are* preferred by some walkers – each personalized trail would produce a haphazard, criss-crossed, higgledy-piggledy sort of cartographic overlay. When walking and collecting happen in happy combination, a spatiality of practice emerges through circumstantial factors, finds its openings in the chance occurrence *and* is simultaneously propelled by the most careful and choreographic of designs.

To better appreciate the resulting collection is to perceive it as a mobile and contingent phenomenon, something immanent in practice and therefore most satisfying when inspected *in situ*. Across 284 mountain summits the permutations by sight and sequence are almost infinite, presenting opportunities to generate an individual topology: only certain visible peaks or high points in a panorama are 'collectables'; not all will yet have been made meaningful by an ascent; and from any one summit other peaks already climbed will be visible, but not the collection in its entirety. From a collector's singular position on any given day, the collection is a constant but one bound forever to re-occur slightly differently. What appears to the eye is unrepeatable. The experience might be compared to discovering a bookmark in the pages of a novel long since put down and re-shelved; or trying to recall the gist of a conversation broken off at some time previously. You might confidently pick up from where you left off. Or, the narrative may be scarcely familiar. Landscape features, perhaps visible only momentarily, interleave into past episodes of a life. From summits and ridges, a collected landscape is inspected according to different skylines. Thus, assemblies of memories, times and places, clear up or cloud over, according to the unique 'event horizon' of a visible-memorable landscape. Auditing and collation are put to work 'on the hoof' as a series of embodied memories and biographical stories that keep feet and eyes working in tandem. It is unsurprising, then, that for many walkers in Scotland, collecting mountaintops offers up a compelling personification of landscape.

Completing and fulfilling

The possibility of completion is fundamental to the appeal of collecting; just as fears of a collection left incomplete must forever be staved off. Being finite in organization, Hugh Munro's system of classification makes wholeness possible. For those who desire it, there is an end point; for them, from the outset, finality beckons. Scotland's long history of geophysical processes has been kind in this regard. The surface area that the walker must cover is reasonably compact; no mountain being *too* far removed from any other included in the system of classification. A total of 284 summits is commonly judged 'just about right'. For the physically fit and committed hill-walker the Munros neatly encapsulate the art of the possible. By scale, number, elevation, arrangement and extent, they are a collection that *can* be finished, but normally only as a reward for years of persistence and effort. Among walkers there is common satisfaction to be had from steady passage leading towards a goal of comprehensive coverage:

> … you can say, well last year I was on that one, that one and that one, and you can piece together the area you walked and it is like a big jigsaw because you are high up looking at the pieces of the jigsaw and trying to slot them into position.

Of course, completion is not for everyone achievable, or always desirable. One-time baggers can discover that interest dissipates, distractions are found, and other pastimes end up being favoured. Many walkers continue to express great enjoyment in climbing mountains, but find their urge to collect to have waned.

The goal of wholeness can be once again differently figured. All of the mountains are located in the Highlands and Islands – geographical imaginary for a Romantic and elemental version of Scotland – and are thus a draw for those who regard walking as a form of political activism or rural militancy over access rights, and those seeking refuge in a wilderness ethic or supporting campaigns for the restoration of indigenous ecological communities. Geographical lore is reassuring in very different claims to holism. The practice of collecting mountains exerts a significant influence on the cultural formation of Scotland's contemporary landscape. Completion does not always lead directly or ultimately to satisfaction, as many different theories of collecting remind us (Belk 1995). There are different kinds of local response to the predicament of running out of Scottish mountains to climb. Walkers will test their powers of endurance by beginning to collect all over again; and then once again, if necessary. Alternatively, there also exist 'subsidiary' systems of topographical classification for the many hundreds of summits and tops that exist between the heights of 2,500 and 2,999 feet above sea level ('The Corbetts'), and 2,000 and 2,499 feet ('The Donalds'). Some walkers find enjoyment collecting summits from each of the collections simultaneously.

Wholeness is a quality that can be embodied in the collector too. To be 'doing the Munros' is a personal statement that can confer a deep sense of fulfilment to practitioners. This aspect of walking echoes other socio-cultural discourses centring on lifestyle management, and motivational strategies based around personal affirmation through target-setting. 'Achievement' and finding 'closure' figure prominently in walkers' descriptions of how collecting can be formative of the self. The drive to *complete* the set can be differently sourced by walkers. Moral wholesomeness and inner confirmation are, for some, bound up in self-determination and identity formation as a Scot. Here, the rhythmic placement of feet sounds a patriotic beat. Rather like other pedestrian determinations of territorial association – such as the ancient custom of 'beating bounds' (Olwig, this volume) – to traverse the country on foot, and according to its very highest points, is to take a stake in certain versions of nationhood: sometimes intensely felt, at other times more diffuse. As collecting happens, pride in belonging is expressed in terms of the sensations of closeness and familiarity, where feet most meaningfully embody a felt connection to land. Unburdened by heavier academic apparatus, there is a lighter sort of rapture experienced in gathering up 'full' geographical knowledge. Such enchantment can take on more spectacular expression. It is increasingly popular for orchestrated and performed shows of patriotism to mark the ascent of a final Munro. These summit celebrations are likely to enrol different theatrical trappings of certain versions of Scottish identity: bagpipers, kilts, whisky toasts and poetry recitals. Sometimes wittingly ironic, occasionally subversive, these heightened expressions of belonging are nevertheless communal investments in the national idea.

If any single summit can offer to a day's walk an end in itself, we must note how it is that walking-collecting as a hobby can be the *means* to wholly different kinds of destination. The places we walk towards need not be identified by claims to sovereignty, or referenced by northing and easting. There is a distant, horizon-hovering openness – a less locatable *elsewhere* – produced in the experience of walking-cum-collecting that enables people to raise to consciousness an aspirant version of their self. Walking is often explained in generative, hopeful terms: taking people on a journey that leads at least part-way towards greater personal security, reviving lapsed aspirations and life ambitions. Most obviously, mountain landscapes are therapeutic, places where people go to put their self more in tune with what are commonly perceived as the timeless rhythms, elements, volumes and surfaces of wild, romantic nature. In such visits, however infrequent or weekend-based, there is the promise of a higher life. Counter-intuitively, belonging and security can be qualities found in places that are *elsewhere*. This form of emotional comfort is not simply a matter of losing your sense of place, nor is there a need for 'non-place' to bring it about. Elsewhere can simply mean landscapes that are *not* workaday. Less obliquely, and certainly more candidly, the Munros are a socially acceptable alternative to placing an ad in the personal columns. If collecting is a subtext, then mountains are the substrate beneath people's longing for love, affection, friendship or a soulmate. Passage on foot presents precious time and the social space for getting to know others, for feeling accepted and for fitting in. Many walkers collect so they can feel (a little more) whole again.

Recording and reporting

For mountaineers and hill-walkers the actual practice of keeping count of the contents of a collection is, on the whole, a domestic affair. Ordinarily, recording the details from a recent outing, and thereby formally cataloguing any new bounty of mountaintops, is an exercise undertaken from the comfort of home. The material form that any collection takes can vary greatly from one to another, and that form has direct bearing on the amount of experiential detail each person chooses to document. At a bare minimum, the accepted practice of acquisition is to record the mountain's name in a notebook, perhaps marking a tick alongside. To such a modest gesture of territorial conquest might then be added: the date of ascent for any peak, the entire distance covered during that day's outing, weather conditions encountered, walking companions and further descriptive notes. For this purpose, many Munroists keep a traditional logbook. Some versions have been designed and published for this specific purpose (for example Butterfield and Baines 1992). Comparably, *The Munros* (Bennet 1999) – the recognized guidebook to climbing Scotland's highest mountains published under the auspices of the Scottish Mountaineering Club – is a recognized source text in which handwritten notes can be added in the marginalia. As a complement, walkers might choose to decorate part of the house (normally a kitchen or study wall) with a custom-made Munroist's map, on which progress is charted by inserting differently-coloured drawing pins. More creative, personal, exercises in documentation and display include scrapbooks, painting or sketch pads and photograph albums, each capturing certain pictorial aspects of successful ascents (Rose 2003). Other walkers have embraced new media and technologies as an alternative means to catalogue achievement. Basic spreadsheets or more elaborate data storage packages are used to keep collections on personal computer. Having the advantage of being transferable for safe keeping in multiple locations, virtual personal property is considered an effective insurance against 'loss' through fire, flood or virus. Recently, personal web-pages arranged to display photo essays from 'bagging' expeditions have become a more explicitly public forum for the presentation of a personal collection. Very few Munroists, it should be noted, are confident enough to entrust their collection to memory alone. Even for the most avid collector recollections of times and places past can slowly erode and thin. Once discrete, outings begin to fuse together, and uneventful climbs lose what little they once held by way of definition. Consequently, worrisome doubts can creep in about having actually been to a particular mountaintop in the first place: 'Me? There? But when?' The play of memory and landscape is always capricious.

Diverse in format, though in character mostly humble and homemade, the material culture of Munro-bagging is a constituent part of the outdoor community's collecting practice. As collections go, what then remains of the many walks undertaken might only amount to sparse textual, or selective visual testimony from a multitude of past experiences. Yet the social functions that these forms of documentation come to serve are little different from those served by more conventional categories of collection in which the material objects acquired are essential, and more immediately proximate, to the endeavour. The prospect of imaginary return to mountain summits is all-important. For some collectors of mountains, the satisfaction taken in compiling a log remains a modest, personal business, with any review of its contents considered an occasional treat, or guilty pleasure. Even so, certain knowledge of the catalogue's continued existence and safe-keeping is essential. If not always the primary locus of memory, it is considered no less than a record of a life. The prospect of undertaking different kinds of excursion can be a different temptation. Some walkers find enjoyment in frequent logbook consultations and inventory updates. Munro-bagging has its own sub-culture of enthusiasts for whom facts are an added bonus from walks, and the more arcane numerical aspects of their pastime are a source of intense interest. Thus recreational book-keeping offers an entry to harmless kinds of diversion based on the statistical analysis of aggregated walking effort. According to different variables (such as car mileage incurred to undertake walks, miles covered underfoot, seasons and calendar months of the year, the frequency of summit views, walking companions, and annual rates of summit acquisition) whole new lists and matters of fact can be extrapolated, and with them additional layers of personal meaning (Campbell 1999). Much of this is esoteric stuff, shot through with a vein of knowing and playful self parody. Walkers-cum-collectors fuel their passion for number games, and celebrate the cultish absurdities of 'Munrology' in the (now web-based) fanzine *The Angry Corrie*.

Ticking a list or keeping a logbook is, of course, done in anticipation of the final mountain walk when a collection will be complete. Considerable encouragement is derived from the fact that a formal mechanism exists to report one's eventual arrival at this personal landmark. Since demand grew in the late 1970s, on completion of the Munros walkers have been welcome to write to the Scottish Mountaineering Club requesting that their name be added to the 'Register of Munroists'. Each walker receives a letter of acknowledgement assigning them a number on the register and thus personal achievement is indexed alongside a college of past and present peers. An ethic of trust prevails in the protocol for reporting a finish 'of the round'. No personal testimonials are taken, and the credibility of any claim is not open to question; in effect walkers are accountable only to themselves. Naturally, some walkers on completing the Munros have no desire to go public with their achievement, and do not join the register. At the last reported count the number of walkers, past and present, to have completed had already surpassed the three thousand mark. The number of walkers completing each year has grown exponentially in the past two decades.

Conclusion – collecting cultures

In this chapter's four pairings of summit-oriented social practice we have tried to respond to two connected questions posed at the outset: namely, how does collecting happen whilst people walk, and how, exactly, is it embodied? As an inquiry into the optics and mechanics of collecting in the open air, we have been mindful of the suggestion of Driver and Martins (2002) that greater efforts be made to 'restore the eye to the body'. Consequently, we have focused on modalities of seeing, feeling and moving that occur as people collect mountain summits during passage on foot. By way of conclusion, three more general points can be sketched out. The first is concerned with the inseparability of the practices of walking and looking; the second, with the continuing social life of collections, and the third with the novelty of spatial formations revealed through 'The Munros' as a specific, sited culture of walking-cum-collecting.

First, while it is difficult to individualize the crowded summit scene, it *is* possible to ground experience and to situate particular versions of seeing geographically. Observant kinds of participation, founded in ethnographic method, are a significant advance here, especially in the light of existing scholarship in geography and cognate disciplines. For very different sorts of intra-disciplinary and epistemic reasons, cognitive mapping (see Laurier and Brown 2005; Laurier and Brown 2008) and feminist critique (Rose 1993) prised practising human subjects apart from theories of seeing. Through close-up observations of praxis, mountain collecting is revealed as an expression of elevated looking, but one always earthed by the walker. Consequently, we argue that perception is attained in a series of correspondences between different sets of eyes and feet. Quite emphatically, neither the ability to look, nor any way of seeing, is detached.

Second, the inherent malleability of a collection like the Munros should alert us to the limitations of treating collecting as a narrowly goal-oriented practice. Acquisition is far from the be all and end all. As we have outlined, at different stages of a mountain walk a personal collection can hove in and out of view. It can reduce to vague aspiration, only to re-merge with far greater urgency than previously anticipated. The very nature of a collection is provisional. It will be recomposed by continued (re)collecting. Collecting cannot be stripped down or rendered passive, left as a backdrop against which social action continually unfolds. But nor is collecting a transcendent, ordering mechanism for walking, always prevailing, determining placement, of one foot in front of the other. Nevertheless, we would readily concede that collecting seems a most British sort of preoccupation, and wonder how it might compare with other European traditions of movement through landscape on foot.

Our third concluding point concerns the recent work of theorists of 'the social' in search of new conceptual motifs for the irrepressible and immanent spatialities currently constituted through assemblages of human and non-human agents, new communication technologies and diverse sorts of auto-mobility (Urry 2001; Thrift 2007). The most ambitious and avant-garde (exploring the properties of fire, smoke, gel or fluid) identify topological figures and complex forms understood to better capture social worlds always in the making, where relations are emergent through conditions of co-presence and the collapse of conventional scales or dimensions (Law and Mol 2001; Law 2004). What we have considered in this chapter will seem, at least in some respects, more steadily paced, sure of foot and positively pedestrian. At least we hope so. While new spatial formations shaping life have their moments, older variants need not be disregarded. The social worlds emerging from walking – that most ordinary and ancient form of movement – produce comparably complex forms of spatial arrangement. Among those recreational hill-walkers who are preoccupied with Scotland's mountains there are a multitude of geometries, cartographies and lifelines to be mapped out across the country's highest points. We might figure these as cartographies of collection which remain dependent on traditional forms of topographical knowledge and well grounded modes of connection, association and attachment.

References

Access Forum (2000), *Care for the Hills: Guidance on the Careful Use of Scotland's Hills and Mountains for Open-Air Recreation* (Edinburgh: Scottish Natural Heritage).

Belk, R. (1995), *Collecting in a Consumer Society* (London: Routledge).

Bennet, D. (ed.) (1999), *The Munros* (Edinburgh: Scottish Mountaineering Club).

Blom, P. (2003), *To Have and To Hold: An Intimate History of Collecting* (London: Penguin).

Butterfield, I. and Baines, D. (1992), *The Munroist's Logbook* (Edinburgh: Scottish Cultural Press).

Campbell. R. (ed.) (1999), *The Munroist's Companion* (Edinburgh: Scottish Mountaineering Trust).

Dempster, A. (1995), *The Munro Phenomenon* (Edinburgh: Mainstream).

Driver, F. and Martins, L. (2002), 'John Septimus Roe and the Art of Navigation, c. 1815–1830', *History Workshop Journal* 54:1, 144-61.

Fowles, J. (1984), 'The Blinded Eye', in Mabey, R., Clifford, S. and King, A. (eds) (1984), *Second Nature* (London: Jonathan Cape).

Highlands and Islands Enterprise (1996), *The Economic Impacts of Hillwalking, Mountaineering and Associated activities in the Highlands and Islands of Scotland* (Internal Report).

Ingold, T. (2004), 'Culture on the Ground: The World Perceived Through the Feet', *Journal of Material Culture* 9:3, 315-40.

Laurier, E. and Brown, B. (2005), 'Maps and Journeys: An Ethnomethodological Investigation', *Cartographica* 4:3, 17-33.

—— (2008), 'Rotating Maps and Readers: Praxiological Aspects of Alignments and Orientation', *Transactions of the Institute of British Geographers* 33:2, 201-216.

Law, J. (2004), 'And if the Global were Small and Noncoherent? Method, Complexity and the Baroque', *Environment and Planning D: Society and Space* 22, 13-26.

Law, J. and Mol, A. (2001), 'Situating Technoscience: An Inquiry into Spatialities' *Environment and Planning D: Society and Space* 19, 609-21.

Lorimer, H. and Lund, K. (2003), 'Performing Facts: Finding a Way over Scotland's Mountains', in Szerszynski B., Heim, W. and Waterton, C. (eds) (2003), 'Nature Performed: Environment, Culture and Performance', *Sociological Review Monographs* (Oxford: Blackwell).

Matless, D. (1999), 'The Uses of Cartographic Literacy: Mapping, Survey and Citizenship in Twentieth-Century Britain', in Cosgrove D. (ed.) (1999), *Mappings* (London: Reaktion).

Rose, G. (1993), *Feminism and Geography* (London: Polity Press).

___ (2003), 'On the Need to Ask How, Exactly, is Geography "Visual"?' *Antipode* 35:2, 212-21.

Solnit, R. (2000), *Wanderlust: A History of Walking* (London: Penguin).

Thrift, N. (2007), *Non-Representational Theory: Space, Politics, Affect* (London: Sage).

Urry, J. (2001), *Sociology Beyond Societies: Mobilities for the Twenty-First Century* (London: Routledge).

Wood, M. (2001), 'The Mountain Panorama and its Significance in the Scottish Context', *Cartographica* 38, 103-118.

Index

Printed in Great Britain
by Amazon